First World War

and Army of Occupation

War Diary

France, Belgium and Germany

46 DIVISION
Divisional Troops
Machine Gun Corps
46 Battalion
28 February 1918 - 31 May 1919

WO95/2679/2

The Naval & Military Press Ltd
www.nmarchive.com
Published in association with The National Archives

Published by

The Naval & Military Press Ltd

Unit 10 Ridgewood Industrial Park,

Uckfield, East Sussex,

TN22 5QE England

Tel: +44 (0) 1825 749494

www.naval-military-press.com

www.nmarchive.com

This diary has been reprinted in facsimile from the original. Any imperfections are inevitably reproduced and the quality may fall short of modern type and cartographic standards.

Contents

Document type	Place/Title	Date From	Date To
Heading	WO95/2679/2 46 Battalion Machine Gun Corps.		
Heading	46 Div Troops 46 Bn. Machine Gun Corps 1918 Mar-1919 May		
Heading	46 Bn M.G. Corps. Vol 1		
Heading	On His Majesty's Service. D.A.G. 3rd. Echelon.		
War Diary	Beaumetz. Lez Aire	28/02/1918	28/02/1918
War Diary	Avchy Aux Bois.	01/03/1918	02/03/1918
War Diary	Fouquieres	03/03/1918	05/03/1918
War Diary	Beauvry	06/03/1918	29/03/1918
War Diary	Les Brebis.	30/03/1918	31/03/1918
Operation(al) Order(s)	46 Battn. M.G. Corps Order No. B.	01/03/1918	01/03/1918
Miscellaneous	March Table For 2nd March 1918 Issued With No. 46 Btn ME. Corps. Order No. 10		
Operation(al) Order(s)	46 Battn. M.G. Corps. Order No 2.B.	02/03/1918	02/03/1918
Operation(al) Order(s)	46th Battn M.G. Corps. Order No. 86		
Miscellaneous	March Table		
Miscellaneous	March Table Issued With 46 Btn. M.G. Corps Order No. 4B		
Operation(al) Order(s)	No. 46th Battalion M.G. Coy. Order No. 48	05/03/1918	05/03/1918
Diagram etc	Identification Trace For Use With Artillery Maps.		
Miscellaneous	With 46 M.G.C. Bt of 1A		
Miscellaneous			
Operation(al) Order(s)	46th Battalion M.G. Order No. 2 A	13/03/1918	13/03/1918
Operation(al) Order(s)	46th. Battalion M.G. Order No. 1.A.	11/03/1918	11/03/1918
Diagram etc			
Miscellaneous	46th. Divisional Machine Gun Scheme.	15/03/1918	15/03/1918
Operation(al) Order(s)	46th Battalion Machine Gun Corps Order No. 3A	17/02/1918	17/02/1918
Operation(al) Order(s)	46th Btn. M.G. Corps, Order No. 4.A.	23/03/1918	23/03/1918
Operation(al) Order(s)	46th Btn. M.G. Corps. Order No. 4.A	23/03/1918	23/03/1918
Operation(al) Order(s)	46th Battalion Machine Gun Order No. 5.A	24/03/1918	24/03/1918
Diagram etc			
Operation(al) Order(s)	46th Battn. Machine Gun Corps Order No. 7.A	25/03/1918	25/03/1918
Operation(al) Order(s)	46th Battn Machine Gun Order No. 6.A.	25/03/1918	25/03/1918
Miscellaneous	1. A Coy. 2. QM. 3. T.O. 4. Signalling Officer.	25/03/1918	25/03/1918
Miscellaneous	March Still Issued With 46th Btn. M.G. Coy Order No. 11		
Operation(al) Order(s)	46th Battn. M.G.C. Order No. 10	27/03/1918	27/03/1918
Operation(al) Order(s)	46th Battalion M.G.C. Order No. 9A	27/03/1918	27/03/1918
Operation(al) Order(s)	46th Battn. M.G.C. Order No. 8A	26/03/1918	26/03/1918
Operation(al) Order(s)	No. 46 Btn M.G. Corps Order No. 11	28/03/1918	28/03/1918
Operation(al) Order(s)	46th Battalion M.G. Corps Order No. 12	23/03/1918	23/03/1918
Miscellaneous	Tracing "G" Will Follous.		
Operation(al) Order(s)	46th Battn. M.G. Corps Order No. 13	31/03/1918	31/03/1918
Heading	War Diary. 46th Battalion Machine Gun Corps April 1918		
War Diary	Les Brebis.	01/04/1918	12/04/1918
War Diary	Bruay.	13/04/1918	14/04/1918
War Diary	Noeux Les Mines.	15/04/1918	23/04/1918
War Diary	Gosnay.	24/04/1918	30/04/1918
Operation(al) Order(s)	46 Battalion M.G.C. Order No. 14	01/04/1918	01/04/1918

Miscellaneous	O.C. A Coy.	04/04/1918	04/04/1918
Diagram etc	Lens & Loos.		
Miscellaneous	Chain of Responsibility		
Operation(al) Order(s)	46th Battalion Machine Gun Corps. Order No. 16	08/04/1918	08/04/1918
Operation(al) Order(s)	48th Battalion Machine Gun Corps Order No. 17	11/04/1918	11/04/1918
Operation(al) Order(s)	46th Battalion Machine Gun Corps Order No. 18	11/04/1918	11/04/1918
Miscellaneous	Relief Table Issued with 46th Battn M.G. Corps Order No. 18	11/04/1918	11/04/1918
Operation(al) Order(s)	46th Battalion Machine Gun Corps Orders No. 19	12/04/1918	12/04/1918
Miscellaneous	March Table. Issued With 46th Battn. M.G. Corps Order No. 19		
Operation(al) Order(s)	46th Battalion Machine Gun Corps Order No. 20	14/04/1918	14/04/1918
Operation(al) Order(s)	46th Battalion Machine Gun Corps Order No. 21	14/04/1918	14/04/1918
Operation(al) Order(s)	46th Battalion Machine Gun Corps. Order No. 22	15/04/1918	15/04/1918
Miscellaneous	March Table Issued With 46th Battn. M.G. Corps Order No. 22	15/04/1918	15/04/1918
Operation(al) Order(s)	46th Battalion Machine Gun Corps Order No. 25	18/04/1918	18/04/1918
Operation(al) Order(s)	46th Battalion Machine Gun Corps Order No. 23 B.	20/04/1918	20/04/1918
Operation(al) Order(s)	46th Battalion Machine Gun Corps Order No. 24	23/04/1918	23/04/1918
Operation(al) Order(s)	46th Battalion Machine Gun Corps Warning Order No. 24 A.	24/04/1918	24/04/1918
Operation(al) Order(s)	46th Battalion Machine Gun Corps Order No. 24 B.	24/04/1918	24/04/1918
Operation(al) Order(s)	March Table to accompany 46th Battn. M.G. Corps Order No. 24 B.	24/04/1918	24/04/1918
Operation(al) Order(s)	46th Battalion Machine Gun Corps Order No. 24.C.	25/04/1918	25/04/1918
Operation(al) Order(s)	46th Battalion Machine Gun Corps Order No. 25	25/04/1918	25/04/1918
Operation(al) Order(s)	46th Battalion Machine Gun Corps Order No. 26	26/04/1918	26/04/1918
Heading	War Diary. 46th Battalion Machine Gun Corps. May 1918		
War Diary	Gosnay.	01/05/1918	31/05/1918
Operation(al) Order(s)	46th Battalion Machine Gun Corps Order No. 27	01/05/1918	01/05/1918
Operation(al) Order(s)	46th Battalion Machine Gun Corps Order No. 28	03/05/1918	03/05/1918
Operation(al) Order(s)	46th Battalion Machine Gun Corps Order No. 29	07/05/1919	07/05/1919
Operation(al) Order(s)	46th Battalion Machine Gun Corps Order No. 30	08/05/1918	08/05/1918
Operation(al) Order(s)	46th Battalion Machine Gun Corps Order No. 30.A.	08/05/1918	08/05/1918
Operation(al) Order(s)	46th Battalion Machine Gun Corps Order No. 31	08/05/1918	08/05/1918
Operation(al) Order(s)	46th Battalion Machine Gun Corps Order No. 32	10/05/1918	10/05/1918
Operation(al) Order(s)	46th Battalion Machine Gun Corps Order No. 33	15/05/1918	15/05/1918
Miscellaneous	46th Division.	21/05/1918	21/05/1918
Miscellaneous	To. O.C. No. 1 Group.	21/05/1918	21/05/1918
Miscellaneous	46th Battn. Machine Gun Corps.		
Miscellaneous	Headquarters, 46th Division., Harassing Fire. Machine Gun Concentration Shoots.	21/05/1918	21/05/1918
Miscellaneous	M.G. Concentration Shoots.	21/05/1918	21/05/1918
Miscellaneous	Harassing Fire Programme.	21/05/1918	21/05/1918
Operation(al) Order(s)	46th Battalion Machine Gun Corps Order No. 34	22/05/1918	22/05/1918
Operation(al) Order(s)	46th Battalion Machine Gun Corps Amendment Order No. 29 A.	23/05/1918	23/05/1918
Diagram etc			
Miscellaneous	Machine Gun Concentration Shoots, Week Commencing Thursday May 30th.	27/05/1918	27/05/1918
Map	Vielle Chapelle.		
Diagram etc	Gorre, Vieille Chapelle.		
Diagram etc	Proposed Grouping of M.Gs.		
Operation(al) Order(s)	46th Battalion Machine Gun Corps Order No. 35	29/05/1918	29/05/1918
Operation(al) Order(s)	46th Battalion Machine Gun Corps Order No. 36	29/05/1918	29/05/1918

Operation(al) Order(s)	46th Battalion Machine Gun Corps Order No. 36. A.	30/05/1918	30/05/1918
Heading	46 Bn M.G. Corps Vol 4		
Heading	On His Majesty's Service. D.A.G. 3rd Echelon.		
Heading	War Diary. 46th Battalion Machine Gun Corps. June 1918		
War Diary	Gorre & Essars Sections. N. La Bassee Canal.	01/06/1918	30/06/1918
Miscellaneous	46th Battn. M.G. Corps. No. 46/2/18	01/06/1919	01/06/1919
Operation(al) Order(s)	46th Battalion Machine Gun Corps Order No. 37	04/06/1918	04/06/1918
Miscellaneous	H.Q. 46th Division.	04/06/1918	04/06/1918
Miscellaneous	Machine Gun Concentration Shoots, Week Commencing Thursday June 6th, 1918	04/06/1918	04/06/1918
Miscellaneous	O.C. No. 1 Group.	09/06/1918	09/06/1918
Miscellaneous	46th Battalion Machine Gun Corps.		
Miscellaneous	Bethune-Canal Bridgehead Line.		
Miscellaneous	Divisional and Brigade Boundaries.		
Miscellaneous	Locality Stores.		
Miscellaneous	Prisoners Of War Cage.		
Miscellaneous	Action In Case Of Attack.		
Miscellaneous	Instructions. regarding warning in Case of hostile gas attack.		
Miscellaneous	Bridges And Roads In The Divisional Area. Prepared For Demolition.		
Map	M.G.D.S. Map. I (Tracing)		
Operation(al) Order(s)	46th Battalion Machine Gun Corps Order No. 38	10/06/1918	10/06/1918
Miscellaneous	H.Q. 46th Division.	11/06/1918	11/06/1918
Miscellaneous	Machine Gun Concentration Shoots, Week Ending June 19th, 1918	11/06/1918	11/06/1918
Operation(al) Order(s)	Order No. 39	13/06/1918	13/06/1918
Operation(al) Order(s)	46th Battalion Machine Gun Corps Order No. 40	16/06/1918	16/06/1918
Miscellaneous	O.C. No 1 Group,	16/06/1918	16/06/1918
Miscellaneous	O.C. No 1 Group, No. 2	17/06/1918	17/06/1918
Miscellaneous	Machine Gun Counter Preparation Scheme.	17/06/1918	17/06/1918
Miscellaneous	Appendix "C"	17/06/1918	17/06/1918
Miscellaneous	Programme Of Machine Gun Concentration Shoots Week Ending June 27th. 1918		
Miscellaneous	H.Q., 46th Division.	21/06/1918	21/06/1918
Miscellaneous	Headquarters, 46th Division.	21/06/1918	21/06/1918
Diagram etc	Vieille Chapelle.		
Miscellaneous	Combined Groups.	21/06/1918	21/06/1918
Miscellaneous	Right Group.	21/06/1918	21/06/1918
Miscellaneous	Left Group.	21/06/1918	21/06/1918
Operation(al) Order(s)	46th Battalion Machine Gun Corps Order No. 41	21/06/1918	21/06/1918
Miscellaneous	H.Q., 46th Division.	26/06/1918	26/06/1918
Miscellaneous	Machine Gun Area Shoots.	26/06/1918	26/06/1918
Miscellaneous	Programme Of Machine Gun Concentration Area Shoots, Ending July 4th, 1918	26/06/1918	26/06/1918
Operation(al) Order(s)	46th Battalion Machine Gun Corps Order No. 42	27/06/1918	27/06/1918
Operation(al) Order(s)	46th Battalion Machine Gun Corps Order No. 45	23/06/1918	23/06/1918
Heading	War Diary Of 46th Battalion Machine Gun Corps July 1918		
War Diary	Gorre & Essars Sections.	01/07/1918	31/07/1918
Miscellaneous	H.Q., 46th Division.	03/07/1918	03/07/1918
Miscellaneous	Programme Of Machine Gun Area & Concentration Shoots Week Ending July 11th, 1918	03/07/1917	03/07/1917
Miscellaneous	O.C. 55th Bn. M.G. Corps.	03/07/1918	03/07/1918
Miscellaneous	Machine Gun Counter Prepartion Scheme.	03/07/1918	03/07/1918

Miscellaneous	Appendix "C"	03/07/1918	03/07/1918
Miscellaneous	H.Q., 46th Division.	03/07/1918	03/07/1918
Miscellaneous	Left Group.	03/07/1918	03/07/1918
Miscellaneous	Combined Groups.	03/07/1918	03/07/1918
Miscellaneous	H.Q., 48th Division. 'D' Coy.	03/07/1918	03/07/1918
Miscellaneous	H.Q., 46th Division.	08/07/1918	08/07/1918
Miscellaneous	Machine Gun Area Shoot "A"		
Miscellaneous	Machine Gun Area Shoot "B"		
Miscellaneous	Machine Gun Area Shoot "C"		
Miscellaneous	Machine Gun Area Shoot "D"		
Operation(al) Order(s)	46th Battalion Machine Gun Corps Order No. 44	04/07/1918	04/07/1918
Diagram etc	DX		
Miscellaneous	H.Q. 46th Division.	08/07/1918	08/07/1918
Miscellaneous	Programme Of Machine Gun Area & Concentration Shoots.	08/07/1918	08/07/1918
Miscellaneous	H.Q., 46th Division. Reference 46/12/314	10/07/1918	10/07/1918
Miscellaneous	H.Q. 46th Division. Ref. Machine Gun Harassing Fire.	18/07/1918	18/07/1918
Operation(al) Order(s)	46th Battalion Machine Gun Corps Order No. 45	09/07/1918	09/07/1918
Miscellaneous			
Miscellaneous	46th Battalion Machine Gun Corps.	21/07/1918	21/07/1918
Operation(al) Order(s)	46th Battalion Machine Gun Corps Order No 46	16/07/1918	16/07/1918
Operation(al) Order(s)	46th Battalion Machine Gun Corps Order No. 48	27/07/1918	27/07/1918
Operation(al) Order(s)	46th Battalion Machine Gun Corps Order No. 47	21/07/1918	21/07/1918
Heading	War Diary Of 46th Battalion Machine Gun Corps. August 1918. Vol 6		
War Diary	Gorre & Essars Sections.	01/08/1918	31/08/1918
Operation(al) Order(s)	46th Battalion Machine Gun Corps Order No. 49	03/08/1918	03/08/1918
Operation(al) Order(s)	46th Battalion Machine Gun Corps Order No. 50	08/08/1918	08/08/1918
Miscellaneous	O.C. No 1 Group.	08/08/1918	08/08/1918
Operation(al) Order(s)	46th Battalion Machine Gun Corps Order No. 51	09/08/1918	09/08/1918
Operation(al) Order(s)	46th Battalion Machine Gun Corps Order No. 52	09/08/1916	09/08/1916
Miscellaneous	H.Q., 46th Division., Machine Gun S.O.S. Lines.	10/08/1918	10/08/1918
Diagram etc	46th Btn. M.G.C. Revised S.O.S. Lines		
Miscellaneous	Administrative Instruction No. 1	12/08/1918	12/08/1918
Miscellaneous	Machine Gun S.O.S. Lines.	12/08/1918	12/08/1918
Operation(al) Order(s)	46th Battalion Machine Gun Corps Order No. 53	14/08/1918	14/08/1918
Miscellaneous	M.G Disposition.		
Miscellaneous	H.Q., 46th Division., Machine Gun Dispositions.	20/08/1918	20/08/1918
Operation(al) Order(s)	46th Battalion Machine Gun Corps Order No. 54	20/08/1918	20/08/1918
Operation(al) Order(s)	46th Battalion Machine Gun Corps Order No. 54A.	21/08/1918	21/08/1918
Operation(al) Order(s)	46th Battalion Machine Gun Corps Order No. 55	23/08/1918	23/08/1918
Operation(al) Order(s)	46th Battalion Machine Gun Corps Order No. 56	23/08/1918	23/08/1918
Heading	War Diary 46th Battalion Machine Gun Corps. September 1918. Vol 7		
War Diary	Essars & Gorre Section.	01/09/1918	04/09/1918
War Diary	Hesdigneul.	05/09/1918	10/09/1918
War Diary	Lozinghem.	11/09/1918	15/09/1918
War Diary	Baisieux.	16/09/1918	19/09/1918
War Diary	St. Quentin Canal.	20/09/1918	30/09/1918
Operation(al) Order(s)	46th Battalion Machine Gun Corps Warning Order No 57	02/09/1918	02/09/1918
Miscellaneous			
Operation(al) Order(s)	46th Battalion Machine Gun Corps Order No. 58	04/09/1918	04/09/1918
Operation(al) Order(s)	46th Battalion Machine Gun Corps Order No 59	20/09/1918	20/09/1918
Operation(al) Order(s)	46th Battalion Machine Gun Corps Order No 60		
Map	Identification Trace For Use With Artillery Maps.		

Operation(al) Order(s)	46th Battalion Machine Gun Corps Order No 61	23/09/1918	23/09/1918
Operation(al) Order(s)	46th Battalion Machine Gun Corps Order No 62	26/09/1918	26/09/1918
Operation(al) Order(s)	46th Battalion Machine Gun Corps Order No. 64	27/09/1918	27/09/1918
Operation(al) Order(s)	46th Battalion Machine Gun Corps Order No. 63	27/09/1918	27/09/1918
Operation(al) Order(s)	46th Battalion Machine Gun Corps Order No. 65	27/09/1918	27/09/1918
Operation(al) Order(s)	46th Battalion Machine Gun Corps Order No 64A.	28/09/1918	28/09/1918
Operation(al) Order(s)	46th Battalion Machine Gun Corps Order No 66	28/09/1918	28/09/1918
Operation(al) Order(s)	46th Battalion Machine Gun Corps Order No 68	28/09/1918	28/09/1918
Operation(al) Order(s)	46th Battalion Machine Gun Corps Order No. 67	28/09/1918	28/09/1918
Operation(al) Order(s)	46th Battalion Machine Gun Corps Order No 69	28/09/1918	28/09/1918
Miscellaneous	Headquarters, 46th Division.	05/11/1918	05/11/1918
Heading	46th Battalion Machine Gun Corps. War Diary. October 1918. Vol 8		
War Diary	Vendelles	01/10/1918	04/10/1918
War Diary	La Baraque.	05/10/1918	05/10/1918
War Diary	Vendelles.	06/10/1918	07/10/1918
War Diary	Magny.	08/10/1918	09/10/1918
War Diary	Fresnoy	10/10/1918	31/10/1918
Operation(al) Order(s)	46th Battalion, Machine Gun Corps Order No. 70	01/10/1918	01/10/1918
Operation(al) Order(s)	46th Battalion Machine Gun Corps Order No. 70A.	02/10/1918	02/10/1918
Miscellaneous	Following From Division 4/10/18	04/10/1918	04/10/1918
Miscellaneous	Following From Division, 5/10/18	05/10/1918	05/10/1918
Miscellaneous	A Form Messages And Signals.		
Operation(al) Order(s)	46th Battalion Machine Gun Corps Order No. 71	15/10/1918	15/10/1918
Miscellaneous	Reference 46th Btn. M.G. Corps Order No 71	16/10/1918	16/10/1918
Miscellaneous	Fire Organization Orders. Attack by 46th Division.	16/10/1918	16/10/1918
Miscellaneous	O.C. "A" Coy.,	16/10/1918	16/10/1918
Miscellaneous	Report On Operations On October 17th, 1918	17/10/1918	17/10/1918
War Diary	Bohain.	01/11/1918	03/11/1918
War Diary	L'Arbre De Guise.	04/11/1918	30/11/1918
Operation(al) Order(s)	46th Battalion Machine Gun Corps Order No. 74	02/11/1918	02/11/1918
Miscellaneous	46th Battalion M.G. Corps F/1 2nd November, 1918	02/11/1918	02/11/1918
Operation(al) Order(s)	Reference 46th Battn. Machine Gun Corps Order No 74. F/2	03/11/1918	03/11/1918
War Diary	Bousies	01/12/1918	06/12/1918
War Diary	Bohain.	07/12/1918	31/12/1918
Operation(al) Order(s)	46th Battalion Machine Gun Corps Order No. 75.A.	06/12/1918	06/12/1918
Operation(al) Order(s)	46th Battalion Machine Gun Corps Order No. 75	06/12/1918	06/12/1918
Miscellaneous	March Table to accompany 46th Battn. M.G. Corps. Order No. 75		
War Diary		01/01/1919	31/01/1919
Miscellaneous	46th Division. M.G. Battalion., Liout-Colonel B.N. Lannowo, D.S.O. Commanding.		
Miscellaneous	46th Battn. M.G. Corps. 46/2/4	05/03/1919	05/03/1919
War Diary	Bohain.	01/02/1919	28/02/1919
Operation(al) Order(s)	46th Battn. Machine Gun Corps. Order No. 76	27/02/1919	27/02/1919
Miscellaneous	March Table to accompany 46th Battn. Machine Gun Corps Order No. 76		
War Diary	Inchy	01/03/1919	31/03/1919
Miscellaneous	D.A.G. British Army of the Rhine.	06/05/1919	06/05/1919
War Diary		01/04/1919	30/04/1919
War Diary	Mechernich.	01/05/1919	31/05/1919

WO/95/2679/2

46 Battalion Machine Gun Corps

46 DIV TROOPS

46 BN. MACHINE GUN CORPS

1918 MAR — 1919 MAY

46 Bn MG Corps
VA 1

On His Majesty's Service.

SECRET

D. A. G.

3rd Echelon

HEADQUARTERS,
3RD BRIGADE,
TANK CORPS.
No. G 4/15.
Date.

Instructions regarding War Diaries and Intelligence Summaries are contained in F. S. Regs., Part II. and the Staff Manual respectively. Title pages will be prepared in manuscript.

WAR DIARY

~~or~~

~~INTELLIGENCE SUMMARY.~~

(*Erase heading not required.*)

46th Battalion Machine Gun Corps.

Army Form C. 2118.

No I

Place	Date	Hour	HAZEBROUCK 5A 1/100000. Summary of Events and Information	Remarks and references to Appendices
BEAUMETZ-LEZ AIRE	28/2/18	–	No 46 Battalion M.G. Corps formed. M.G. Coys absorbed were 137, 138, 139 & 178.	1 B. R
			Lieut Colonel Hewitt A.B. D.S.O. M.C. took over Command	
		2.15pm	Order No 1. B. issued (copy attached).	
AUCHY AUX BOIS	1/3/18		Move to AUCHY AUX BOIS completed without incident.	R
			1 Coy marched from CAPELLE SUR LA LYS } to AUCHY AUX BOIS	
			1 " " " PETIGNY }	
			2 " " " BEAUMETZ LEZ AIRE. }	
			Battn HQ " }	
"	2/3/18	6pm	Order No 2 B issued (copy attached) Lieut. K McAlpine RAMC posted.	2 B. R
			1 OR. Evacuated (Sick).	
FOUQUIERES	3/3/18		Move to FOUQUIERES completed by 3pm without incident.	
–		11am	Inspected volunteers in 139 Inf Bde for transfer to M.G. Corps to complete new establishment	R
			Preliminary reconnaisance by Commanding Officer of positions in line to be taken over	
	4/3/18		Reconnaisance of line by Commanding Officer & all Coy Commanders.	
			Order 3 B. issued (copy attached) 2/LIEUT R.E Robinson posted.	3 B. R

(A7092). Wt W12839/M1293 750,000. 1/17. D. D. & L., Ltd. Forms/C.2118/14.

Instructions regarding War Diaries and Intelligence Summaries are contained in F. S. Regs., Part II. and the Staff Manual respectively. Title pages will be prepared in manuscript.

WAR DIARY 46th Battalion M G Corps

~~INTELLIGENCE SUMMARY.~~

(*Erase heading not required.*)

Army Form C. 2118.

No 2.

Place	Date	Hour	Summary of Events and Information HAZEBROUCK 5A. 1/100000. LA GORRE 1/20000.	Remarks and references to Appendices
FOUQUIERES	5/3/18	7am	Companies designated ABCD Coys. (from 137, 138, 139 & 178 Coys respectively)	
			C.O. delegated full powers to Coy. Cmdrs. vide K.R. 501.	
			A Coy moved into billets at BEUVRY	R
"	"		B " into the line to take over part CAMBRIN SECTION from 11th Battn. M G Corps	
			C " moved into billets at BEUVRY	
			D " " " " " BETHUNE	
			HQ " " " " " BEUVRY	
BEUVRY	6/3/18	9 am	Order No B issued (copy attached)	4 B. R
			A Coy move into line to take over part CAMBRIN Section from 55th Battn. M G Corps	
			1/2 C Coy " " ANNEQUIN into reserve	
			D Coy " " BEUVRY.	
			C.O. visited line with I Corps Machine Gun Officer	
"	7/3/18		8 Men reported from 42 M G Battalion to reconnoitre reserve positions	
			Lieut & QM Sommerfield M S posted. 3 OR^s evacuated (sick)	R
			Inspection of volunteers from 1st Monmouth Regt for transfer to M G Corps to complete new establishment.	
			" " " 137th & 138th Bde " " " " "	
"	8/3/18		Fired 1,500 rounds on to enemy's roads & light railway in area A23a.	R
			4 OR^s posted 1 OR evacuated sick	

(A7092) Wt W12839/M1293 750,000 1/17. D. D. & L., Ltd. Forms/C.2118/14.

Army Form C. 2118.

Instructions regarding War Diaries and Intelligence Summaries are contained in F. S. Regs., Part II. and the Staff Manual respectively. Title pages will be prepared in manuscript.

WAR DIARY

~~or~~

~~INTELLIGENCE SUMMARY.~~

(Erase heading not required.)

46th Battn. M.G. Corps

No 3

Place	Date	Hour	Summary of Events and Information	Remarks and references to Appendices
			~~BF~~ GORRE 1/20000	
BEUVRY	9/3/18		Remaining ½ C Coy. moved from BEUVRY into ANNEQUIN	
			Fired 41,000 rounds M.G. fire on to enemys roads & tracks & light railway in areas A22 & A23a	2
			CSM of the A.G. Staff posted	
	10/3/18		M.G.s fired 10,500 rounds harassing fire on to x roads & tracks in area A23a	2
	11/3/18		Order 1A issued (copy attached)	1 A.
			68 men reported for 3 weeks trial course from Infantry Battalion of 46 Div. to complete new establishment	2
			M.G.s fired 6,500 rounds harassing fire on to enemy areas round LA BASSEE CANAL	
	12/3/18		Course started in BEUVRY for 63 new recruits. duration to be 3 weeks.	
			Our M.G.s fired 10,000 rounds harassing fire on to enemys light railways, roads & tracks.	2
			1 OR Evacuated (Sick) Major E.A. Ellwood DSO MC struck off on posting to VII Corps	
			1 " Transferred 1 OR Wounded in Action	
	13/3/18		Order 2A issued copy attached 1 OR Wounded in Action. 4 OR Evacuated (Sick)	2 A 2
			M.G.s fired 8,500 rounds harassing fire on enemys dumps & communications	
	14/3/18		Our M.G.s fired 4,000 rounds harassing fire on enemys roads & tracks & 1,500 rounds at E.A.	2
			1 OR evacuated 1 OR reinforcement	

(A7092). Wt. W12839/M1293. 750,000. 1/17. D. D. & L., Ltd. Forms/C.2118/14.

Instructions regarding War Diaries and Intelligence Summaries are contained in F. S. Regs., Part II. and the Staff Manual respectively. Title pages will be prepared in manuscript.

WAR DIARY 46th Battn. M.G. Corps.
or
~~INTELLIGENCE SUMMARY.~~
(Erase heading not required.)

Army Form C. 2118.

No. 4.

Place	Date	Hour	Summary of Events and Information	Remarks and references to Appendices
			GORRE 1/20000.	
BEUVRY	15/3/18	-	46th Divisional Defence Scheme submitted to Division. (copy attached) M.G.s fired 4,500 rounds harassing fire on enemy communications. 1 O.R. evacuated (sick) 2 O.R. reinforcements	X
	16/3/18	-	M.G.s fired 3,000 rounds on to Enemy communications during the night and 2,500 rounds at E.A. We fired 3,000 rounds to cover Infantry Patrols in front of Chateau Alley A15d 22.55. 1 O.R. Wounded in Action. Lieut. D.R. Wildblood Wounded in Action 30 O.R.s Reinforcements 2/Lieut. B Kidd " " " (Died of Wounds 19-3-18)	
	17/3/18	-	Order No 3A issued (copy attached) M.G.s fired 5,000 rounds harassing fire on to enemys communications 1 O.R. Killed in action 1 O.R. Wounded in Action	3A.
	18/3/18	-	M.G.s harassed suspected enemy raiding spot at A28 a 2.6. 1,500 rounds fired at A20 d.9.7. 1 O.R. Evacuated sick. Rev. T Harper C.F. reported	
	19/3/18	-	M.G.s fired 4,000 rounds on enemys communications & gaps in enemys wire in conjunction with the Artillery. We fired 1,000 rounds at each LES BRIQUES A28b and SPOTTED DOG A22 b. 3. O.R.s Evacuated (sick).	
	20/3/18	-	M.G.s in conjunction with the artillery fired 5,000 rounds harassing fire on to enemy's communications, also 1,000 rounds on A23a 43.64 and 1,000 rounds on A22 b 47.45, 1,000 rounds	

(A7092). Wt W12839/M1293 750,000. 1/17. D. D. & L., Ltd. Forms/C.2118/14.

Army Form C. 2118.

Instructions regarding War Diaries and Intelligence Summaries are contained in F. S. Regs., Part II. and the Staff Manual respectively. Title pages will be prepared in manuscript.

WAR DIARY

~~or~~

~~INTELLIGENCE SUMMARY.~~

(*Erase heading not required.*)

46 Battn M.G. Corps

No 5.

Place	Date	Hour	Summary of Events and Information GORRE 1/20000.	Remarks and references to Appendices
BEUVRY	20/3/18 (Contd)		on Les Briques A28b and 1,000 rounds on X Roads at A23 C 14.42. 1. OR Evacuated (sick) Lieut/Capt. T.C. Low to Base Depot.	2
	21/3/18		9 ORs Reinforcements. M.G.s fired 1,000 rounds on to enemys communications	2
	22/3/18		Lieut Colonel J. Harington. DSO. Rifle Brigade appointed to succeed Lieut Colonel C.C. Hewitt. DSO. MC S.O.S. sent up at 12.30 am same MGs fired 90,000 rounds on to M.G. S.O.S. targets Lieut. Saunders 4.V.B. killed in action. B Battery knocked out of one forward gun, 1 man was killed & 2 wounded during the heavy bombardment. After bombardment, about 10 Germans appeared 10 yds in front of this gun & by throwing bombs caused the remainder of the team to retire. One man eventually won their way back, but no trace could be found of the Vickers gun, which it is presumed was captured. 2,000 rounds harassing fire on to enemys communications at A27d. 2. OR. killed in action. 3. OR. Wounded.	2
	23/3/18	7pm.	Order No 4A issued & tracing G. (copy attached) 5,500 rounds fired on to enemys communications 19 ORs reinforcements.	4 A
	24/3/18.	8.15pm.	Order 5A. & tracing H issued. (copy attached). 1. OR. Wounded in Action. 2 ORs Evacuated. (Sick) B Coy. relieved A Coy. in the line A Coy. moving into rest billets in BEUVRY.	5 A

(A7092). Wt. W12839/M1293 750,000. 1/17. D. D. & L., Ltd. Forms/C.2118/14.

Instructions regarding War Diaries and Intelligence Summaries are contained in F. S. Regs., Part II. and the Staff Manual respectively. Title pages will be prepared in manuscript.

WAR DIARY

or ~~INTELLIGENCE~~ SUMMARY. 46 Battn. M.G. Corps

(Erase heading not required.)

No. 6.

Army Form C. 2118.

Place	Date	Hour	Summary of Events and Information GORRE 1/20000 + ST NAZAIRE RIVER 1/20000.	Remarks and references to Appendices
BEUVRY.	24/3/18 (Contd)		2,250 rounds harassing fire on enemy's communications. Lieut Colonel C.C. Hewitt DSO MC proceeded for duty as M.G. Officer Third Army.	
	25/3/18.	6. am.	Order No 6A issued (copy attached) 2,500 rounds fired on to enemy's communications	6 A
		11.45 am	" " 7A " (" ") 2/Lieut. A.L. Smith posted.	7 A
			2/Lieut. J Mosley attached from 6th N. Staffs. Reg. for duty as Signalling Officer	
	26/3/18	1 am.	Order No 8.A. issued (copy attached)	8 A
			2 OR. Evacuated (Sick) 2/Lieut E. Holden / " E. Lamb } posted.	
	27/3/18	9.30 pm	Order No 9A issued. (copy attached)	9 A
			" " 10 " (" ")	10
	28/3/18	7 am.	Order No 11 issued. (copy attached)	11
			Battalion marched to LES BREBIS without incident + 3½ Coys direct into the line to relieve 4th Canadian Machine Gun Battalion.	
	29/3/18	9. am	Order No 12 issued (copy attached)	12
			2/Lieut. E.H. Lane posted.	

(A7092). Wt W12539/M1293 75,0.0. 1/17. D. D. & L., Ltd. Forms/C.2118/14.

Instructions regarding War Diaries and Intelligence Summaries are contained in F. S. Regs., Part II. and the Staff Manual respectively. Title pages will be prepared in manuscript.

WAR DIARY 46 Batt. M G Corps

~~or~~

~~INTELLIGENCE SUMMARY.~~

(*Erase heading not required.*)

No 7

Army Form C. 2118.

Place	Date	Hour	Summary of Events and Information	Remarks and references to Appendices
			ST NAZAIRE RIVER 1/20,000	
LES BREBIS	30/3/18	-	5,500 rounds fired on to enemys communications	
	31/3/18	1-0pm	Order No 13 issued. (Copy attached)	13
			2,000 rounds fired on to enemys communications	
			1. OR Wounded in Action	
			1 OR Reinforcement	
				[illegible signature] Capt

Secret

Copy No. 8

46 Battn. M.G. Corps Order No. 1. B

Reference 1/100.000 HAZEBROUGH 5.A. & LENS. 11. Sheets

1 General — The 46th Battn. M.G. Corps will move tomorrow from the BOMY area to take over a portion of the 1st Corps front from 11th & 55th Divisions

2 Situation — On completion of moves the 138th INFANTRY BRIGADE will hold the CAMRIN Section and 137th INFANTRY BRIGADE the CUINCHY Section 139th INFANTRY BRIGADE will be in Divisional Reserve. Details regarding the divisional and brigade boundaries will be issued later

3 Reliefs — The relief of the CAMBRIN Section is to be completed by 6.am 5th MARCH, and that of the CUINCHY Section by 6 am 6th MARCH.
Machine Guns will be relieved 24 hours after the Infantry reliefs. orders for which will be issued later

4 March Table — March Table for MARCH 2nd is attached

5 Billetting — Each Coy will send forward 1 Officer and 1 Cyclist ~~runner~~ to report to the Btn Billetting Officer (Lt Moody) at AUCHY AU BOIS at 10 am tomorrow.
The cyclists will meet their respective Coys at the point where LIGNY by AIRE-ARMETTES road crosses the WESTREHEM - St HILAIRE road.

6 Horse Lines — The o/c D Coy will send 1 Officer and the o/c A Coy one N.C.O. (Cpl) tomorrow to the Horse Lines vacated by 11th Div. S.A.A. Section of D.A.C. at F.2.c.d.1.1 (sheet 36.B 1/40000.)
Seperate instructions have been issued

Order No 1 B. continued. Sheet No 2

7 Certificates Coys will render a certificate immediately on arrival AUCHY AU BOIS Area regarding Billets etc vacated in BOMY Area stating:-

A. All Latrines filled in correctly

B. -"- Billets left clean

C. -"- Stables -"- -

D. Ground in vicinity of A.B.C. cleaned up.

E. No Damage to report or if any damage, list of same with full particulars

F. All Billetting claims submitted

Copies issued to

1 A. Coy

2 B

3 C

4 D

5 Qr. Mr

6 Lt. MOODY

7 46th Division

8 War Diary

R. Hickens

Capt & Adjt

46 M Gun. Battn.

1-3-1918

Time 2.15 pm

MARCH TABLE FOR 2ND MARCH 1918 ISSUED WITH No 46 BTN M G CORPS ORDER No [illegible]

COMPANY	STARTING POINT	TIME	ROUTE	REMARKS
"B"	1st [illegible] CAPELLE SUR LA LYS	9 45 AM	RECLINGHEM - BEAUMETZ LES AIRE - LAIRES - FEBVIN PALFART - WESTREHEM - AUCHY AU BOIS Area	
"A"	900x S E BEAUMETZ CHURCH BEAUMETZ LES AIRE, LAIRES ROAD	11 20 AM	LAIRES - FEBVIN PALFART - WESTREHEM - AUCHY AU BOIS Area	
"D"	- ditto -	11 30 AM	- ditto -	To follow A Coy at 500x interval Btn H Q will move with D Coy
"C"	400x SE PETIGNY on North Road PETIGNY - BOMY	11 25 AM	BOMY - thence via road on Southern slope HILL 105 to road [illegible] of ST JULIEN - CUHEM - LIGNY LES AIRES - to point where LIGNY LES AIRE - ARMETTES road crosses the WESTREHEM - ST HILAIRE road AUCHY AU BOIS Area	

SECRET. COPY No. 8

46 Battn: M.G. CORPS. ORDER No. 2.B

Reference:- 1/100.000 HAZEBROUCK 5A and
LENS 11 sheets
1/20.000 36c N.W. and 36b N.E.

2nd MARCH 1918.

I MOVE The Battalion will move from AUCHY-au-BOIS to FOUQUIERES tomorrow March 3.

2 STARTING POINT. Where the 100 metres contour crosses the ESTREE-BLANCHE = FERFAY ROAD at a point South of B in AUCHY-AU-BOIS.

3 ROUTE. Starting point = FORFAY = CAUCHY-A-LA-TOUR = AUCHEL = LOZINGHEM = MARLES-LES-MINES = LABUISSIERE = FOUQUIERES.

4 TIMES TO PASS STARTING POINT.

'A' Coy. at 9.30 A.M.
D " " 9.40 " x (To include Btn: H.Q.)
C " " 9.50 "
B " " 10.0 "

5 RATIONS. For this march a Haversack Ration will be carried by each man. This will be consumed at the third halt.

6. Baggage. One Baggage Wagon to convey Blankets, Stoves, Baggage etc will be detailed by the Q.M. to report to Coy H.Q. by 8.0 A.M. tomorrow Mch 3.

Continued

SHEET 2 Order 28.

7 BILLETTING PARTIES Each Coy will detail a billetting party of 1 Officer and 1 cyclist to report to Btn Billetting Officer (Lt MOODY) at Starting point given in para I above at 9.10 AM tomorrow 3/3

The Btn Billetting Officer will allot areas of FOUQUIERES to COYS & the Coy Cyclists will be detailed to meet respective Companies at a point 400 metres SW of the entrance to FOQUIERES and to conduct Coys to such areas.

8 BILLETTING RETURNS.

Billetting returns for the present will be rendered by O/c Coys.

9 LOCATION COY HQ The location of Coy HQ at FOQUIERES will be notified without delay to Btn HQ

10 CERIFICATE O/c COYS will render the usual certificate regardingave from Billets to Btn HQ by 5 PM March 3

Copies issued to
1 A Coy.
2 B –
3 C –
4 D –
5 QM
6 Lt Moody
7. 46 Div
8 War Diary

Acknowledge

2 3 1918

R. Hickson
Capt & Adjt
46 Btn MG Corps

SECRET

COPY No. 9

46th BATTn M.G. CORPS ORDER No 38

Reference:- 1/40,000 BETHUNE Combined Sheet and Secret Trench Map

4 March /18

1. MOVE The Batty will move by Companies from FOUQUIERES tomorrow 5th inst as follows

A Coy (less 4 sub-sections) to BEUVRY

B " (with 4 " A Coy) into the line to take over CAMBRIN sector

C Coy to BEUVRY

D " " BETHUNE

MARCH TABLES as attached

Billeting Parties will be detailed as follows:-

From A & C Coys to report to Lt MOODY at Bn HQ at 10.0 AM March 5th. A representative will meet respective Coys on arrival at outskirts of BEUVRY on the BEUVRY – BETHUNE road

D Coy will send forward a Billeting party to BETHUNE to ascertain location of Billets from Town Major BETHUNE

The Group Commander will arrange for Billets with the Town Major at SAILLY-LABOURSE

Billetting Claims will be rendered by Coys

Baggage etc 1 G.S. Wagon and 2/3 Limber ... Carts will report FOUQUIERES

(Continued)

Sheet 2 Continued

46 Bn. H.Q. Coy. Order [illegible]

Baggage etc. continued at 1 P.M. March 5th to Company Blankets, Baggage, [illegible] etc. Small trading [illegible] will be detailed to [illegible] & the [illegible] [illegible] The N.C.O. i/c these parties will report to [illegible] for instructions at 12.0 noon March 5th

Bn. H.Q. will close at [illegible] at 11.0 A.M. March 5th

All Q.M. Stores will be located at F 20 Central

2 RELIEFS "B" Coy less 1 platoon of "A" Coy will [illegible] [illegible] the [illegible]

Bn. [illegible] Coy [illegible] [illegible] [illegible] [illegible] [illegible] will be [illegible] [illegible] [illegible] the [illegible] [illegible] [illegible] [illegible] [illegible] of "A" Coy will [illegible] [illegible] [illegible] [illegible] "A" Coy [illegible] [illegible] [illegible] [illegible] [illegible] the [illegible] Coy [illegible]

Communication [illegible] [illegible] [illegible] ([illegible]) [illegible]

Bn. H.Q. will be [illegible] [illegible] [illegible] [illegible]

Requirements for communication [illegible] [illegible]

[illegible] [illegible] [illegible] [illegible] [illegible] [illegible]

[illegible] [illegible] [illegible]

[illegible] [illegible] [illegible] [illegible] [illegible] [illegible]

[illegible] [illegible] [illegible]

[illegible] [illegible] [illegible]

[illegible] [illegible] [illegible] [illegible] [illegible]

[illegible] [illegible] [illegible]

[illegible] 2nd Bn. M.G. Corps Orders
[illegible] 28

TRANSPORT STORES: All Transport and other stores, including stores on M.G. Equipment [illegible] must be taken over and quantities so taken over reported to Bn. H.Q.

INFORMATION

A. The Company Commanders will report to Bn. H.Q. as early as possible:-

1. S.O.S. Lines for forward guns.
2. S.O.S. Barrage " Rear "
3. Battle line " forward "
4. Battle lines " Rear "
5. Position of any M.G. Observation posts
6. Position of Section depots
7. Work programme for first 24 hours
8. Ammunition requirement to complete

B. The Company Commanders will report to Bn. H.Q. within 24 hours

1. [illegible] out accumulation at each gun and Battery location stating whether [illegible]
2. Requirement [illegible] Section orders and maps [illegible]
3. Position [illegible] to be [illegible] out of S.O.S. including the 12th [illegible]
4. Deficiency, if any, in any stores such as Gun Boots - Patent Thermos etc.

Ackn.

[illegible]
Capt. & Adjutant
2nd Bn. M.G. Corps

Issued at 7.0 A.M. [illegible]

Copies issued to:-

1 A Coy
2 B "
3 C "
4 D "
5 [illegible]
6 [illegible] Division
7 [illegible]
8 [illegible]
9 Retained H.Q.

MARCH TABLE issued with 4th Bath M.G. Coys Order No. 3B.

COY	STARTING POINT	TIME	ROUTE	REMARKS
B	N. end of FOUQUIERES on the BETHUNE – [illegible] Road	4.30 A.M.	BETHUNE – BEUVRY – X roads N of L in ANNEQUIN – into the LINE	The 1 mule section from A Coy will travel & proceed with B Coy and arrangements to be made by the Coy concerned
A	– ditto –	11.0 A.M.	BETHUNE – BEUVRY	Less 1 mule section as above
C	– ditto –	11.10 A.M.	– ditto –	Bn H.Q. mule proceeds with C Coy
D	– ditto –	11.20 A.M.	BETHUNE	

NOTE Coy Transport (less Travelling Kitchen) will be parked at the Bn Transport lines F 20 CENTRAL and will report to the Bn Transport Officer (Lt [illegible]) on arrival.

//

MARCH TABLE ISSUED With 46 Btn: M.G.Corps ORDER No 4 B

Coy	STARTING POINT	TIME	ROUTE	REMARKS
A	Junction of BEUVRY - SAILLY LABOURSE and BEUVRY-ANNEQUIN Road	12 Noon	ANNEQUIN	
C	— ditto —	2·30 PM	ANNEQUIN	½ Coy remain at BEUVRY
D	Junction of BETHUNE - BEUVRY and BETHUNE - ANNEQUIN, Road	2·30 PM	BEUVRY	

Note. ALL TRANSPORT (LESS TRAVELLING KITCHEN) WILL BE PARKED AT THE BTN. TRANSPORT LINES F20 CENTRAL AND WILL REPORT TO THE BTN TRANSPORT OFFICER (LT. MOODY) ON ARRIVAL.

330
80

SECRET. COPY NO. 7

NO. 46th BATTALION M. G. COY. ORDER NO. 48.

REFERENCE. 1/100.000 HAZEBROUCK 5A and

1/20.000 36 B N.E. and 1/10.000 36 C N.W. 1.

5th March 1918.

1. MOVE. 1. The following moves will take place tomorrow.

A. A. Coy (less 1 sub section) will move into the line to take guns in CAMBRIN SECTION.

B. ½ of C Coy into reserve at ANNEQUIN. Remaining ½ of C Coy will remain in present billets.

C. D. Coy will move from BETHUNE to BEUVRY.

2. MARCH TABLE. is attached.

3. Billetting.
A. The billetting for the ½ of C Coy at ANNEQUIN will be arranged direct between O.C. Coy and Town Major. ANNEQUIN.
B. D. Coy will be met on arrival at the northern outskirts of BEUVRY and will be conducted to their billets which will be arranged by the R.S.M.

4. Baggage.
The Transport Officer will arrange for transport for blankets, baggage, etc of D. Coy.
O.C. C. Coy will make own arrangements.

2 RELIEFS 2. RELIEFS.
1. A. Coy (less 1 sub section) will take over gun positions from the 55th Btn M.G. Corps tomorrow as arranged.
Completion of relief will be notified to Btn H.Q. by the Code Word GREEN.
The 1 sub section of A Coy at present in the line will be taken over by O.C. A. Coy under arrangements to be made by O.C. Coys Concerned.

2. Communications.
A. Communications between Group Commanders(Capt Nurse M.C.) and Btn H.Q. has been arranged for.
B. The location of O.C. Forward and O.C. Rear Guns will be notified to Batn H.Q. as early as possible in order that arrangements can be made to connect these Officers with the Group Commander.

3. Rations.
The Q.M. will arrange to deliver rations for A. Coy as follows.
8 Teams to A. 14 D. 21. 75.
8 Teams to A. 20 D. 12. 48.
Reference. 1/10.000. LA BASSEE 36. C N.W.1.
To be delivered at dusk.
This Coy will carry rations for up to and including 7th.

4. Trench Stores.
All Trench and Area Stores, rations and stores in M.G. Emplacements. armour piercing S.A.A. ammunition will be taken over and quantities so taken over reported to Btn H.Q.

5. Report

A. The Group Commander will report to the Btn H.Q. as early as possible.

1. S.O.S. lines for forward guns.
2. S.O.S. Barrage for rear Guns
3. Battle lines for forward guns.
4. Battle lines for rear guns.
5. Position of any M.G. observation posts.
6. Position of Section Depots.
7. Work programme for first 24 hours.
8. Ammunition required to complete.

B. The Group Commander will report to Btn H.Q. within 24 hours

1. Dug-out accomadation at each gun and battery position stating whether mined or concrete.
2. Requirements as to sentries orders and maps also fighting maps
3. Routine firing to be carried out up to and including the 18th March.
4. Deficiency if any in any items such as gum boots. petrol tins, ets,

---

Issued at 9 am 6.3.18 to.

1. A. Coy.
2. B. Coy.
3. C. Coy.
4. D. Coy.
5. Q.M.
6. 46th Division.
7. War Diary.
8. Transport Officer.
9. Btn Signalling Officer.
10. Medical Officer.
11. Retained at H.Q.

Chkg.

Blickens
Capt: Adjt
46th: Btn: M.G. Corps

1 : 10,000.

SECRET TRACING A.

Identification Trace for use with Artillery Maps.

NOTE.—(1). These traces are intended to facilitate the communication of information as to the position of targets, which have been located on a squared map.

(2). The squares on this trace are 500 yards in length on the 1/10,000 scale, 1,000 yards in length on the 1/20,000 scale, and 2,000 yards in length on the 1/40,000 scale.

(3). The squares on the trace are fitted to the squares of the map showing the targets, which are then drawn on the trace. Sufficient letters and numbers must also be added to enable the recipient to place the trace in the correct position on his own map. A little detail may also be traced, but this is not essential. The name and scale of the map to which the trace refers must be always given. The trace can be used for the 1/10,000, 1/20,000, or 1/40,000 scale.

G.S.C.S. 3023.

Tracing taken from Sheet ....

of the 1: .... *map of* ....

Signature .... *Date* ....

SECRET.

With 46 M.G.C Bt 7 - 1A

①

Coy.	No of gun	Present Location	New Location.	Time to move	Remarks.
A	F 2	A21B 98·93	No change	—	Work to be commenced to admit of fire N.E. if required.
A	F 4	A15d 98·52	A15d 22·59	7 am	To duplicate R66 gun
A	R 66	A15d 22·59	NO CHANGE	—	
A	F 1	A21b 70·55	A21c 95·62	8 am	
A	S 1	A21c·91·62	A21c 91·60	7 am	
A	A27·3	A27a 95·65	A27b 18·67	7·30 am	
A	R 63	A27b 08·05	NO CHANGE		
A	R 62	A27c·92·80	A21c·91·60	8 am	To duplicate F1 gun
B	R 58	G.4a·10·12	A27c·92·80	7 am	To relieve gun of A Coy (R62)
B	R 61	A27d 35·15	No CHANGE		
B	R 60	A27a 40·08	" "		
B	R 59	G3b 79·75	" "		
B	R 57 A	G3a 75·75	" "		
B	R 56	G4c 35·30	G10a 55·52	8 am.	
B	V 39 A	G3d 60·10	NO CHANGE		
B	Central Keep.	G3d·65·15	" "		

SECRET.

Coy.	No of gun	Present Location	New Location.	Time to move	Remarks.
A.	PF 4	A 14 d. 58. 96.	A 14 d 66 20.	10 am	To form E Battery
A	PF 1.	A 14 d 36 60.	= ditto =	10-30 am	
A	V. 55.	A 20 b 90.71	= ditto =	11. am	
A	V 56.	A 20 b 91.79.	= ditto =	11-20 a	
A	VH8	A 26 b 55.31.	No change	–	
A	VH7	A 26 b 35.11	ditto	–	
B	A. Battery	G 3 a. 30 40.	G 2 b. 32 14.	10 am	To form "B" Battery
B	W. Battery	G 9 a 60.90.	No change	–	" " "A" "
C	2 guns RESERVE.	ANNEQUIN	A 26 d. 37 25.	9.30 am.	To Man V 13 and V 14
C	"B" Battery	G 2 b 32. 14	A 26 d 37.57	11 am	To form "C" Battery
C	"E" Battery	A 30 c 65.75	No change	–	" " "D" Battery

Secret   Copy No 11.

46th Battalion M.G. Order No 2 A.

Reference 1/10,000 Maps sheets 36.C.NW1 & 36.NW3 and Tracing A issued with M.G. Order 1A dated 11.3.18.

1. The following move and relief will be carried out on the 15th 16th inst.
   1. D Coy will take over D Battery & No 18 position from C Coy on the 16th March.
   2. C Coy will take over 5 Gun Positions from A Coy and 2 from B Coy on the 16th March.
   3. A Coy will take over D Battery & No 11 Position on the 16th March.
   4. D Coy will take over from B Coy remaining Positions on the 11 Mar.
   5. B Coy will move to BEUVRY on completion of relief.

   All details will be arranged between O.C. Companies concerned.

   On completion of the above relief there will be three groups of Machine Guns in the line disposed as follows.

No 1 Group (O.C. Capt Wood. M.C.)

R 59	- 1	Gun
R 57A	- 1	"
R 56	- 1	"
CENTRAL KEEP	- 2	"
R 60	- 1	"
V 44	1	"
V 43	1	
D. BATTERY	4	"
A	4	"
TOTAL	16	Guns

No 2 Group (O.C. Capt Baker M.C.)

F1	- 1	Gun (Firing S.E.)
A 27 3	- 1	"
R 63	- 1	"
R 62	- 1	"
R 61	- 1	
V 48	- 1	
V 47	1	
C BATTERY	4	
ANNEQUIN LOCALITY	4	
CAMBRIN	"	
Total	16	Guns

P.T.O.

No 3. Group (O.C. Capt Nurse M.C.)

F2 – 1 Gun
R66 " 2 "
F1 " 2 "
V52 " 1 "
V51 " 1 "
E BATTERY 4 "
D " 4 "
CAMBRIN. 18 1 "
TOTAL 16 Guns

3. All maps, stores, ammunition, fighting lamps etc. will be handed over.

4. Completion of reliefs will be notified to Battalion Hqrs. by the Code word "LION"

5. Acknowledge.

13.3.18

[signature]
Capt Adjutant
46 Battalion M.G. Corps

Distribution.
Copy No.

1 A Coy
2 B
3 C
4 D
5 46 Division
6 137 Bde
7 138
8 139
9 Signal Officer
10 File
11 War Diary

SECRET

Copy No......12.

46th. BATTALION M.G.ORDER No 1.A. 11th. March 1918.

Reference 1/10,000 Maps sheets 36c N.W.1. and 36c N.W.3. and Tracing A. (attached).

1. Dispositions. The Machine Guns of Companies in the line will be disposed at 12 noon tomorrow as shown on attached table
Changes from present positions will be carried out at the times stated.

2. Tasks Guns will be allotted tasks as follows:-
Forward Guns.

(a) Direct or Indirect fire in front of selected Infantry Posts in the Front Line.
Details of this task will be issued later.

(b) Direct fire to form a screen between the Front and Reserve Lines in the event of a penetration of the Front Line.
This task is shown on Tracing A.

Rear Guns.

(a) Indirect Fire to provide a S.O.S. Barrage on selected localities in front of our Front Line.

(b) Direct or Indirect Fire to engage targets of opportunity in the event of a hostile penetration.

(c) Direct fire to form a screen between the Reserve and VILLAGE LINES" as shown on Tracing A.
Temporary tasks for (a) and (b) will be arranged by each Group Commander in accordance with the wishes of the Brigade Commander, until further instructions are received.

3. Reserve Guns. The two positions in the CAMBRIN and four positions in the ANNEQUIN LOCALITIES respectivily will continue to be manned by "C" Company.
The O.C. "C" Coy will acquaint the Officers Commanding these localities as to dispositions and tasks.

4. Ammunition. Reference Para 2:-
Forward Guns.
7. Belt boxes per gun for task (a).
7 " " " " " (b).
5 Boxes of S.A.A. per gun.
Rear Guns.
7. Belt boxes per gun for task (a).
2 Belts in S.A.A. boxes " " (a).
7 Belt boxes per gun for tasks (b) and (c).
15 Boxes of S.A.A. per gun.

5. Water and Oil. 4 Gallons of water, and ½ pint of Lubricating oil will be provided for each rear gun.

6. Grenades. 2. Boxes Mills Grenades at each Forward position
4. Per Battery of Rear Guns.

7. A.P. Ammunition. Armour piercing ammunition will be allotted to the following positions.:-
R.66F1., S 12 guns in vicinity of PARK LANE
R.63. R.62. R 59. R. 57 A. CENTRAL KEEP "A" Battery "B" Battery. "D" Battery.

8. Completion of moves will be reported to Battn Hqs By the word "PASSED".

9. ACKNOWLEDGE.

B.H. McBain
CAPT and ADJUTANT.
46th. Battn.M.G.Corps.

ISSUED at 4 Coys + 46. 5.15 PM
Other 8.25 PM

Distribution.

Copy No 1. XX 1ith. Battalion.
2. 55th "
3. A. Coy.
4. B. Coy.
5. C. Coy.
6. D. Coy.
7. 46th. Division.
8. 137th . Bde.
9. 138th Bde.
10. 139th Bde.
11. FILE.
12. War Diary.

SECRET
TRACING B.

1:10,000 LA BASSÉE AND LOOS.

Identification Trace for use with Artillery Maps.

COPIES TO A COY.
" " B "
" " C "
" " D "
" " R.A. AND FILE.

14 15 16

B
C
D

20 21 22

V47 & V48
V43 & V44
A
E

A

26 27 28

D
V 47 & V48
V43 & V44

C

C
B

2 3 4

NOTE.—(1). These traces are intended to facilitate the communication of information as to the position of targets, which have been located on a squared map.

(2). The squares on this trace are 500 yards in length on the 1/10,000 scale, 1,000 yards in length on the 1/20,000 scale, and 2,000 yards in length on the 1/40,000 scale.

(3). The squares on the trace are fitted to the squares of the map showing the targets, which are then drawn on the trace. Sufficient letters and numbers must also be added to enable the recipient to place the trace in the correct position on his own map. A little detail may also be traced, but this is not essential. The name and scale of the map to which the trace refers must be always given. The trace can be used for the 1/10,000, 1/20,000, or 1/40,000 scale.

G.S.G.S. 3025.

═══ S.O.S. BARRAGE AT PRESENT AVAILABLE.

NOTE:- IN CASE OF A GENERAL ATTACK.

'B' FIRES SOUTH. | 'C' FIRES NORTH. | 'D' FIRES SOUTH.
'V43' 'V44' } " NORTH. | 'V47' 'V48' } " " | 'E' " "

Tracing taken from Sheet ....

of the 1 .... *map of* ....

Signature .... *Date* ....

46 M.G/T.102

SECRET

COPY NO. 8

46th. DIVISIONAL MACHINE GUN SCHEME.

(Reference ~~Map A~~ tracing 'A' issued also tracing 'B' attached.)

The Machine Gun Defence of the Divisional Sector is organized as follows:-

Forward Guns 1. (a) Forward Guns are allotted to definite Battle positions to form a screen between the Front and Reserve Lines in the event of a penetration of the Front Line. These tasks are carried out by direct fire.

(b) In addition to the role described in the preceeding paragraph, S.O.S Lines will be laid down for all Guns so as to cover selected positions of the Front as close as possible to our Front Line.

These tasks will be carried out by direct or indirect fire, the lines of fire passing obliquely between posts in the Front Line.

These lines will be laid in order to supplement the Artillery Barrage in case of raids or minor attacks.

These tasks can only be performed if the conditions described in Part I S.S.192, Section 26, paras 3,4,5, and 6 exist.

When tasks in (b) above have been arranged by Group Commanders, the lines of fire will be tested by firing on them by day.

The fire will be observed from that ~~position~~ portion of the Front Line it is intended to cover.

O.C. Forward Guns will inform Infantry Battalion Commanders concerned that the test is being carried out. The Infantry Company Commander on whose Front the S.O.S. line is laid must then accompany the O.C. Forward Guns so as to satisfy himself where the fire is directed and from what direction it comes.

Directors or other devices must be provided for each Gun to assist Machine Gun sentries in recognizing the S.O.S. signal on the Company front they are covering. These directors will be fixed a few yards from the Gun and be laid on the S.O.S. rocket stands of the Company the Machine Gun is to cover.

Group Commanders will make themselves acquainted with all Infantry posts in the Front Line, and any alterations which may take place from time to time in the position of these posts, as changes in these posts may demand changes in ~~the~~ S.O.S. Lines.

It is of the utmost importance that all Forward Guns should be warned of all raids, otherwise Guns from an adjacent Front might fire on their S.O.S. lines into one of our own raiding parties. The Forward Machine Gun Officer is responsible for the ~~co-ordination~~ communication of this information to his Group Commander for transmission to neighbouring groups,

Forward Guns will open on their S.O.S. lines in case of heavy shelling on the Front ~~Line~~ they are covering, except when notice of a raid or attack to be carried out by us on that front has been received.
Traversing stops and electric lamps will be used to maintain the requisite direction and elevation.
Atmospheric corrections (Part II S.S. 192) must be carefully studied and applied, especially those affecting deflections.

Rear Guns. 2. The Rear Guns are organized in Batteries, and are sited to perform the following tasks:-

(a) To form a screen between the Reserve and VILLAGE Lines in the event of the former being penetrated.
(b) To provide an Indirect S.O.S. Barrage coordinated with the Artillery to disorganize an enemy attack by engaging it in its origin.
(c) To engage targets of opportunity in the event of a hostile penetration by direct or indirect fire.

In order to carry out task (b) each Battery has been allotted one switch to meet the case of an attack on our portion of the Divisional Front.
In the case of a general attack Batteries have been given orders to fire as shewn on ~~Map A~~ × Tracing B. These S.O.S. lines will not be changed without reference to O.C. M.G. Battalion.
Each Gun in a Battery will be provided with a lamp and posts to enable fire to be opened by night with the minimum of delay and greatest degree of accuracy.
The O.C. Rear Guns is responsible that fire is opened on S.O.S. or in the case of heavy firing on the front his guns are covering.
To enable this to be done independently of telephonic communication, the O.C. Rear Guns will arrange for an observation post to be established from which the S.O.S. signal can be seen, and relayed to his ~~Battalion~~ Batteries.
All S.O.S. lines will be tested periodically by the Group Commander and the time taken to open fire noted.
In order to perform task (c) O.C. Rear Guns, Battery Commanders, and Group Commander will prepare " Fighting Maps"(Part II S.S. 192)

3.
Stores and Equipment at Gun Positions.

Every Machine Gun Position will be provided with the following in addition to the usual equipment and stores :-

(1) An Order Board defining clearly the action of the Gun numbers on S.O.S. and in case of a bombardment of the Front Line, Also orders regarding change from S.O.S. to Direct Lines.
(2) A range card shewing S.O.S. line and direct line, each being clearly marked for direction and elevation.
(3) A night firing lamp per gun (These will be provided later for Forward Guns).

(4) Ammunition.

Forward Guns.

7 Belt Boxes per gun for task (b)
7 " " " " " " (a)
5 S.A.A. Boxes per gun reserve.

Rear Guns.

7 Belt Boxes per gun for task (b)
2 Belts in S.A.A. Boxes" " (b)
7 Belt Boxes per gun for task (a) and (c)
15 S.A.A. Boxes per gun reserve.

(5) Water and Oil.

For Rear Guns. 4 gallons of water and ½ pint of lubricating oil per gun.

Drill 4. To ensure guns firing when and where required, all duties must be carefully rehearsed as a drill, Hours for this will be laid down in the daily programme for each Battery or Gun position.

C. C. Hewitt.

LIEUT COLONEL.
Commanding,
46th, Battalion M.G.Corps.

15-3-18.

Copies issued
1 46th Division
2 A. Coy
3 B. "
4 C. "
5 D. "
6. File.
7 War Diary

SECRET.

COPY NO. 9

46th BATTALION MACHINE GUN CORPS ORDER NO. 3A

~~[illegible]~~.

1. Rear Guns will open fire as under on receipt of the following calls, in place of or in addition to S.O.S. rockets, or heavy bombardments.

(a) S.O.S. HOHENZOLLERN.
ATTACK HOHENZOLLERN

B. Battery on Right switch.
C. " " " "
D. " " " "
V.47 and V.48 " "
V.43 and V.44 " "

(b) S.O.S. CAMBRIN.
ATTACK CAMBRIN.

A. Battery on Left switch.
E. " " Right "
V.47 and V.48 Left "
V.43 and V.44 " "

(c) S.O.S. CUINCHY.
ATTACK CUINCHY.

B. Battery on Left switch.
C. " " " "
D. " " " "

NOTE :- A. Battery will fire on Right switch in accordance with instructions already received, on Right Brigade Front of Division on our right.
Instructions as regards Left switch of E. Battery will be issued later.

2. Acknowledge.

[signature]
LIEUT COLONEL.
COMMANDING
46th BATTALION M.G.CORPS.

17-8-18.

Copies issued to,

1. 46 ~~[illegible]~~.
2. 11th Battn M.G.C.
3. 55th " " " "
4. A. Coy.
5. B. Coy.
6. C. Coy.
7. D. Coy.
8. File.
9. War Diary.

Relief

SECRET. Copy No....2.....

46th Btn.M.G.Corps,Order No 4.A.

Reference 1/10,000 Maps sheet 36.c.N.W.1.and 36.c.N.W.3. and tracing G.(attached).

1. Relief. 'B' Coy will relieve 'A' Coy in the line on the 24th March.

2. Duties. The O.C. 'B'Coy will take over the duties of O.C. No 3 Group on the 24th March and will arrange for relief of Forward and Rear Gun Officers within the Group.

3. Positions. The positions and tasks to be taken over will be as shewn on the attached tracing marked 'G' which cancels tracings A & B issued with order 1 A dated 11th inst. and 46.M.G./102 dated 15th inst.

4. Stores etc. All maps, stores, ammunition, night firing lamps, etc will be handed over to 'B' Coy. Receipts will be obtained.

5. Billetting. 'A' Coy will report at once to Battn H.Q. what number of Billets are required under headings 1.Officers, 2 N.C.O's, 3 O.Ranks. A list of Billets to be occupied will then be issued.

6. Report. Completion of the relief in the line will be wired to Battn.H.Q. by the code word "READY"

7. Acknowledge.

Lieut-Colonel.

Commanding 46th Bn.M.G.Corps.

Distribution.
1. 46th Division
2. C.R.E.
3. 137 Infy Bgde.
4. 138 Infy Bgde
5. 139 Infy Bgde
6. Signalling Officer
7. A. Coy
8. B "
9. C "
10. D. "
11. 55th Btn.M.G.C.(without tracing)
12. File
13. War Diary.

Issued at:- 10.0 P.M.

23.3.18.

SECRET. Copy No....12....

46th Btn.M.G.Corps, Order No 4.A.

Reference 1/10,000 Maps sheet 36.c. N.W.1.and 36.c.N.W.3. and tracing G.(attached).

1. Relief. 'B' Coy will relieve 'A Coy' in the line on the 24th March.

2. Duties. The O.C. 'B'Coy will take over the duties of O.C.No 3 Group on the 24th March and will arrange for relief of Forward and Rear Gun Officers within the Group.

3. Positions. The positions and tasks to be taken over will be as shown on the attached tracing marked 'G' which cancels tracings A & B issued with order 1 A dated 11th inst. and 46.M.G./102 dated 15th inst.

4. Stores etc. All maps, stores, ammunition, night firing lamps, etc will be handed over to 'B'Coy. receipts will be obtained.

5. Billetting. 'A' Coy will report at once to Battn H.Q. what number of Billets are required under headings 1.Officers, 2.N.C.O's, 3.O.Ranks. A list of Billets to be occupied will then be issued.

6. Report. Completion of the relief in the line will be wired to Battn.H.Q. by the code word "READY".

7. Acknowledge.

C. C. Stewitt.

Lieut-Colonel.

Commanding 46th Bn.M.G.Corps.

Distribution.

1. 46th Division.
2. C.R.E.
3. 137 Infy Bgde.
4. 138 Infy Bgde.
5. 139 Infy Bgde.
6. Signalling Officer
7. A. Coy
8. B, Coy
9. C, "
10. D. "
11. 35th Btn.M.G.C.(without tracing)
12. File
13. War Diary.

Issued at:- 10.0 P.M.

23.3.18

SECRET. Copy No. 6

46th BATTALION MACHINE GUN ORDER No 5.A. 1/20.000 GORRE

1. Until further orders the Company in Reserve will be held in readiness to move at ½ hours notice. All limbers (including S.A.A.) belonging to this Company will be packed seperately to the remainder.
The remaining S.A.A. limbers will be packed in readiness for an immediate move.

2. The Officer Commanding the Reserve Company will detail 1 Officer and 1 N.C.O. to reconnoitre gun positions and routes thereto as follows :-

   A. Position for 2 guns at L.4.C.04
   B. Position for 2 guns at F.27.B.73
   C. Position for 2 guns at F.21.D.99
   D. Position for 2 guns at Le Preol Locality.

   The lines of fire for these guns are shewn on attached tracing. 'H'

3. The Quartermaster will arrange for 10 boxes of ammunition and 2 gallons of water to be stored at positions.

4. The Signalling Officer will arrange and prepare for communication to be established.

5. On the word "Action"being received from these Headquarters:-
   (a) The Company will fall in on its "alarm post" which will be situated clear of BEUVRY and marched to the Transport lines at F.20 Central.
   On arrival the Subsections detailed to man positions A, B, and C, and D, will move off to their allotted positions using limbers or pack animals according to the situation.
   The remainder of the Company will stand by and await further orders.
   (b) The Transport Officer will at once have all animals harnessed up in stables but not hooked in.
   (c) The Q.M. will be prepared to issue at once 2 days rations.
   (d) Those men doing elementary course will fall in at F.20 Central.

6. Acknowledge.

Issued at:- 8 15 PM

J Harington Lieut-Colonel.

24/3/18. Commanding 46th Battn.M.G.Corps.

Copies to
1. A. Coy
2. Q.M
3. T.O.
4. Signalling Officer
5. File
6. War Diary
7. 46th Division
8. Lt Robinson
9

Issued only to 'A' Coy

46th Div

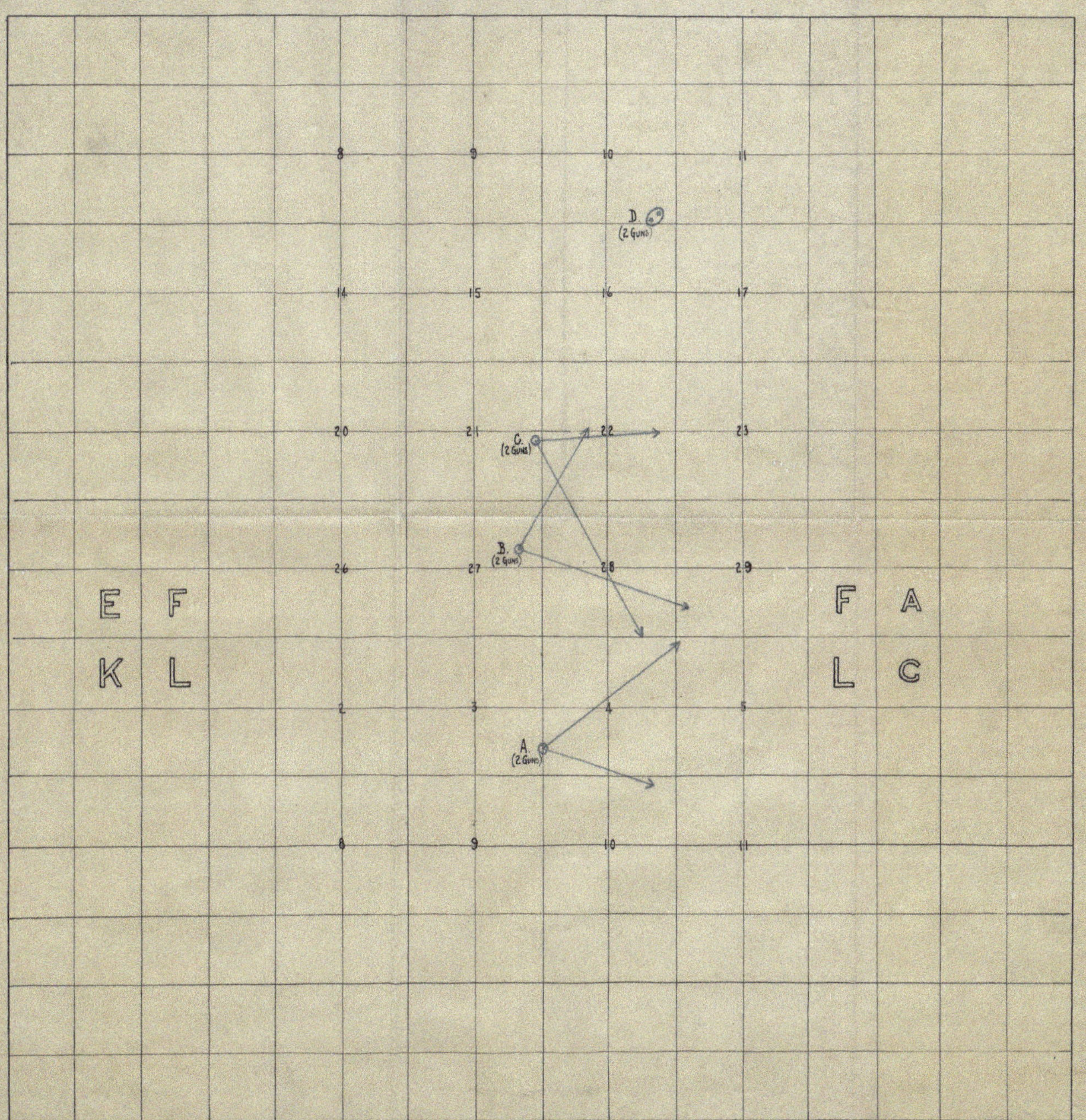

SCALE 1/20,000.
GORRE
SECRET TRACING H.
D. (2 GUNS)
C. (2 GUNS)
B. (2 GUNS)
A. (2 GUNS)
E F
K L
F A
L C

S E C R E T

Copy No 11

48th Battn. MACHINE GUN CORPS ORDER No.7.A.

Reference 48/M.G.B57. All preparatory action so as to be ready to move tonight in case of necessity will be taken forthwith; this will include the following items:-

1. Handing over certificates will be prepared.

2. Officers Kits will be packed and ready to be put on limbers immediately the order is given.

3. Apart from the item in 2, all limbers will be packed with the exception of any items, stores etc required in the line or required for actual use in the Transport lines, Coy Offices etc.

4. Each Company will notify the Transport Officer what limbers are required to convey stores etc which cannot be collected until the relief is definitely ordered. The Transport Officer will have these wagons parked separately by Coys, drivers detailed, horses harnessed up in stables but not hooked in so there is no delay in moving to collect when ordered.

5. The Q.M. Stores will also be packed to move. The dump for surplus stores, if any will be at F.20 Central. In case this is used details of the items dumped and the exact location of the dump will be submitted at once.

6. The M.O. will arrange direct with the Transport Officer re the Maltese cart will be in readiness to move as above.

7.A. Should the order to carry out the relief be given, Coys would move in order "Action expected". – when relief completed.

B. The men on course under Lieut. Robinson would move with Hqrs.

8. The above is merely a preparatory warning of action that will be taken so as to ensure the relief be carried out smoothly and correctly. Guides will be detailed.

9. Acknowledge by wire.

Issued at :- 11.45 am

[illegible] Capt. & Adjt: for

Lieut-Colonel.

25/9/18

Commanding 48th M.G. Corps. (Battn)

Distribution:-

Copy No 1. A. Coy
2. B. "
3. C. "
4. D. "
5. T.O.
6. Q.M.
7. M.O.
8. Lieut. Robinson
9. File
10.)
11.) War Diary.

SECRET

Copy No 6.

46th Battn Machine Gun Order No 6A.

With reference to 46th Bn M G Corps Order No 5 A and amendment issued under 46 MG/359 d/- 25.3.18

Letter No 46 MG/359 d/- 25.3.18 is cancelled and the following issued to substitute para 1 of Order 5A

1 All troops in billets will be held in readiness to move at one hours notice

2. All first line Transport will be held in readiness to move at 2 hours notice. All limbers (including S.A.A limbers) of the Company in Reserve will be parked separately to the remainder

3. Acknowledge

R. Dickens.

Capt & Adjt

46th Bn M G Corps

Issued at - 6.15 p.m.
25/3/18

Distribution To all recipients of Order 5 A and 46 MG/359

SECRET

COPY NO 6

46 MG/359.

To/
1 A Coy
2 QM
3 T O
4 Signalling Officer
5. File
6 War Diary
7 46th Division
8 Lt Robinson.

Amendment to 46 Batt. MG Order No 5a. issued 24.3.18.

1/ Delete para 1 & substitute. Para 1. Until further orders the Coy in reserve will be held in readiness to move at 2 hours notice.

All limbers (including SAA limbers) belonging to this Coy will be parked seperately to the remainder.

All S.A.A. limbers will be packed in readiness to move as above

Issued at :-
12 30 pm

25.3.18.

[signature]
Capt & Adjutant
46 Batt. M G Corps

March Table issued with 46th Btn: M.G. Corps Order No. 11.

COY.	Starting point	Time	Route
B.	ROAD JUNCTION at:-	1.30 P.M.	Cross Roads L.3.C 10.60
			NOEUX-LES-MINES.
C	F 26. B 35.95	1.45 "	BRACQUEMENT.
			Cross Roads PETIT SAINS.
D	=	2.0 "	-"- L.28.A 90.35
	ditto		Road Junction L 28.C 45.75
A		2.15 "	Cross Roads L 34 B 55 50
	=		
H.Q.	F 13. D 10.80	2.30 "	LES BREUIS.

Arrangements will be made for teas to be prepared on the march.

Companies will move off at 200x interval between

Coy. H.Q. and each section which interval will be maintained

27.3.1918

SECRET

COPY NO 6

46th Battn MGC Order No 10

1. Orders 5A & 6A still apply to A Coy whilst A Coy is in this area

2. B C & D Coys will be held in readiness to move at one hours notice.

3. All Transport will be held in readiness to move at 2 hours notice. All Limbers (including SAA Limbers) will be packed in readiness.

4. Men may be issued with one Blanket if necessary arrangements are made and instructions issued.
The remaining blankets will be rolled in bundles of 10

5. Please acknowledge at once

Issued at 9.30 pm.

[illegible]
Capt Adjutant
46th Battn MGC

27 3 18

Distribution

Copy 1 A Coy
2 B "
3 C "
4 D "
5 TO & QM.
6 War Diary
~~7 [illegible]~~
7

Seen [illegible] 27/3/18

SECRET

Copy No 9

46th Battalion M.G.C. Order No 9A

Reference 1/20,000 GORRE

In continuation orders Nos 7A & 8A

1. Reliefs. A. The relief of 'B' Coy by 55th Battn M.G.C. and 'C' & 'D' Coys by 11th Battn M.G.C. will be completed by 6 a.m. tomorrow 28th inst.

B. All emplacements and all stores therein including those emplacements and positions not actually being taken into use by 11th & 55th Battn M.G.C. will be handed over.

C. 'A' Coy will hand over to 55th Battn M.G.C. the following positions and all stores etc therein:-

A	Position at	L.A.c.	02.35	for 2 guns
B	" "	F.27 b	70.30	" 2
C	" "	F.21 d	80.52	" 1 "
		F.21 d	90.90	" 1
D	" "	F.10 d	52.07	" 1
		F.10 d	45.12	" 1 "

2. Notification Completion of reliefs and handing over will be wired to these H.Q. by code word 'FINISH'

3. Reports Receipts for all stores rations A.P., S.A.A. and S.A.A. etc etc handed over duly completed will be submitted to these H.Q. as soon as possible after reliefs are completed

It will also be stated what positions have been handed over -

Under 'A' on being relieved by guns of 11th & 55th Bn M.G.C.

Under 'B' M.G. Emplacements or positions handed over only

Great care must be taken in handing over rations & all other details

4. Guns The 2 Guns of 'A' Coy at present with 'B' Coy will be returned to 'A' Coy when relief completed

5. Billeting Orders will be issued later

6. Acknowledge

R. Dickens.
Capt & Adjt
46th Bn M.G. Corps

Issued at:-
27/5/18

Distribution
1 A Coy
2 B "
3 C "
4 D Coy
5 11th Bn M.G.C.
6 55th "
7 [illegible]
8 War Diary
9 "
10 [illegible]

SECRET

11th Batt. M.G. Order No. 8 A — Copy No 8.

(Warning Order)

Ref [illegible] GORRE.

1 Relief (a) C & D Coys will be relieved in the line tomorrow 13/14 inst by one company of the 11th Batt. M.G. Corps.

The following ~~guns~~ positions only will be taken over by the 11 Batt. M.G. Corps.

(b) From C Coy
[illegible] A. C. Battery (4 guns)

(c) From D Coy
R60, R59, R57a R56 Central Keep (4 guns) A. Battery (4 guns)

(d) B Coy will be relieved by the 55 Batt. M.G.C. Details will be issued later

2 Guides 11 Batt. M.G.C. will arrange direct with O.C. C & D Companies regarding guides.

3 Trench Stores
Receipts for all trench stores [illegible] M.G. emplacements [illegible] S.A.A. Maps [illegible] will be [illegible] with receipts [illegible] H.Q.

4 Notification.
Completion of relief will be notified to H.Q. by the code word FINISH.

5 Further Orders
Further Orders will be issued later.

6 Acknowledge

B. [illegible]
Capt & Adjt.
41 Battalion M.G. Corps

26-3-18

Issued at -

Copies to 1 ar 27.3.18.

No 1. A Coy
2 B
3 C
4 D
5 41 Battn. M.G.C.
6 File
7 War Diary
8

SECRET. COPY No: 9

No. 46. Btn. M.G. Corps Order No. 11.

Reference 1/20.000 GORRE and ST NAZAIRE RIVER.

1. MOVE. A. The Battalion will move from BEUVRY to LES BREBIS tomorrow 28th March. B. March Table is attached.

C. Companies will move by sections complete with limbers Coy: H.Q.rs will move separately.

D. Battn. H.Q. and the men on course under Lt. Robinson will move separately in 2 parties at 200^x interval.

2. BAGGAGE. The Transport Officer will arrange for G.S. Wagons or Coy: H.Q. Limbers to do a double journey if required.

3. BILLETING. A billeting party of 1 Officer, 1 NCO, 1 Transport NCO, and 3 men (bicycles) per Coy: will report to the Second in Command at Transport lines F.20. Central at 9.30 A.M. tomorrow ready to proceed to LES BREBIS. Full kits and haversack rations will be carried. Billeting parties will meet sections at L 35. A. 20.20 on arrival to conduct to Billets and lines.

4 CERTIFICATE. Coys. QM and T.O. will render a certificate by 6.0 P.M. 28th. that all Billets and Latrines and Offices ^vacated^ at BEUVRY have been left clean, and that apart from items notified, if any, no damages are for reporting. The T.O. will include in the certificate rendered by him that all horse and wagon lines have been left clean.

5 REPORTS. On arrival at LES BREBIS Coys QM & TO will notify H.Q. of their location and Coys. will detail a runner with kit to report to Btn: H.Q.

6. H.Q. Battn. H.Q. will close at BEUVRY 2.30 P.M. 28th. and will open at LES. BREBIS same time.

7. Acknowledge.

Blickson. Capt: & Adjt:
46th: Btn: M.G. Corps.

Issued at 7.0 A.M. 28.3.18

Copies to:-

1. 46th Div
2. A Bty
3. B -
4. C -
5. D -
6. Q.M. & T.O.
7. War Diary
8. File
9. C.O.

SECRET

COPY NO. 10

46th BATTALION M. G. CORPS ORDER NO 12.

REF. 1/20,000 ST NAZAIRE RIVER.

28th MARCH 1918.

1 MOVE The Battalion moved from BEUVRY to LES BREBIS this day to take over the line from the 4th Canadian M.G. Batt.

2 RELIEFS.

'D' Coy will take over LENS Section from 16th Canadian M.G. Coy
'C' " " " " ST. EMILE " " 10th "
'D' " " " " HILL 70 " " 11th "
8 Guns 'A' Coy " " " " " 12th "

Verbal orders have been issued regarding these reliefs.

3/ GROUPS.

'B' Coy is designated No 1 Group.
'C' " " " " 2 "
'D' Coy with
8 Guns 'A' Coy " " 3 "

4 REPORTS. A copy of inventory of all trench and area stores, ammunition, maps, schemes, photographs Instructions, etc etc. taken over will be submitted to these Hqs.

5 NOTIFICATION Completion of reliefs will be notified to these Hqs by Group Commanders by the Code word 'PURPLE'.

6 DISPOSITIONS Group Commanders will submit as early as possible the map location of the disposition of the Guns.

7 ACKNOWLEDGE

Issued at 9 am

29. 3. 18.

[signature]
Capt Adjt.
46 Batt. M.G. Corps.
(Sgd 29. 3. 18).

P.T.O.

Distribution

Copy No	1	46 Division
	2	4th Canadian Div
	3	A Coy
	4	B "
	5	C "
	6	D "
	7	137 Inf Bde
	8	138 " "
	9	139 " "
	10	File
	11	} War Diary
	12	}
	13	Signalling Officer
	14	QM/TO/MO.

Tracing "G" will follow.

SECRET   Copy No 1

46th Battn M. G. Corps Order No 13

1. Reliefs. On the night 1/2 April 'A' Coy will relieve 'C' Coy in the line on the ST. EMILE Sector and reliefs in the following order will take place.
   (a) The 8 guns of 'A' Coy at present in reserve will relieve 8 guns of 'C' Coy in the ST. EMILE Sector.
   (b) The 8 guns of 'C' Coy thus relieved will relieve 8 guns of 'A' Coy now under the Command of O.C. No 3 Group in the HILL 70 Sector and will come under the Command of O.C. No 3 Group.
   (c) The 8 guns of 'A' Coy thus relieved ~~and~~ will then relieve the 8 remaining guns of 'C' Coy in the ST. EMILE Sector
   (d) The 8 guns of 'C' Coy thus relieved and 'C' Coy H.Q. will then move into Billets in LES BREBIS

2 Details. All further details will be arranged between O.C. Groups & Coy concerned

3. Billets. The O.C. 'C' Coy will notify these H.Q. at once the number of (1) Officers (2) N.C.Os (3) Other Ranks that will require to be billeted under para 1 (d) when billet will be arranged and notified, and, if necessary guides can be made available at Battalion H.Q.

4. Notification. Relief will be completed by 6 a.m. on April 2nd and communicated to Battn H.Q. by the code word "SEPIA"

5. Acknowledge

Issued at:- 1.0 pm

B. [illegible]
Capt & Adjt
46th Battn M. G. Corps

31/3/18

P. T. O.

W A R   D I A R Y.
****

46th BATTALION MACHINE GUN CORPS.

APRIL 1918.

****

Army Form C. 2118.

WAR DIARY

or

~~INTELLIGENCE SUMMARY~~

(Erase heading not required.)

46th BATTALION MACHINE GUN CORPS.

Instructions regarding War Diaries and Intelligence Summaries are contained in F. S. Regs., Part II. and the Staff Manual respectively. Title Pages will be prepared in manuscript.

APRIL 1918.

No 1.

Place	Date	Hour	Summary of Events and Information ST NAZAIRE RIVER 1/20,000 LOOS 36 c.N.W. 1/10,000 GORRE 1/20,000. LACOUTURE 1/20,000 LENS 11. 1/100,000 HAZEBROUCK 5 A. 1/100,000	Remarks and references to Appendices
LES BREBIS.	1st.	7.a.m.	Order No 14 issued; (copy attached) 2 other ranks evacuated(sick) M.Gs fired 2,500 rounds on enemy communications.	Order No 14.
	2nd.		2 M.Gs damaged by shell fire. 1 unrepairable, 1 will be repaired by Battalion Armourer. 4 reserve Guns movedinto MOROC, 60 guns in the line. M.Gs fired 8,500 rounds on enemy's tracks in N.3.c.	
	3rd.		As all guns in line but 4, started a two days rest in billets in LES BREBIS for 1 Officer and 25 men per Company. 67 Recruits from Infantry, after three weeks course, posted to Companies, 1 other rank evacuated (sick), 2 M.Gs damaged by shell fire, 1 returned unrepairable. M.G.s fired 3,250 rounds on enemy's dumps, tracks, C.Ts, etc.,	
	4th.		Tracing "A" issued (copy attached), 1 N.C.O. rejoined after evacuation Letter No M.50 issued (copy attached) 1 O.R. evacuated (sick) 1 O.R. reinforcement M.Gs fired 12,000 rounds harassing fire.	Tracing "A" Letter M.50
	5th.		M.Gs fired 10,000 rounds harassing fire on enemy's communications.	
	6th.		Lieut.L.F.BOURNE wounded at duty, 1 O.R. wounded at duty. M.Gs fired 3,500 rounds in conjunction with our Gas projection.	
		11.35 a.m.	2/Lieut H.W.RUDLAND reported to have brought down an enemy plane,which was flying low over our lines at about N.2.d.	
	7th.		2 O.Rs evacuated (sick) M.Gs fired 7,000 rounds on roads and tracks.	
	8th.		4 M.Gs placed in defended locality positions making 64 guns in the line. 1 O.R. reinforcement, 1 O.R. evacuated (sick), 4 O.Rs wounded (GAS) M.Gs fired 7,000 rounds harassing fire. Lieut.R.H.PEACOCK posted to 37th Battalion Machine Gun Corps as Adjutant, 1 O.R. struck off as Batman to Lieut.PEACOCK.	
		5.0 pm.	Order No 16 issued (copy attached)	Order No 16.

2449 Wt. W14957/M90 750,000 1/16 J.B.C. & A. Forms/C.2118/12.

Army Form C. 2118.

WAR DIARY

Instructions regarding War Diaries and Intelligence Summaries are contained in F. S. Regs., Part II. and the Staff Manual respectively. Title pages will be prepared in manuscript.

APRIL 1918. ~~INTELLIGENCE SUMMARY~~ 46th BATTALION MACHINE GUN CORPS.

(Erase heading not required.)

No 2.

Place	Date	Hour	Summary of Events and Information ST NAZAIRE RIVER 1/20,000 LOOS 36 c.N.W. 1/10,000 GORRE 1/20,000. LACOUTURE 1/20,000. LENS 11. 1/100,000 HAZEBROUCK 5 A. 1/100,000	Remarks and references to Appendices
LES BREBIS.	9th.		M.Gs fired 9,000 rounds on to C.Ts, roads, etc. 1 O.R. reinforcement. 1 O.R. to Base under age. R.Q.M.S. Smith W.F. to Base Depot. 2 O.Rs wounded in action (Gas)	
		1.p.m.	Order No 15 issued and cancelled same day.	
	10th.		4,000 rounds fired on to Cross roads and C.Ts. Lieut.L.F.BOURNE admitted to Hospital after wounded at duty. 1 O.R. wounded (Gas) 1 O.R. killed in action. 2 O.Rs evacuated (sick) 1 O.R. reinforcement. Lieut A.R.M.DARBY MC reinforcement.	
	11th.		M.Gs fired 4,000 rounds harassing fire, 1 O.R. evacuated (sick)	
		7 a.m.	Order No 17 issued (copy attached)	Order No 17.
		1.45 p.m.	Order No 18 issued (copy attached)	Order No 18.
	12th.		1 O.R. wounded in action 1 O.R. evacuated (sick)	
		4 a.m.	Order No 19 issued (copy attached) Battalion relieved in the line on nights 11/12th and 12/13th April by the 3rd Canadian Machine Gun Battalion (see Order No 17).	Order No 19
BRUAY.	13th		Battalion moved to BRUAY.	
	14th	7 p.m.	Order No 20 issued (copy attached)	Order No 20.
		11.0 p.m.	Order No 21 issued (copy attached)	Order No 21
NOEUX LES MINES	15th		2 O.Rs evacuated (sick) 1 O.R. reinforcement.	
		10.0 a.m	Order No 22 issued (copy attached) Battalion moved to NOEUX LES MINES.	Order No 22
	16th		1 O.R. evacuated (sick)	
	17th		5 O.Rs evacuated (sick)	
	18th	3.30 a.m.	Order No 23 issued (copy attached) Guns in positions stated by 5.30 a.m. 4 O.Rs wounded (Gas) 1 O.R. reinforcement.	Order No 23

(A7092) Wt W12839/M1293 750,000 1/17. D. D. & L., Ltd. Forms/C.2118/14.

Instructions regarding War Diaries and Intelligence Summaries are contained in F. S. Regs., Part II. and the Staff Manual respectively. Title pages will be prepared in manuscript.

Army Form C. 2118.

WAR DIARY

APRIL 1918.

46th BATTALION MACHINE GUN CORPS.

(Erase heading not required.)

No 3.

Place	Date	Hour	Summary of Events and Information ST NAZAIRE RIVER 1/20,000 LENS 11. 1/100,000 LOOS 36 c.N.W. 1/10,000 GORRE 1/20,000. LACOURTURE 1/20,000. HAZEBROUCK 5 A. 1/100,000	Remarks and references to Appendices
NOEUX LES MINES.	19th.		1 O.R. evacuated (sick) 2 O.R. reinforcements.	
	20th.		1 O.R. wounded	
		12.0 noon.	Order No 23 B.issued (copy attached)	Order No 23B
	21st.		1 O.R. reinforcement.	
	22nd.		2 O.Rs evacuated (sick) 1 O.R. reinforcement.	
	23rd.		1 O.R. evacuated (sick)	
		10.0 p.m.	Order No 24 issued (copy attached)	Order No 24.
GOSNAY.	24th.		2 O.Rs reinforcements	
		1.15 a.m.	Order No 24 A.issued (copy attached)	Order No 24A
		11.45 a.m.	Order No 24 B.issued (copy attached) 32 Guns moved into line in ESSARS Sector to relieve 3rd Battalion Machine Gun Corps.	Order No 24B
	25th.		1 O.R. wounded (Gas)	
		10.40 a.m.	Order No 24 C.issued (copy attached)	Order No 24C
		11.30 p.m.	Order No 25 issued (copy attached)	Order No 25
	26th.		1 O.R. wounded (Gas) 2 O.Rs Evacuated (sick)	
		6.0 p.m.	Order No 26 issued (copy attached)	Order No 26
	27th.		1 O.R. wounded 2 O.Rs evacuated (sick) 24 Guns moved into GORRE Sector to relieve 55th Battalion Machine Gun Corps.	
	28th.		6 O.Rs evacuated (sick) 1 O.R. reinforcement.	

(A7092). Wt W12839/M1293 75,0.0. 1/17. D. D. & L., Ltd. Forms/C.2118/14.

Army Form C. 2118.

WAR DIARY

Instructions regarding War Diaries and Intelligence Summaries are contained in F. S. Regs., Part II. and the Staff Manual respectively. Title pages will be prepared in manuscript.

APRIL 1918.

~~INTELLIGENCE SUMMARY~~
(Erase heading not required.)

46th BATTALION MACHINE GUN CORPS.

No 4.

Place	Date	Hour	Summary of Events and Information LENS 11. 1/100,000 HAZEBROUCK 5 A. 1/100,000 GORRE 1/20,000 LACOUTURE 1/20,000	Remarks and references to Appendices
GOSNAY.	29th.		M.Gs fired 4,250 rounds harassing fire between the hours of 10.30 p.m. and 4.30 a.m. 7 O.Rs wounded 1 O.R. wounded at duty 2 O.Rs evacuated (sick)	
	30th.		2 O.Rs evacuated (sick) 1 O.R. rejoined after desertion (Awaiting trial by F.G.C.M.)	

J Harington
Bt.Lieut.Colonel,
Commanding 46th Battn.Machine Gun Corps.

(A7092). Wt W12839/M1293. 75 ,0.0. 1/17. D. D. & L., Ltd. Forms/C.2118/14.

SECRET

COPY No. 1

46 BATTALION M.G.C. ORDER NO 14.

1 Cancel para 1 (d) of 46' Battn MGC. Order No 13 and substitute.

A. The 8 guns of 'C' Coy thus relieved will then be disposed as follows.

B. 4 Guns (of 'C' Coy, as a battery) will join No 3 Group on the HILL 70 Section and will come under the command of O/C No 3 Group.

C. Remaining 4 guns and 'C' Coy Hq will move into Billets in MAROC.

2 The final distribution on April 2nd will be:-

No 1 Group	LENS SECTION	–	16 guns
" 2 "	ST. EMILE "	–	16 "
" 3 "	HILL 70 "	–	28 "
In reserve MAROC		–	4 "

3 The M.G. Limber Wagons for the 4 guns in reserve will move to MAROC April 1st under arrangements to be made by T.O. in direct communication O/C 'C' Coy.

4 The Signalling Officer will arrange for reserve guns Hq. to be in telephone communication with their req. by 6 pm April 1st.

5 Billets for reserve guns at MAROC will be arranged for by O.C. 'C' Coy. direct with Town Major MAROC.

6 All the reliefs and moves referred to in Order No 13, as amended by Order No 14 will be completed by 6 a.m April 2nd.

7 Completion will be notified to Battalion Hq by code word "SEPIA"

8 Acknowledge.

Issued at 7 am.

[signature]
Capt & Adjutant
46 Batt MG Corps.

1. 4. 18.

To all Recipients of Order No 13.

M. 50

O.C. A Coy
O.C. B Coy
O.C. C Coy
O.C. D Coy

War Diary 1 — 2

1. The attention of Coy Commanders is directed to 46th Divisional Letter No. 3121/26/G. dated the 2nd March 1918. (Copies of which were issued to all Coys under 147 dated 4/3/18 and 365 dated 26/3/18) which must be strictly complied with both by Coy Commanders when acting as Group Commanders and by all Officers serving under their Command

2. Group Commanders will in addition to the above mentioned general instructions be responsible for the discipline and the proper carrying out of their duties by all ranks serving under their Command.

3. They will ensure:-

A. That the correct map reference and lines of fire and ranges are given for all guns and batteries in their group.

B. That Section and Gun Commanders are thoroughly conversant with their duties and tasks and carry them out correctly.

C. That the necessary sentries are posted in the proper manner.

D. That order boards are kept at all gun positions.

E. That the proper amount of belt boxes, SAA, water and rations is kept at each emplacement.

F. That teams especially in CHAMPAGNE emplacements are daily practised in mounting the guns. A record of the time taken should be kept.

G. That each dugout occupied by a teams has a sufficient supply of candles and Tommy Cookers. All requirements must be indented for at once.

H. That a daily inspection is made by an Officer of the guns, tripods, and equipment of the teams.

P.T.O

I That the dugout and emplacements are kept clean and in a sanitary condition.

J That the men get their proper rations and that the conditions under which the teams live are made as comfortable as possible, compatible with efficiency.

K That the dress, turn out, clothing, and equipment of the men receives constant attention.

L A chain of responsibility for the guidance of all concerned is attached.

4 Please acknowledge.

Bliken Capt & Adjt

for Lieut - Colonel.

Commanding.

46th Battn MG Corps.

4.4.18.

Secret Tracing A.

LENS & LOOS.

Hill 70 Section.
Provisional M.G. Defense Scheme:-
1. Showing direct lines of fire.
2. S.O.S. Lines of fire.

Identification Trace for use with Artillery Maps.

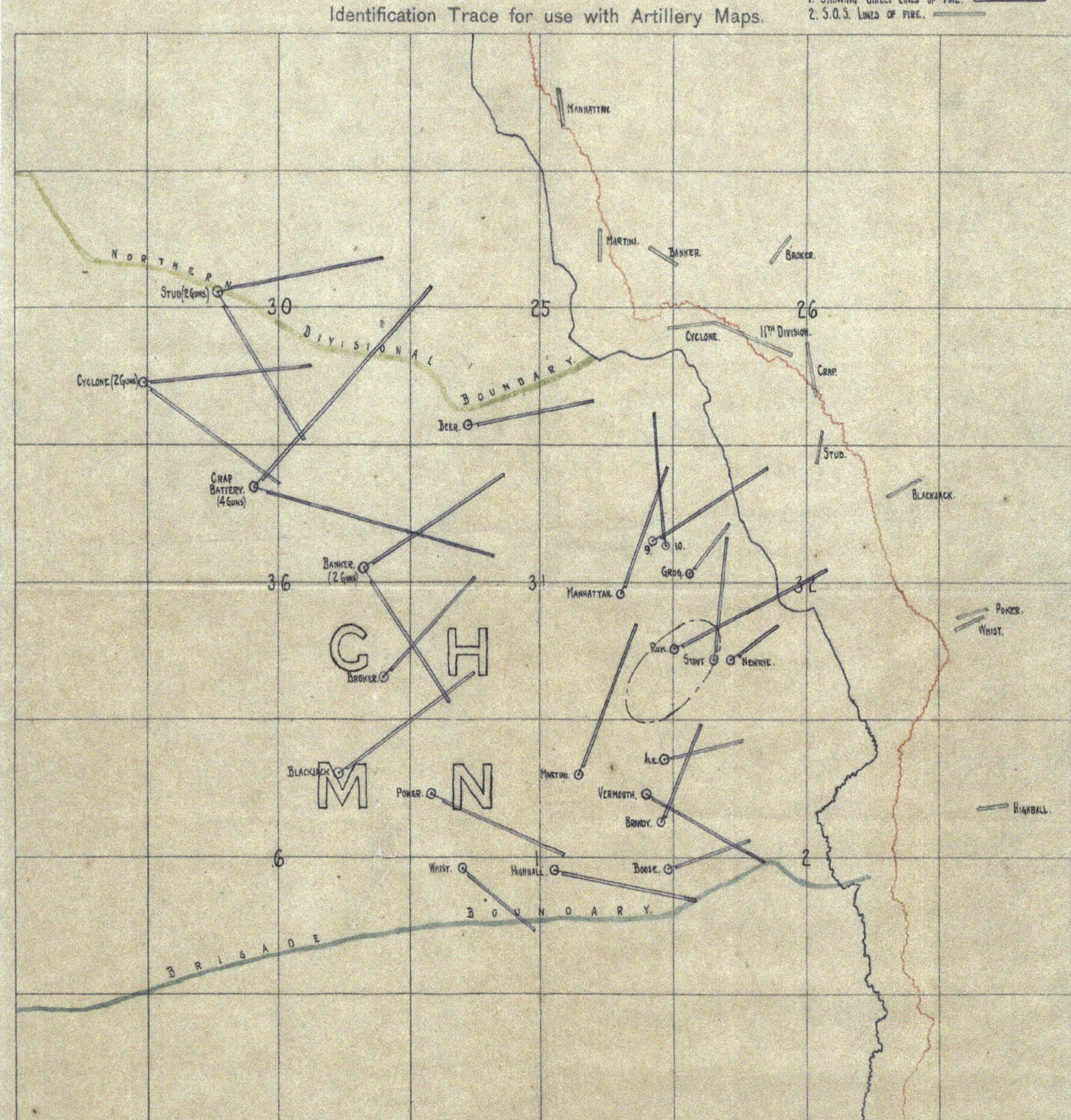

NOTE.—(1). These traces are intended to facilitate the communication of information as to the position of targets, which have been located on a squared map.

(2). The squares on this trace are 500 yards in length on the 1/10,000 scale, 1,000 yards in length on the 1/20,000 scale, and 2,000 yards in length on the 1/40,000 scale.

(3). The squares on the trace are fitted to the squares of the map showing the targets, which are then drawn on the trace. Sufficient letters and numbers must also be added to enable the recipient to place the trace in the correct position on his own map. A little detail may also be traced, but this is not essential. The name and scale of the map to which the trace refers must be always given. The trace can be used for the 1/10,000, 1/20,000, or 1/40,000 scale.

G.S.G.S. 3023.

Tracing taken from Sheet 36c S.W.1. & 36c N.W.3.

of the 1:10,000. map of LENS & LOOS.

Signature .... Date ....

Chain of Responsibility

A. In the line.

O/c Group } to Battalion Commander.
O/c Reserve Guns }

O/c Forward Guns } to Group Commander.
O/c Rear Guns }

O/c Section to O/c Forward or Rear Guns
or Group Commander.

O/c Sub-Sections to Section Commander.

Gun Commanders to Subsection Commander.

B. Out of the line

Coy Commander to Battalion Commander
Section Commanders to Coy Commander.
Gun Commanders to Section Commanders.

/

SECRET   Copy No. 1

46th Battalion Machine Gun Corps Order No 16 (16)

April 8th.1918.

Reference. 1/10,000 LOOS 36.c.N,W.3.

1. 4 Guns of C,Coy now in Divisional Resere will move into the following emplacements.

Position	Location	Remarks.
MATTHEW	G.28.c.95.42	To fire N.E, direction
CROSS POST	G.29.c.10.47	to protect Spur in
HAYSTACK	G.29.a.06.20	G.28.d. and G.28.a & b.
MACKAY	G.34.b.50.92	

2. At each of the above positions the following will be placed forthwith. 10,000 rounds of S.A.A. (over and above the 14 belts) water,2 gallons, Rations, 2 days supply in sealed boxes. The ammunition can be arranged by O.C. No.3 Group from dumps now being cleared. The rations will be demanded. The O,C, 'C'Coy will be responsible that these positions are occupied forthwith.

3. When the guns are in position they will come under the Command of the O.C. No 3 Group.

4. Completion will be notified to Battalion H,Q, by the code word "SPUR"

5. O.C.'C'Coy will reconnoitre positions for the two reserve guns whose positions are now occupied. The emplacements to be reconnoitred are:-
   G.23 location G.27.d.17.93
   G.20A location G.27.d.39.41
   G.20B location G.27.d.31.28

At the two positions selected 10,000 rounds of S.A.A. and 2 gallons of water will be placed.

O.C.'C' Company will report as soon as possible which two positions have been selected and will send in a certificate that the ammunition and water as directed has been placed at these positions.

7. Acknowledge.

Issued at:- 5 p.m.

8/4/1918.

Blicker
Capt.& Adjt.
46th Battn.Machine Gun Corps.

Copies to:-

1.)
2.)War Diary.
3. File
4. C.Coy
5. No 3.Group
6. 138th Inf.Bde.
7. 46th Division.
8. Signalling Officer
9. Q.M.
10. 11th Bn.M.G.C.

SECRET

Copy No. 15

46th BATTALION MACHINE GUN CORPS ORDER No 17

Reference LENS 11 and Secret Map.
In continuation of Warning Order No 16 (Issued only within the Battn.

1. The Battalion is to be relieved in the line by the 3rd Canadian Machine Gun Battalion as follows:-

   LENS Group on night 11/12th April

   HILL 70 " " " 11/12th "
   ST.EMILE " " " 12/13th "

   Details will be arranged in conjunction with O.C. relieving Coys: and Brigade Commander concerned.

2. On relief by 3rd Canadian M.G.Battn completed march table for night 11/12th April will be as follows:-

   'B' Coy (1 Group) will move to AIX NOULETTE
   'C' ")
   'D' ") (3 Group) " " " BRACQUEMONT.

   Transport for night 11/12th will remain as at Present.
   Headquarters " " 11/12th " " " " "
   Men at LES BREBIS in rest will join Coys: when reliefs are completed under arrangements to be made by O.C., Coys:
   Orders for march table, 'A' Coy, ST.EMILE Section for night 12/13th will be issued later.

3. Billetting at BRACQUEMONT and AIX NOULETTE will be arranged by 2/Lt.Smith 1 Officer and 4 other ranks per Company (to be taken from men in rest) will meet 2/Lieut.Smith at Town Major's Office at places stated as follows:-

   'C'Coy)
   'D' ") BRACQUEMONT at 10.30 a.m. April 11th.
   'B' " AIX NOULETTE at 12 noon April 11th.

   Of these details four will be detailed by the Officer i/c respective parties to proceed to their Coy:H.Q. in the line to conduct Coys: by sections or sub-sections to billets when the reliefs is completed.

4. Handing over certificates will be prepared and will in due course be submitted to Battn:H.Q. duly consolidated and completed by an Officer, showing the details handed over, by positions.

5. Signalling equipment in use in the line will be brought away by 'fighting'limbers. It will be divided amongst these limbers and only stored in the rear portions. A signaller will be detailed to each limber concerned under arrangements to be made by the Signalling Officer

6. Company Commanders will arrange direct with Transport Officer regarding the time and place for fighting limbers to report.

7. Completion of the above reliefs will be wired to Battn.H.Q. by code words as follows:-

   LENS Section Code word:- "COLD"
   HILL 70 " " " :- "WARM" WARM.
   ST.EMILE " " " :- "HOT "

8. Acknowledge.

Issued at 7 AM

11/4/18

Capt & Adjt.
46th Battn M.G.Corps.

P.T.O.

Distribution:-

1. A.Coy
2. B. "
3. C. "
4. D. "
5. 46th Division
6. 11th Bn.M.G.C.
7. 3rd Canadian Div.
8. T.O.
9. Q.M.
10. Signalling Officer
11. 137th Inf.Bde.
12. 138th " "
13. 139th " "
14.)
15.) War Diary
16. File
17. 2/Lieut.Smith.

SECRET   Copy No 10

46th BATTALION MACHINE GUN CORPS ORDER No 18.

Reference LENS 11 and Secret Trench Map.
In continuation of 46th Battn.M.G.Corps Order No.17.

1. The Q.M. will make arrangements so that the three Companies moving to-night will each have one Travelling Kitchen, and that hot tea or soup is prepared for issue to the men on arrival at their destinations. Subject to amendment the times of arrival at destinations are as follows.(approximately)

   B.Company 12.30 a.m. 12th April.
   C. and D. Coys, 1.30 a.m. 12th April.

   Q.M. will make necessary preparations regarding the issue of one blanket per man for use in the billets at the above destinations, and also for Rations for the 12th April.

2. Relief Table is attached.
   One guide per gun position will be detailed as directed therein.

3. The guns of C.Coy now in the line and under the Command of O.C., No 3 Group will on being relieved by the Canadian Guns come under the Command of O.C.,C.Company. C.Coy H.Q. in MAROC will not be taken over by the Canadians. The Section in reserve at MAROC will be free to move under the orders of the O.C.,C.Coy when the relief of C.Coys guns in the line has been fully completed. The O.C., C.Coy will work in conjunction with O.C., No 3 Group.

4. Reference Para.2 of 46th Bn.M.G.Corps Order No 17. Company Commanders will move by any route to their allotted destinations.

5. Acknowledge by wire. On arrival destination, please notify immediately location your H.Q.

Issued at 1.45 p.m.

11/4/18   Capt & Adjt.
46th Battn.Machine Gun Corps.

Distribution:-

1. A.Coy
2. B. "
3. C. "
4. D. "
5. 46th Division.
6. T.O.
7. Q.M.
8. Signalling Officer
9. } War Diary.
10. } War Diary.
11. File.

Relief Table 11/4/18

Issued with 46th Battn M. G. Corps Order No 18

Date	Coy	Relieving Coy	No of Guns	Guides at	Time & Date
11	'D'	19th Can. Coy	16	Water Tank 100 yds W. of 3 Group H. Q.	8-30 p.m. 11th
11	'C'	'C' Battery	8	ditto	ditto
11	'C'	'F' Battery	4	ditto	ditto
11	'B'	17th Can Coy	16	Chateau 1 Group H. Q.	ditto
12	'A'	B & D. Battery	16	M. 12 C. 70. 70	8-30 p.m. 12th

1 Guide for each Gun position will be detailed to report as above.

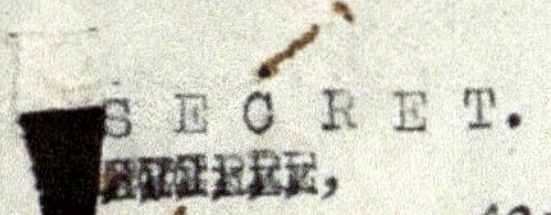

SECRET. Copy No. 10

46th BATTALION MACHINE GUN CORPS ORDER No.19

Reference LENS 11 and Secret Trench Map.
In continuation of 46th Battn.Machine Gun Corps Order Nos.17 and 18 of April 11th, 1918.

1. The following moves will take place as stated:-

A. Night 12/13th April No.2 Group ('A'.Coy) will be relieved in the line by 3rd Canadian Machine Gun Battation, and will move into billets in MAZINGARBE when relief completed.

B. 'B' Coy will move from AIX NOULETTE to BRUAY April 12th.

C. 'C' Coy)
D. 'D' Coy) " " " BRACQUEMONT to BRUAY April 12th.

E. 'A' Coy " " " MAZINGARBE to BRUAY April 13th.

F. H.Q. " " " LES BREBIS to BRUAY April 13th.

2. March table for above moves is attached.

3. Billeting for 'A' Coy at MAZINGARBE for the night 12/13th April will be arranged for by O.C. 'A' Coy who will render direct the necessary claims and certificates.

4. Billeting claims for the night 11/12th April for B, C, & D.Coys: will be submitted direct by O.C.,Coys:

5. The T.O. will make all the necessary arrangements re accommodation for Transport and animals in accordance with the attached march table.

6. Billeting for B,C,& D.Coys from night 12/13th and 'A' Coy and H.Q. from night 13/14th at BRUAY will be arranged by 2/Lieut.W.L.Smith who will report to Town Major, BRUAY 10.0 a.m. April 12th.
B, C, and D.Coys: will send forward usual Billeting Parties to report to Lieut.Smith at the Town Major's Office at BRUAY at 11.0 a.m. April 12th.
Lieut.Smith will make all arrangements re H.Q.billets.
'A' Coy will detail a billeting party to report Battalion H.Q.,BRUAY at 10.0 a.m. April 13th.

7. The Q.M. will make the necessary arrangements regarding the issue of Rations.

8. Meals will be prepared under Coy: arrangements for issue to men on arrival at destination.

9. March Formation will be decided by O.C.,Coys: accordingly with the situation.
Dress will be full marching order.
Steel Helmets will be carried by all troops after passing W. of LES BREBIS.

P.T.O.

10. Company Commanders will arrange any further details.

11. The location of Coy: H.Q. BRUAY (also MAZINGARBE) for night 12/13th April in case of 'A' Coy.) will be notified without delay to Battn.H.Q.
Battalion H.Q. will close at LES BREBIS 10.0 a.m. April 13th and will open at BRUAY same hour.

12. Acknowledge.

[signature]

12/4/18.

Capt & Adjt.
46th Battn.Machine Gun Corps.

Issued at 4.0 p.m.

Distribution:-

1. A.Coy
2. B. "
3. C. "
4. D. "
5. T.O.
6. Q.M.
7. Signals
8. 46th Division
9. 3rd Canadian Div.
10. War Diary
11. " "
12. File.

MARCH TABLE. Issued with 49th Battn. M.G.Corps Order No 19

Coy.	Date	From	To	Route	Transport	Remarks.
A.	Night 12/13th	The line	MAZINGARBE	Any	Remain as at Present	On relief by 3rd Cdn M.G.Battn.
B.	13th	AIX NOULETTE	BRUAY	HERSIN BRUAY.	With Coy:	Time to leave Present billets 2.15 p.m.
C.	13th	BRACQUEMONT	BRUAY	NOEUX LES MINES HERSIN, BRUAY.	do	do 2.15 p.m.
D.	13th	do	do	do	do	do 2.45 p.m.
A.	13th.	MAZINGARBE	BRUAY	do	do	do 9.30 a.m.
H.Q.	13th	LES BREBIS	do	do	With H.Q.	do 10.0 a.m.

Billeting Parties will meet Coys: on arrival at BRUAY and conduct to Billets.
H.Q. men will carry haversack rations, which will be arranged by Q.M.

SECRET. Copy No. 11

46th BATTALION MACHINE GUN CORPS ORDER No.20.

Reference GORRE 1/20,000
" LENS 11
" HAZEBROUCK 5.A.

1. In the event of a hostile attack on the I Corps front South of LA BASSEE Canal 46th Battalion Machine Gun Corps will be prepared to occupy the following Battery Positions.

A.Coy.	SAILLY Battery SAILLY Defences SAILLY POST Battery	Each a Battery of 4 guns
C.Coy.	MUCKHEAP Battery RAILWAY POST Battery NOEUX Battery	
B.Coy.	LES QUESNOY Locality - 12 guns.	

2. Necessary reconnaisance of the above Positions will be carried out by Company Commanders concerned under verbal instructions issued this morning.

3. A copy of information regarding the above Positions giving location, showing direction in which to fire etc is attached.

4. All Personel and Transport of this Battalion is placed under orders to be held in readiness to move at two hours notice.

5. Acknowledge.

Issued at:- 7pm.

14/4/18.

R. Dickens.
Capt & Adjt.
46th Battn. M.G.Corps.

Note. The copy of information attached ~~as~~ only in case of A. B. & C.Coys:

Distribution:-

1. A.Coy
2. B. "
3. C. "
4. D. "
5. Signalling Officer
6. Q.M.
7. T.O.
8. T.O.M.
9. 46th Division
10. Corps M.G.O.
11. X
12.) War Diary
13. File.

S E C R E T,　　　　　　　　　　　　　　　　Copy No. 11.

46th BATTALION MACHINE GUN CORPS ORDER No.21.

Reference GORRE 1/20,000
　　"　　LENS 11.

1. The Battalion will move from BRUAY to NOEUX LES MINES tomorrow 15th April 1918.

2. March table will be issued later, but in the meantime necessary preparations for this move will be made by all concerned. The probable hour for first Company to leave BRUAY will be 2 p.m., therefore early dinners should be arranged.

3. Bathing arrangements tomorrow morning will be carried out.

4. The Battalion is required to work on various Machine Gun Battery Positions in SAILLY locality, NOEUX locality, BEUVRY locality on the 16th inst: regarding which further orders will be issued later stating the various positions of Batteries and the work required on each.

5. Billetting. 2/Lieut.Smith and a billetting party from each Company will leave Battalion Orderly Room tomorrow morning at 8 a.m. to arrange for billets at NOEUX LES MINES with the Town Major.
The Transport Officer or representative will also proceed with this party to arrange Horse and wagon lines, also billets for Transport Personnel. Guides will be detailed from above parties to meet Coys on & conduct Billets.

6. Acks

Issued at:- 11.0 PM

14/4/18.

[signature]
Capt & Adjt.
46th Battn.M.G.Corps.

Distribution:-

1. A.Coy
2. B. "
3. C. "
4. D. "
5. Q.M.
6. T.O.
7. Signalling Officer
8. M.O.
9. 2/Lt.Smith
10. 46th Division
11.) War Diary
12.)
13. File.

S E C R E T.

Copy No. 11

46th BATTALION MACHINE GUN CORPS ORDER No 22.

Reference LENS 11 and HAZEBROUCK 5.A.

15/4/18.

In continuation of 46th Battn.M.G.Corps Order No 21.

1. March table for move today from BRUAY to NOEUX LES MINES is attached.

2. Dress, Marching Order.

3. Battalion Headquarters close BRUAY 5.0 p.m.. Open NOEUX LES MINES same hour.

4. Coys:, T.O., Q.M. M.O. Signals will render a certificate to reach Battn. Orderly Room 6.0. p.m. this day that all Billets, Horse Lines, Latrines, etc, etc, as occupied have been left in a clean and sanitary condition.

5. Acknowledge.

Issued at:- 10.0 A.M.

15/4/18

[illegible]

Capt & Adjt.

46th Battn.M.G.Corps

Distribution:-

1. A.Coy
2. B.Coy
3. C.Coy
4. D.Coy
5. T.O.
6. Q.M.
7. M.O.
8. Signals
9. 2/Lt.Smith
10. 46th Division
11.
12. War Diary.
13. File.

March Table issued with 46th Battn. M.G. Corps Order No 22 d/- 15/4/18

<table>
<tr><th>Coy..</th><th>Time to Pass:-</th><th>Starting Point.</th><th>Route</th><th>Remarks.</th></tr>
<tr><td>H.Q. Transport only</td><td>1.45 P.m.</td><td rowspan="6">Transport Lines</td><td rowspan="6">To Cross Roads. MARLEY-LES-MINES - HALLICOURT-OURTON - BETHUNE thence direct NOEUX-LES-MINES taking road just South of HOUCHIN</td><td rowspan="6">Teas will be PrePared on the way for issue on arrival at destination.
'D' Coy will PrePare teas for H.Q.. Personnel.</td></tr>
<tr><td>A. Coy</td><td>2.0. P.m.</td></tr>
<tr><td>B. Coy</td><td>2.15 P.m.</td></tr>
<tr><td>C. Coy</td><td>2.30 P.m.</td></tr>
<tr><td>D. Coy</td><td>2.45 P.m.</td></tr>
<tr><td>H.Q. Personnel</td><td>2.55 P.m</td></tr>
</table>

Coys: will move off by sections at 100 yards ~~interval~~ distance between sections.
Coy: H.Q. will move off with the resPective Coys: leading section.
Dress for all ranks full Marching Order.

SECRET — Copy No. 9

[illegible] BATTALION MACHINE GUN CORPS [illegible]

Reference [illegible] 1/[illegible]

With reference to [illegible] dated 14th, 17th, and 18th inst:

1. The following [illegible] will be [illegible] in accordance with [illegible] below.

A Coy [illegible] [illegible]

C Coy [illegible]

2. Completion will be [illegible] to Battalion Headquarters [illegible] word "[illegible]".

3. The [illegible] will be [illegible] 1918.

4. Previous instructions [illegible] are hereby cancelled.

5. Acknowledge.

Issued at [illegible]

18/[illegible]/1918.

[illegible]

[illegible]

Distribution [illegible]

[illegible]

S E C R E T. Copy No. 12

46th BATTALION MACHINE GUN CORPS ORDER No.23 B.

Reference GORRE 1/20,000

1. With reference to order No 23 and 23 A. the 12 (twelve) guns of A.Company in SAILLY Locality, also the 4 (four) guns of C.Coy at MUCKHEAP BATTERY will be withdrawn at 5.0 p.m. to join Battalion at NOEUX LES MINES this day under arrangements to be made by Company Commanders.

2. Completion will be wired to Battalion Headquarters by the wode word "SATURDAY".

3. Para.2 of order No 23 A. will still stand and the Battalion is placed under orders to move at 4 (four) hours notice.

4. Acknowledge.

Issued at :- 12 noon

20/4/18.

Capt.& Adjt.
46th Battn.M.G.Corps.

Distribution:-
1. A.Coy 4. D.Coy 7. Signalling Officer
2. B.Coy 5. T.O. 8. 46th Division
3. C.Coy 6. Q.M. 9. 11th Battn.M.G.Corps.

Added:- Ammunition at MUCKHEAP will be left there and notice board put up.

SECRET. Copy No. 15

[illegible] BATTALION MACHINE GUN CORPS ORDER No.34.

Reference 1/20,000 [illegible] and [illegible].

1. 16 (Sixteen) guns from each C and D.Coys: of the [illegible] Battalion M.G.Corps will take over 32 (Thirty two) gun Positions in the line from 3rd Battalion Machine Gun Corps on night 24/25th April 18.
To be completed by 6.0 a.m. 25th April, 1918

2. The approximate boundaries are K 14.A.10.90 ([illegible] River exclusive) to K [illegible] central.

3. The O.C.'D' Coy will be Group Commander of the above 32 (Thirty two) guns. (Major K.B.Wood, M.C.)
The O.C.'C' Coy will be O.C. Rear guns. (Capt, T.W.Boughey)
C.& D.Coys guns will be disposed in the line as follows :-
C.Coy, 12 Forward Guns,
1 Battery of 4 guns.

D.Coy, 4 Batteries of 4 guns.
Group Headquarters will be at [illegible].30.90 (approximate)

4. A return stating disposition of guns and fields of fire (grid bearings and ranges), and copies of battery charts will be rendered to Headquarters as soon as possible.
Map references of Headquarters of O.C., Group, O. C., Forward Guns, O.C., Rear Guns, Battery and Section Commanders will be given in this return.

5. Further details regarding this relief will be arranged direct between Group Commanders concerned.

6. At each Forward gun Position there will be 16 Belt boxes and 10 boxes of S.A.A. per gun.
At each Battery of 4 guns there will be 18 Belt boxes and 10 boxes S.A.A. per gun.
At each Battery position at least 10 Belt boxes per gun will be reserved for direct fire.

7. A consolidated inventory of trench area and other stores and rations taken over will be rendered to Battalion Headquarters as soon as possible.

8. Completion of this relief will be notified by wire to Battalion Headquarters by the code word "[illegible]".

9. Acknowledge.

Issued at :- 10.0 p.m.

[illegible]/4/18.

[signature]
Capt & Adjt.
[illegible] Battn. M.G.Corps.

Distribution :-

1. A.Coy
2. B. "
3. C. "
4. D. "
5. T.O.
6. Signals
7. Q.M.
8. [illegible] Inf: Bde.
9. [illegible] Inf: Bde.
10. [illegible] Division
11. [illegible] Division
12. [illegible] Division
13. 3rd Bn.M.G.Corps
14.) File.
15.)
16.) War Diary.

SECRET.　　　　　　　　　　　　Copy No. 13

48th BATTALION MACHINE GUN CORPS WARNING ORDER NO 24 A.

Reference 1/20,000 GORRE and LACOUTURE.

1. The following moves will take place today April 24th, 1918.

2. C. & D.Coys into the line vide Order No 24.

3. B.Coy and two sections of A.Coy will move into Billets at BETHUNE.

4. Remaining two sections and Headquarters of A.Coy will move into Billets FOUQUIERIES.

5. Transport and Quartermaster will move to FOUQUIERIES, also one water cart from Headquarter Transport.

6. Battalion Headquarters and Headquarter Transport less one water cart will move to GOSNEY.

7. March tables will be issued later.

8. A billeting party from A.& B. Companies, also from Transport Officer and Quartermaster will proceed to respective destinations, leaving NOEUX LES MINES by 9.0 a.m. this day to arrange accommodation.
2/Lieut W.L.Smith will proceed to GOSNEY to arrange Headquarters Billets.
Each of the above parties will arrange to have guides to meet incoming troops.

9. Acknowledge.

Issued at :- 1.15 a.m.

24/4/18.

Capt & Adjt.
48th Battn.M.G.Corps.

Distribution:-
1. A.Coy
2. B. "
3. C. "
4. D. "
5. T.O.
6. Q.M.
7. Signals
8. M.O.
9. 48th Division
10.)
11.) File
12)
13) War Diary.

S E C R E T.   Copy No. 12

46th BATTALION MACHINE GUN CORPS ORDER No.24 B.

Reference 1/20,000 GORRE and LACOUTURE.

1. With reference to order No 24 A, March table is attached for moves today, the 24th April, 1918.

2. Battalion Headquarters will close at NOEUX LES MINES 1.0 p.m. this day and will open at GONNEHEM same hour.

3. Quartermaster will make necessary arrangements direct with O.C., Companies and Details regarding blankets, packs and stores. All Companies Stores will be at FOUQUIERES.

4. Acknowledge.

Issued at :- 11.45 a.m.

Capt & Adjt.
46th Battn. M.G.Corps.

24/4/18.

Distribution:-

1. A.Coy	7. Signals
2. B. "	8. M.O.
3. C. "	9. 46th Division
4. D. "	10.)
5. T.O.	11.) File
6. Q.M.	12.)
	13.) War Diary.

MARCH TABLE to accompany 46th BATTN. M.G.Corps Order No 24 B.
issued 24/4/18.

No.	Unit.	Starting Point.	Time.	Route.	Destination.	Remarks.
1.	H.Q.	K.18.a.70.70	1.0 p.m.	VAUDRICOURT-HESDIGNEUL.	GOSNAY.	Less 1 water cart to move with Transport to FOUQUIERIES Dress; Marching Order.
2.	2 Sections A.Coy & A.Coy H.Q.	do	1.30 p.m.	VAUDRICOURT.	FOUQUIERIES.	Dress Marching Order
3.	2 Sections A.Coy B .Coy	K.18.b.20.90	2.0 p.m.	direct	BETHUNE.	Dress; Battle Order.
4.	C and D Coys.	———	———	——	Into the line under orders to be issued by the O.C. Group (Major K.B.Wood, MC Dress; Battle Order.	
5.	The Transport of 2 sections 'A' Coy and 'B' Coy.	K.18.a.70.70		VAUDRICOURT.	FOUQUIERIES.	Under arrangements to be made by T.O. direct with O.C.'A' Coy & 'B' Coy. Dress; Marching Order.

P.T.O.

6.	Any men of all Coys marked E.D. or L.D. by R.M.O.	K.18.A.70.70	2.0 p.m.	VAUDRICOURT. FOUQUIERES.	Dress Battle Order

*To march off from Bn.H.Q. at 1.40 p.m. under an Officer to be detailed by O.C.'B' Coy. The R.M.O. will accompany this Party.

Note. The O.C. Group (Major H.B.Wood, M.C.) will distribute the men of C and D. Coys as is found necessary to ensure a team is with each gun.

S E C R E T.   Copy No. 9

46th BATTALION MACHINE GUN CORPS ORDER No.24.C.

Reference 1/20,000 GORRE and LACOUTURE.

1. The two sections and Headquarters of A.Coy in reserve are placed under orders to move at one hours notice, and every preparation will be made accordingly.

2. The limbers for these sections will always be packed and will be parked separately.

3. Acknowledge.

Issued at :- 10.40 a.m.

25/4/18.

Capt & Adjt.
46th Battn. Machine Gun Corps.

Distribution :-
1. A.Coy   5. T.O.
2. B. "   6. Q.M.
3. C. "   7. Signals
4. D. "   8. File
9.
10. } War Diary.

76

49th BATTALION MACHINE GUN CORPS ORDER No.55.

Reference 1/20,000 GORRE and LACOUTURE.

1. 16 (Sixteen) guns from B.Company and 8 (Eight) guns from A.Company of the 49th Battalion Machine Gun Corps will take over 12 (Twelve) gun Positions in the line from the 55th Battalion Machine Gun Corps and in addition will occupy the following Battery Positions, each with 4 (Four) guns :- LE QUESNOY EAST, F.3.d.45.20 and F.2.d.65.40 on the night 24/25th April, 1918. Relief to be completed by 5.0 am. 25th April, 1918.

2. All necessary work on the above Battery sites will be commenced forthwith under arrangements to be made by the Group Commander.

3. The O.C."B"Company (Major H.P.Bailey) will be Group Commander of the above 24 (Twenty Four) guns.

4. A return stating disposition of guns and fields of fire (grid bearings and ranges), and copies of Battery charts will be rendered to Headquarters as soon as possible.
Map references of Headquarters of O.C., Group, O.C., Forward Guns, O.C., Rear Guns, Battery and Section Commanders will be given in this return.

5. Further details regarding this relief will be arranged direct between Group Commanders concerned.

6. At each Forward Gun Position there will be 16 Belt boxes and 10 boxes of S.A.A. per gun.
At each Battery of 4 (Four) guns there will be 16 Belt boxes and 15 boxes S.A.A. per gun.
At each Battery Position at least 10 belt boxes per gun will be reserved for direct fire.

7. A consolidated inventory of trench area and other stores and rations taken over will be rendered to Battalion Headquarters as soon as possible.

8. Completion of this relief will be notified by wire to Battalion Headquarters by the code word "BRANDY".

9. Acknowledge.

Issued at :- 11.30pm.

23/4/18.

Capt & Adjt.
49th Battn.M.G. Corps.

Distribution:-

1. A.Coy	10. 33rd Division
2. B. "	11. 49th Division
3. C. "	12. 55th Division
4. D. "	13. 55th Bn.M.G.Corps
5. T.O.	14. File.
6. Signals.	15)
7. Q.M.	16) War Diary.
8. 148th Inf:Bde.	
9. 147th " "	

S E C R E T.　　　　　　　　　　　　　　　　　　　　Copy No 16

46th BATTALION MACHINE GUN CORPS ORDER No.26.

Reference to 46th Bn.M.G.Corps Orders Nos 24 & 25.

1. Major N.P.Bailey, Commanding the Machine Guns in the GORRE Sector is designated the O.C., No 1 Group.

2. Major K.E.Wood,M.C., Commanding the Machine Guns in the ESSARS Sector is designated the O.C., No 2 Group.

3. Acknowledge.

Issued at :- 6pm

26/4/18.

Capt & Adjt,
46th Battn.M.G. Corps.

Distribution :-

1. A.Coy	7. Q.M.	13. 55th Bn.M.G. Corps
2. B. "	8. 139th Inf.Bde.	14. File.
3. C. "	9. 137th " "	15.)
4. D. "	10. 3rd Division.	16.) War Diary.
5. T.O.	11. 46th Division.	
6. Signals.	12. 55th Division.	

****

W A R   D I A R Y.

46th BATTALION MACHINE GUN CORPS.

MAY 1918.

****

Army Form C. 2118.

WAR DIARY

or

~~INTELLIGENCE SUMMARY.~~

(*Erase heading not required.*)

Instructions regarding War Diaries and Intelligence Summaries are contained in F. S. Regs., Part II. and the Staff Manual respectively. Title pages will be prepared in manuscript.

MAY 1918.

46th BATTALION MACHINE GUN CORPS.

No 1.

Place	Date	Hour	Summary of Events and Information GORRE 1/20,000 VIEILLE CHAPELLE 1/20,000 BETHUNE COMBINED SHEET 1/40,000 36A. S.E., 36. S.W., 36B.N.E.,36C.N.W.	Remarks and references to Appendices
GOSNAY.	1st.		Lient.E.LAMB, wounded in action (Gas) 47 O.R. wounded in action (Gas) 3 O.Rs. wounded in action.	
		3.30 pm.	Order No 27 issued (copy attached) 52 Guns in the line. M.G's fired 10,500 rounds harassing fire during night on enemy cross roads and tracks In response to S.O.S. from Division on our left our M.G's fired 2,000 rounds on S.O.S.Lines on to that front.	Order No 27
	2nd.		4 O.Rs.wounded in action (Gas) 48 Guns in the line. 16 Guns in Divisional Reserve. M.G's fired 13,500 rounds harassing fire during night on to enemy's cross roads, tracks,etc.	
	3rd.	2.30 pm.	Order No 28 issued (copy attached) M.G's fired 14,000 rounds harassing fire during night on enemy's communications, tracks, etc. 4 O.Rs.evacuated sick. 1 O.R. to 15th Battn.M.G.Corps,as Armourer Sgt. 2/Lieut.R.V.Jenner from Base Depot.	Order No 28
	4th.		In response to S.O.S. call at 5.0 a.m. on our front M.G's fired 29,500 rounds on S.O.S.lines. M.G's fired 12,000 rounds harassing fire on to enemy's cross roads, tracks, and dumps. Capt.J.B.BABER, M.C., transferred to 1/16th London Regt. 1 O.R. evacuated sick 2 O.Rs.wounded in action (Gas)	
	5th.		M.G's fired 11,000 rounds harassing fire during night on to enemy's tracks etc. M.G's fired 110 rounds at enemy aircraft. 2/Lieut. A.J.CASSON,) 2/Lieut. J.F.THORPE,) From Base Depot. 2/Lieut. G.F.RENWICK,) 40 O.Rs. from Base Depot.	
	6th.		M.G's fired 10,000 rounds harassing fire during night on to enemy's roads, tracks etc. M.G's fired 350 rounds at enemy aircraft. 8 O.Rs.evacuated sick.	
	7th.	7.0	Order No 29 issued (copy attached) M.G's fired 10,000 rounds harassing fire during night on to enemy's tracks etc. M.G's fired 100 rounds at enemy aircraft. Major A.LYBURN to III Corps. 1 O.R. as batman to III Corps.	Order No 29.

D. D. & L., London, E.C. (A8001) Wt. W1 71/M2031 750,000 5/17 Sch. 52 Forms/C2.118/14

Army Form C. 2118.

WAR DIARY
or
~~INTELLIGENCE SUMMARY~~
(Erase heading not required.)

Instructions regarding War Diaries and Intelligence Summaries are contained in F. S. Regs., Part II. and the Staff Manual respectively. Title pages will be prepared in manuscript.

MAY 1918.

46th BATTALION MACHINE GUN CORPS.

No 2.

Place	Date	Hour	Summary of Events and Information GORRE 1/20,000 VIEILLE CHAPELLE 1/20,000 BETHUNE COMBINED SHEET 1/40,000 36A.S.E.,36.S.W., 36B.N.E.,36C.N.W.	Remarks and references to Appendices
GOSNAY.	7th.		2/Lieut.J.ROWLEY returned to 1/6th North Staffords. 1 O.R. from Divisional Training Battalion. 3 O.Rs.arrived after evacuation.	
	8th.	2.30 pm.	Order No 30 issued (copy attached) Order No 30A issued (copy attached)	Order No 30 Order No 30A
		2.45 pm.	Order No 31 issued (copy attached) M.G's fired 12,000 rounds during night on to enemy's tracks,communications, etc. M!G's fired 1,250 rounds at enemy aircraft., 2 O.Rs.evacuated sick.	Order No 31
	9th.		M.G's fired 7,500 rounds during night on to selected enemy targets. 1 O.R.evacuated sick 1 O.R. evacuated after evacuation. 27 O.Rs. from 1st Monmouth Regt.,pending transfer to M.G.Corps.	
	10th.	7.30 pm.	Order No 32 issued (copy attached) M.G's fired 7,500 rounds during night on to selected enemy targets 3 O.Rs.wounded in action. 1 O.R. evacuated sick. Major G.A.WADE, M.C. from 57th Battn.M.G.Corps. 1 O.R. as batman from 57th Battn.M.G.Corps. 20 O.Rs. from Base Depot.	Order No 32
	11th.		M.G's fired 7,600 rounds during night on to selected enemy targets. M.G's fired 500 rounds at enemy aircraft. Capt E.B.WOODFORDE to 1/5th Notts & Derbys. 1 O.R. evacuated sick. 1 O.R. arrived after evacuation.	
	12th.		M.G's fired 10,000 rounds during night on to selected enemy targets. 1 O.R. killed in action. 1 O.R. wounded in action.	
	13th.		M.G's fired 14,000 rounds during night on to selected enemy targets. 1 O.R. wounded in action. 1 O.R. evacuated sick. 1 O.R. arrived after evacuation.	
	14th.		M.G's fired 8,500 rounds during night on to selected enemy targets. 2 O.R's evacuated sick. 3 O.R's arrived after evacuation. M.G's fired 1,000 rounds at enemy aircraft.	

D. D. & L., London, E.C.
(A8001) Wt. W1-71/M2031 750,000 5/17 Sch. 52 Forms/C2118/14

Army Form C. 2118.

WAR DIARY
or
~~INTELLIGENCE SUMMARY.~~

(Erase heading not required.)

Instructions regarding War Diaries and Intelligence Summaries are contained in F. S. Regs., Part II. and the Staff Manual respectively. Title pages will be prepared in manuscript.

MAY 1918.

46th BATTALION MACHINE GUN CORPS.

No 3.

Place	Date	Hour	GORRE 1/20,000 VIEILLE CHAPELLE 1/20,000 — Summary of Events and Information — BETHUNE COMBINED SHEET 1/40,000 36A.S.E.,36.S.W.,36B.N.E.,36C.N.W.	Remarks and references to Appendices
GOSNAY.	15th.	3.0 pm.	Order No 33 issued (copy attached) M.G's fired 8,500 rounds during night on to selected enemy targets. M.G's fire successfully drove off many enemy aeroplanes. 2 O.Rs.evacuated sick.	Order No 33
	16th.		M.G's fired 14,000 rounds during night on to selected enemy targets. M.G's fired 1,200 rounds at enemy aircraft. 1 O.R. evacuated sick.	
	17th.		M.G's fired 11,000 rounds during night on to selected enemy targets. M.G's fired 500 rounds at enemy aircraft. 1 O.R. evacuated sick. 3 O.Rs.returned to Base Depot. 30 O.Rs. from Base Depot.	
	18th.		M.G's fired 12,000 rounds during night on to selected targets. M.G's fired 500 rounds at enemy aircraft. 1 O.R. wounded in action. 2 O.Rs. wounded in action (Gas).	
	19th.		M.G's fired 13,000 rounds during night on to selected targets. M.G's fired 200 rounds at enemy aircraft. 1 O.R. evacuated sick.	
	20th.		M.G's fired 11,000 rounds during night on to selected targets. 1 O.R. evacuated sick. 1 O.R. from Divisional Training Battalion.	
	21st.		Letter X issued sheets X1, X2, X3, X4.(copies attached) } Letter XA issued sheets 1, 2, 3, 4, (Copies attached) } See Tracing 46/20/67 issued 27/5/18. M.G's fired 7,250 rounds during night on to selected targets. M.G's fired 600 rounds at enemy aircraft. 1 O.R.evacuated sick.	Letter X Tracing X4 Letter XA
	22nd.	7.0 am.	Order No 34 issued (copy attached) 33 O.Rs. wounded in action (Gas). 1 O.R.evacuated sick. M.G's fired 5,000 rounds during night in accordance with programme,see letter XA. M.G's fired 1,000 rounds at enemy aircraft. Lieut.H.W.BROWN, wounded in action (Gas) No 15204 C.S.M.ODLUM J. from 29th Battalion M.G.Corps.	Order No 34

D. D. & L., London, E.C.
(A8001) Wt. W1 71/M2031 750,000 5/17 Sch. 52 Forms/C2.118/14

Army Form C. 2118.

WAR DIARY

~~or~~

~~INTELLIGENCE SUMMARY.~~

(Erase heading not required.)

Instructions regarding War Diaries and Intelligence Summaries are contained in F. S. Regs., Part II. and the Staff Manual respectively. Title pages will be prepared in manuscript.

MAY 1918. 46th BATTALION MACHINE GUN CORPS.

No 4.

Place	Date	Hour	GORRE 1/20,000 VIEILLE CHAPELLE 1/20,000 Summary of Events and Information BETHUNE COMBINED SHEET 1/40,000 36A.S.E.,36.S.W.,36B.N.E.,36C.N.W.	Remarks and references to Appendices
GOSNAY.	23rd.	7.0 pm.	Order No 29A issued (copy attached) 2 O.Rs.Evacuated sick. 2 O.Rs.arrived after evacuation. M.G's fired 4,500 rounds during night vide programme in letter XA.	Order No 29A.
	24th.		M.G's fired 6,000 rounds during night vide programme in letter XA. 6 O.Rs.wounded in action (Gas). 1 O.R. arrived after evacuation.	
	25th.		M.G's fired 13,000 rounds during night vide programme in letter XA. 2 O.Rs. arrived after evacuation.	
	27th.		Tracing 46/20/67 issued (copy attached) M.G's fired 10,000 rounds during night vide programme in letter XA. 7 O.R.wounded in action (Gas) 1 O.R. wounded in action and gassed. 1 O.R.evacuated sick. 1 O.R. arrived after evacuation.	Tracing 46/20/67.
	28th.		M.G's fired 15,500 rounds during night vide programme in letter XA. 4 O.Rs.evacuated sick.	
	29th.	12.0 noon.	Order No 35 issued (copy attached) By this order guns in line grouped by Companies i.e. 1 Coy Left Forward, 1 Company Right Forward, 1 Company Rear Guns, these again divided into 2 Groups (1 Group each Brigade) the rear guns being one half with each group. M.G's fired 10,000 rounds during night vide programme in letter XA. 1 O.R.evacuated sick. Lieut. G.D.HAMILTON, and 2/Lieut.C.WITT, from Base Depot. 50 O.Rs. from Base Depot.	Order No 35.
	30th.	4.45 pm.	Order No 36 issued (copy attached) M.G's fired 16,000 rounds during night vide programme in letter XA. At 2.15 a.m.enemy attempted raid on ROUTE 'A'KEEP, S.O.S. was sent up, M.G.Batteries and guns opened fire in 10 seconds on their S.O.S.lines in front ROUTE 'A'KEEP and fired 16,000 rounds, this attack was repulsed.	Order No 36.
	31st.		M.G's fired 1,000 rounds at enemy aircraft. Lieut.C.A.R.HOGGAN killed in action. 7 O.Rs.evacuated sick. 1 O.R.arrived after evacuation.	

J. Harington

Bt.Lieut-Colonel,

Commanding 46th Battn.M.G.Corps.

D. D. & L., London, E.C.
(A8093) Wt. W1 71/M2031 750,000 5/17 Sch. 52 Forms/C2118/14

S E C R E T.

Copy No. 15

46th BATTALION MACHINE GUN CORPS ORDER No.27.

Reference 1/20,000 GORRE and VEILLE CHAPELLE.

1. The following 4 (four) guns in the ESSARS Section will be withdrawn this day.
   F5 ~~F.1.~~ ~~[illegible]~~ X.14.a.87.24
   F6. ~~F.2.~~ ~~[illegible]~~ X.14.a.64.28.
   F.3.)
   F.4.) X.25.a.50.70.
   This will allow one section of 'C' Company to be withdrawn, and this Section will move into Billets at FOUQUIERIES tonight.

2. The 4 (four) guns at LE QUESNOY EAST Battery in the GORRE Section will be withdrawn today. Locations of these guns are as follows:-
   LE QUESNOY EAST.
   F.8.b.35.20.
   F.8.b.30.20.
   F.8.d.55.10. (F.8.d.55.10)
   F.8.d.55.18. (F.8.d.55.18)
   This will allow one section from this Group to be withdrawn, and this will be one section of 'A' Company, which will move tonight to the Transport lines situated at BOIS DES MONTAGNES, E.27.c.90.90.

3. Tomorrow the 2/5/18 one section of 'C' Company, which moved into billets at FOUQUIERIES this day will relieve in No. 1 Group the remaining section of 'A' Company, and the section of 'A' Company thus relieved will proceed to the Battalion TransportLines, location as above.

4. Any further details, Guides, etc., will be arranged between Company and Group Commanders concerned.

5. Billets for the section of 'C' Company at FOUQUIERIES tonight have been arranged, and 'C' Company Rear Headquarters informed of their location. The second in command at 'C' Company's Rear Headquarters will arrange for the section of 'C' Company coming into billets tonight to have a bath tomorrow morning.

   Completion of these reliefs and withdrawals will be notified to this Office by wire by the code word "FIRST", and will also be notified by Group Commanders to the Brigade Commander concerned.

7. Acknowledge.

   Issued at:- 3.30 pm

[signature]
Capt & Adjt.
46th Battn. Machine Gun Corps.

1/5/18.

Distribution:-

1. A. Coy.	9. 137th Inf. Bde.
2. B. "	10. 3rd Battn M.G.C.
3. C. "	11. 46th Division.
4. D. "	12. 55th Battn. M.G.C.
5. T.O.	13. File.
6. Signals	14.)
7. Q.M.	15.) War Diary.
8. 139th Inf.Bde.	

S E C R E T.   Copy No 14

46th BATTALION MACHINE GUN CORPS ORDER No 28.

Reference 1/20,000 GORRE and VEILLE CHAPELLE.

1. 12 (twelve) guns of 'A' Company and 'A' Company Headquarters now in Divisional Reserve at Transport lines will relieve 12 (twelve) guns of 'B' Company and 'B' Company Headquarters in No 1 Group, GORRE Section, on the night 4/5th May, 1918.

2. 12 (twelve) guns of 'B' Company and 'B' Company Headquarters thus relieved will move into the accommodation at the Transport lines vacated by 'A' Company.

3. Immediately the above relief is completed Major E.R.Nurse, M.C. will take over the Command of No 1 Group from Major N.P.Bailey.

4. Any further details, such as guides, etc., will be arranged between Company Commanders concerned.

~~4~~.5. Completion of this relief will be notified to Battalion Headquarters by wire by the code word "SECOND".

~~5~~.6. Completion of this relief will also be notified by the Group Commander to the Brigade Commander concerned.

~~6~~.7. When this relief is completed the guns in No 1 Group under the Command of Major E.R.Nurse, M.C., will be as follows :-

'A' Company   16 (sixteen) guns
'C' Company   4 (four) guns

~~7~~.8 Divisional Reserve will ~~xxxxx~~ consist of 16 (sixteen) guns of 'B' Company situated at the Battalion Transport lines.

9.~~8~~. Acknowledge.

Issued at 2.30 p.m

3/5/18.

Bliebens
Capt & Adjt,
46th Battn.M.G. Corps.

Distribution :-

1. A.Coy
2. B.Coy
3. C.Coy
4. D.Coy
5. T.O.
6. Signals
7. Q.M.
8. 138th Inf:Bde.
9. 139th Inf:Bde.
10. 3rd Bn.M.G.Corps
11. 55th Bn.M.G.Corps
12. 46th Division.
13. File
14. } War Diary.
15. }

S E C R E T. Copy No 9

46th BATTALION MACHINE GUN CORPS ORDER No.29.

Reference 1/20,000 GORRE and VIEILLE CHAPELLE.

1. All guns in reserve are placed under orders to move at one hour's notice.

2. The transport of the guns in reserve will be kept packed, and will be parked by Sections, separate to other transport.
All animals concerned will be kept separate and drivers will be detailed off for respective duties.

3. In the event of warning being received by Battalion Headquarters indicating an attack on the Divisional front, or neighbouring Divisional front, Battalion Headquarters will issue the order "move reserves".
On receipt of this message the following action will be taken.

4. A. The Guns in reserve will move to an assembly position about E.28.d.
B. All other animals will be harnessed but not hooked in, and all transport wagons will be loaded.

5. Battery positions at the following positions will be reconnoitred on or before the day following any Guns moving into reserve with a view to their occupation in the event of the situation demanding it.

A.	LE QUESNOY WEST	F.8.d.10.30.
B.	DOCK BATTERY	F.7.c.4.3.
C.	HEDGE BATTERY	X.25.a.60.70.
D.	BETHUNE LOCALITY BATTERY	F.13.c.20.30.

6. The following positions will also be reconnoitred :-

E.	LE QUESNOY EAST BATTERY	F.8.b.40.40.
F.	ONE POSITION	E.[illegible].a.00.90
G.	ANOTHER AT	E.29.b.90.30.

7. The Officer Commanding any Company in reserve will ensure that at positions A, B, E, 15 (fifteen) boxes S.A.A. for each gun will be maintained.

Please acknowledge.

R. Gibson

Issued at :- 7 pm

7/8/1918.

Capt & Adjt,
46th Battn.Machine Gun Corps.

Distribution :-
1. A.Coy
2. B.Coy
3. C.Coy
4. D.Coy
5. T.O.
6. Signals
7. Q.M.
8. File.
9.)
10.)War Diary.

SECRET. Copy No(13

46th BATTALION MACHINE GUN CORPS ORDER No.39.

Reference 1/20,000 GORRE and VIEILLE CHAPELLE.

1. 'B' Company and 'B' Company Headquarters will relieve in No 2 Group, 3 (three) sections of 'D' Company at Battery positions D, E, & G, one section of 'C' Company at 'C' Battery position and 'D' Company Headquarters, in the line, on the night 9/10th May 1918.

2. After the relief of one section of 'C' Company at 'C' Battery is completed this section will relieve 1 section of 'D' Company at CANAL BATTERY.

3. 'D' Company and ~~HQ~~ 'D' Company Headquarters thus relieved will move into reserve at the Transport lines and will take over accommodation vacated by 'B' Company.

4. Immediately the above reliefs are completed Major H.P.Bailey will take over the Command of No 2 Group from Major K.B.Wood, MC.

5. Any further details will be arranged direct between O.C., Companies concerned.

6. Completion of this relief will be wired to Battalion Headquarters by the code word "THIRD".

7. Completion of this relief will also be notified to the Brigade Commander concerned.

8. When this relief is completed :-
   A. No 2 Group will consist of
   16 (sixteen) Guns of 'B' Coy, and
   12 (twelve) Guns of 'C' Coy. Total 28 (Twenty eight) guns.

   B. Divisional Reserve at Battalion Transport lines will consist of 16 (sixteen) guns of 'D' Company.

9. Acknowledge.

Issued at :- 2.30 pm

8/5/1918.

[signature]
Capt & Adjt,
46th Battn.Machine Gun Corps.

Distribution :-
1. A.Coy
2. B.Coy
3. C.Coy
4. D.Coy
5. T.O.
6. Q.M.
7. Signals
8. 46th Division
9. 3rd Bn.M.G.Corps
10. 137th Inf: Bde.
11. 139th Inf: Bde.
12. File
13.)
14.)War Diary.

SECRET. Copy No 13

46th BATTALION MACHINE GUN CORPS ORDER No.30.A.

Reference 1/20,000 GORRE and VIEILLE CHAPELLE.

1. The relief ordered in 46th Battalion Machine Gun Corps order No 30 is postponed until further orders

Issued at :- 7 and 9 d

8/5/18.

Bleiben
Capt. & Adjt,
46th Battn.M.G. Corps.

Distribution :-

1. A.Coy	8. 46th Division.
2. B.Coy	9. 3rd Bn.M.G. Corps
3. C.Coy	10. 137th Inf:Bde.
4. D.Coy	11. 139th : :
5. T.O.	12. File.
6. Q.M.	13.)
7. Signals.	14.)War Diary.

SECRET.

Copy No 5

46th BATTALION MACHINE GUN CORPS ORDER No. 31.

Reference 1/20,000 GORRE and VIEILLE CHAPELLE.

1. The O.C., No 1 Group will arrange for the Section of 'C' Coy now attached to No 1 Group to occupy 'B' Battery position forthwith i.e. if this section is not already occupying that position.

2. As soon as this is completed the O.C.,No 1 Group will notify the O.C., No 2 Group and under arrangements to be made between Group Commanders, exchange will be made forthwith to leave the position as follows :-

At 'B' Battery No 2 Section complete of 'C' Company under Lieut.C.D.Pound.

At C.5. & C.6., 1 sub-section of No 3 section of 'C' Company under Lieut.R.J.C.Shipley.

3 (see below)

4 ~~3.~~ Each Group will report completion to Battalion Headquarters by wire by the code word "ADJUSTED".

5 ~~4.~~ Acknowledge.

Issued at :- 2 45 pm

8/5/1918.

Capt & Adjt,
46th Battn.Machine Gun Corps.

Distribution :-

1. No 1 Group,
2. No 2 Group,
3. Q.M.
4. File.
5.)
6.)War Diary.

3. 3. Each Group Commander will notify these Headquarters and the Brigade Commander concerned detail of any actual reliefs that will take place to comply with this order.

S E C R E T.   Copy No 14

46th BATTALION MACHINE GUN CORPS ORDER No.32.

Reference 1/20,000 GORRE and VIEILLE CHAPELLE.

With reference to 46th Battalion Machine Corps Orders Nos 30 and 30.A.

1. 'B' Company and 'B' Company Headquarters will relieve in No 2 Group, 3 (three) sections of 'D' Company at Battery positions D, E, & G, one section of 'C' Company at 'C' Battery position and 'D' Company Headquarters, in the line, on the night 11/12th May, 1918.

2. After the relief of one section of 'C' Company at 'C' Battery is completion this section will relieve 1 section of 'D' Company at CANAL BATTERY.

3. 'D' Company and 'D' Company Headquarters thus relieved will move into reserve at the Transport lines and will take over accommodation vacated by 'B' Company.

4. Immediately the above reliefs are completed Major N.P.Bailey will take over the Command of No 2 Group from Major K.B.Wood, M.C.

5. Any further details will be arranged direct between O.C.,Companies concerned.

6. Completion of this relief will be wired to Battalion Headquarters by the code word "FOURTH".

7. Completion of this relief will also be notified to the Brigade Commander concerned.

8. When this relief is completed :-
   A. No 2 Group will consist of :-
      16 (sixteen) Guns of 'B'Coy, and
      12 (twelve) Guns of 'C' Coy. Total 28 (Twenty eight) guns.
   B. Divisional Reserve at Battalion Transport lines will consist of 16 (sixteen) guns of 'D' Company.

9. Acknowledge.

Issued at :- 7.30 PM

10/5/1918.

Capt & Adjt,
46th Battn.Machine Gun Corps.

Distribution :-
1. A.Coy
2. B.Coy
3. C.Coy
4. D.Coy
5. T.O.
6. Q.M.
7. Signals
8. 46th Division
9. 3rd Bn.M.G. Corps
10. 137th Inf:Bde.
11. 139th Inf:Bde.
12. File.
13.)
14.)War Diary.

S E C R E T.   Copy No 16

46th BATTALION MACHINE GUN CORPS ORDER No. 33.

Reference 1/20,000 GORRE and VIEILLE CHAPELLE.

1. 'D' Company and 'D' Company Headquarters will relieve 'C' Company and 'C' Company Headquarters in the line on the night 17/18th May as follows :-
   - A. In No 1 Group one section of 'C' Company at 'B' Battery.
   - B. In No 2 Group three sections of 'C' Company and 'C' Company Headquarters.

2. 'C' Company and 'C' Company Headquarters thus relieved will move into reserve at the Transport lines, and will take over accommodation vacated by 'D' Company.

3. Any further details, also guides etc., will be arranged direct between Os.C.,Companies and Groups concerned.

4. Completion of this relief will be wired to Battalion Headquarters by the code word "FIFTH".

5. Completion of this relief will also be notified to the Brigade Commanders concerned by Os.C. No 1 and 2 Groups.

6. When this relief is completed guns will be distributed as follows :-
   No 1 Group, 16 (sixteen) guns 'A' Coy.
   4 (four) guns 'D' "
   Total 20 (Twenty) guns.
   No 2 Group, 16 (sixteen) guns 'B' Coy.
   12 (twelve) guns 'D' "
   Total 28 (Twenty eight)guns.
   Divisional Reserve, 16 (sixteen) guns of 'C' Coy situated at Battalion Transport lines.

7. The O.C.,'C' Company will arrange for preliminary reconnaisance of the reserve positions to take place before this relief commences, and in communication direct with the O.C.'D' Coy who will hand over to the O.C.'C' Company all the necessary documents and correspondence.

8. Acknowledge.

Issued at 3.0 p.m.

15/5/1918.

Blister
Capt & Adjt,
46th Battn.Machine Gun Corps.

Distribution :-

1. A.Coy
2. B.Coy
3. C.Coy
4. D.Coy
5. T.O.
6. Q.M.
7. Signals
8. 46th Division.
9. 3rd Bn.M.G. Corps.
10. 55th Bn.M.G. Corps.
11. 137th Inf:Bde.
12. 138th Inf:Bde.
13. 139th Inf:Bde.
14. File.
15.) War Diary.
16.)

War Diary 1

= = 2

X1

S E C R E T.

To:-
46th Division,
137th Inf:Bde.
138th Inf:Bde.
139th Inf:Bde.
O.C.,No 1 Group,
O.C.,No 2 Group,

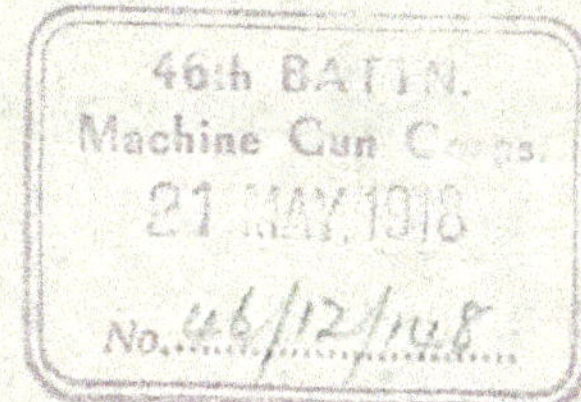

Subsidiary Machine Gun Barrage on areas in front of LIVERPOOL LINE.

1. As the number of guns available is not sufficient to put down an annihilating barrage in front of the whole LIVERPOOL LINE, the area immediately in front of it has been divided into seven zones, letteredA to G as shown on the attached tracing.

2. The batteries now in position will bring fire to bear on any zone with the number of guns indicated thereon, upon receipt of orders to do so, e.g. if the order is given to fire on A sixteen guns will function, on E twenty guns, and so on.

3. Safety clearance is allowed over the whole length of the LIVERPOOL LINE.

4. All arrangements will be made by Group Commanders for this scheme to come into operation at any time after 6.0 p.m. 24th inst:

21/5/1918.

Bt.Lieut-Colonel,
Commanding 46th Battn.M.G. Corps.

X 2

S E C R E T.

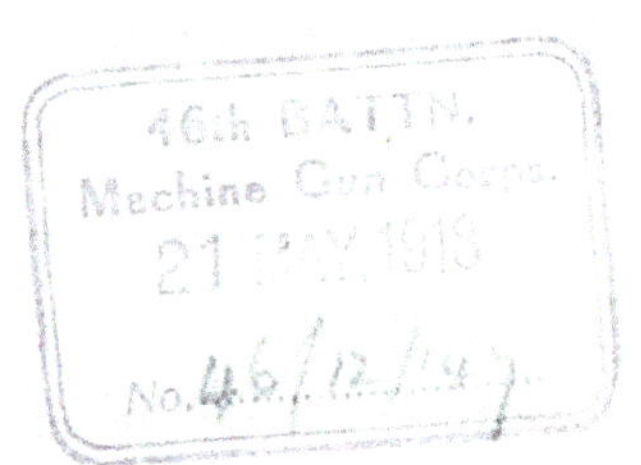

To O.C. No. 1 Group,
: 2 :

1. From 4 p.m. 24th inst: OWL, HAWK, WREN, ROBIN, THRUSH, and PIGEON Batteries will be prepared to fire on the zones detailed in Table enclosed, in accordance with the attached letter.

2. These zones will only be fired upon when ordered by the Brigade concerned.

3. Rates of fire will vary according to circumstances.

4. Group Commanders are responsible that no firing is done which has not the required safety clearance.

5. All calculations and Fighting Maps will be at once prepared and copies of the former sent to these Headquarters as soon as possible.

6. ACKNOWLEDGE.

Lieut-Colonel,
Commanding 46th Battn. Machine Gun Corps.

21/5/1918.

X 3

SECRET.
****

BATTERY.	ZONE.	TASK.
HAWK.	A.	X.29.c.25.00 to X.29.c.15.20.
	B.	X.28.d.65.90 to X.28.b.52.00.
	C.	X.22.c.60.18 to X.22.c.22.28.
	D.	X.22.c.22.38 to X.22.c.01.29.
	E.	X.21.b.10.42 to X.21.b.30.55.
OWL.	A.	X.28.d.98.18 to X.28.d.90.50.
	B.	X.28.d.40.94 to X.28.b.26.15.
	C.	X.22.c.55.05 to X.22.c.25.30.
	D.	X.22.c.25.30 to X.21.d.90.60.
	E.	X.21.b.61.10. (Concentration).
WREN.	A.	X.28.d.72.10 to X.28.d.79.27.
	B.	X.28.d.71.84 to X.28.b.71.00.
	F.	X.15.c.62.15 to X.15.c.99.20.
	G.	X.8.c.28.15 to X.8.c.64.32.
ROBIN.	B.	X.28.d.40.70 to X.28.d.40.90.
	C.	X.28.a.79.49 to X.28.a.75.87.
	D.	X.22.c.20.45 to X.22.c.05.80.
	E.) F.)	X.21.b.15.86 to X.15.c.86.08.
	G.	X.14.a.45.92 to X.14.a.82.92.
THRUSH.	C.	X.28.a.45.90 to X.22.c.46.32.
	D.	X.21.d.95.45 to X.21.d.95.85.
	E.	X.21.b.35.40 to X.21.b.27.65.
	F.	X.15.c.65.52 to X.15.c.35.85.
	G.	X.14.b.60.59 to X.14.b.05.75.
PIGEON.	D.	X.21.d.76.60 to X.21.d.80.92.
	E.	X.21.d.37.90 to X.21.b.39.35.
	F.	X.15.c.70.12 to X.15.c.59.49.
	G.	X.14.b.11.91 to X.8.c.68.20.

XA 1

SECRET.

War Diary I
" " 2 ✓

Headquarters,
46th Division.
137th Inf:Bde.
138th Inf:Bde.
139th Inf:Bde.
55th Bn.M.G. Corps.
3rd Bn.M.G. Corps
O.C.No 1 Group
O.C.No 2 Group.

46th BATTN.
Machine Gun Corps.
21 MAY 1918
No. 46/12/142

Harassing Fire. Machine Gun Concentration Shoots.

1. In future it is proposed that the indirect fire of Machine Guns shall take the form of concentrations of as many guns as possible on to each target.

2. Watches will be synchronized and definite times laid down for firing. One minute before scheduled time guns will be ready to fire, a central battery will set the time and the instant it is heard to fire every gun detailed will fire one belt rapid.

3. The intervals between concentrations will be irregular, but will be of sufficient duration to allow the belts just emptied to be refilled ready for firing in the next concentration.

4. Guns having S.O.S.lines will be prepared to switch on to them instantly should the S.O.S. signal be observed while guns are engaged in a Concentration Shoot.

5. All guns will fire through screens of wet canvas.

6. Attached is a list of targets, numbered according to the square they are situated in and distinguished by letters.
The list also shows the number of guns which can be focussed on to each target.

7. A programme for the week commencing Wednesday May 22nd is enclosed.

8. ACKNOWLEDGE.

21/5/1918.

J Harington
Bt.Lieut-Colonel,
Commanding 46th Battn.M.G. Corps.

S E C R E T.

M.G. C O N C E N T R A T I O N   S H O O T S.

TARGET. GUNS ABLE TO FIRE. Batteries

No.	Map Reference.	C1.	C2.	C3.	C4.	C5.	C6.	C7.	C8.	5.	6.	Tuning Fork West.	9.	10.	11.	15.	THRUSH.	PIGEON.	WREN.	HAWK.	TOTAL.	DIRECTING GUNS.
3A.	X.3.d.20.10	1		1		1		1													4	C 3.
3B.	X.3.d.70.65			1	1	1		1													4	C 3.
8A.	X.8.b.92.48	1		1		1		1									4	4			12	THRUSH Bty.
8B.	X.8.b.35.49	1		1		1		1									4	4			12	THRUSH Bty.
10A.	X.10.d.65.02		1		1	1		1		1	1				1	1			4		12	WREN Bty.
10B.	X.10.d.65.20	1		1		1		1		1	1				1	1			4		12	WREN Bty.
10C.	X.10.c.05.15		1		1	1		1									4		4		12	THRUSH Bty.
10D.	X.10.d.00.90			1		1		1	1				1	1							6	C 5.
10E.	X.10.b.12.23	1		1			1	1					1	1							6	C 1.
15A.	X.15.b.08.94					1	1	1					1	1			4	4	4		17	PIGEON Bty.
16A.	X.16.d.30.00			1	1	1	1	1				2							4	4	15	HAWK Bty.
16B.	X.16.d.80.90	1		1		1		1		1	1	2	1	1	1	1			4	4	20	WREN Bty.
16C.	X.16.d.29.93		1		1			1	1	1	1	2	1	1	1	1			4	4	20	WREN Bty.
16D.	X.16.b.12.90	1		1		1		1		1	1		1	1					4		12	WREN Bty.
16E.	X.16.a.83.97	1	1	1	1		1	1		1	1		1	1	1	1			4		16	WREN Bty.
17A.	X.17.c.19.09			1		1	1	1	1	1	1	2	1	1	1	1			4	4	21	HAWK Bty.
17B.	X.17d.43.52.	1		[illegible]	1				1	1	1	2	1	1	1	1			4	4	19	HAWK Bty.
17C.	X.17.d.39.83.	1	1	1					1	1	1	2	1	1	1	1			4		16	WREN Bty.
19A.	S.19.c.30.63									1	1	2	1	1							6	TUNING FORK WEST
19B.	S.19.c.24.92									1	1	2	1	1							6	TUNING FORKWEST.
19C.	S.19.a.08.70									1	1	2	1	1							6	TUNING FORK WEST
23A.	X.23.a.95.20			1	1				1						1	1			4	4	13	HAWK Bty.
23B.	X.23.a.75.92			1	1	1			1			2			1	1			4	4	16	WREN Bty.
24A.	X.24.a.86.22									1	1	2			1	1				4	10	HAWK Bty.
24B.	X.24.a.03.47	1	1	1					1	1	1	2			1	1			4	4	18	WREN Bty.
24C.	X.24.a.18.88	1	1						1	1	1	2			1	1				4	13	HAWK Bty.

21/5/1918.

J. Harrington
Bt.Lieut-Colonel,
Commanding 46th Battn.M.G. Corps.

XA 3

SECRET.

HARASSING FIRE PROGRAMME.

NIGHT.	TARGET.	TIME.	ROUNDS PER GUN.	REMARKS.
Wednesday. 22/23rd. May 1918.	16 A.	3.0 am.	250	
	16 A.	3.15 am.	250	
	17 A.	3.42 am.	250)	
	17 A.	4.5. am.	250)	
	16 A.	4.25.am.	250)	Only if visibility low
	~~mx~~		)	
	17 A.	4.50 am.	250)	
Thursday. 23/24th May 1918.	17 B.	10.30 pm.	250	
	16 E.	10.45 pm.	250	
	23 A.	11.20 pm	250	
	17 B.	11.40 pm	250	
	16 E.	12.30 am	250	
	17 B.	1.10 am	250	
	16 E.	2.55 am	250	
Friday. 24/25th May 1918.	15 A.	11.0 pm	250	
	3 A	12.15 am	250	
	16 C.	12.30 am.	250	
	15 A.	12.55 am	250	
	16 C.	1.55 am	250	
	3 A.	2.15 am	250	
	16 C.	3.10 am	250	
	15 A.	4.15 am	250	-------Only if visibility low
Saturday. 25/26th May 1918.	17 A (	10.15 pm	125	
	(	10.18 pm	125	
	24 B	10.35 pm	250	
	17 C	12.0 mid:	250	
	24 B	1.30 am	250	
	17 C	1.45 am	250	
	17 C	3.15 am	250	
	24 B	3.30 am	250)	Only if visibility low
	24 B.	4.20 am	250)	
Monday. 27/28th May 1918.	8 A		250	
	23 B	2.59 am	(125	
	23 B	3.2 am	(125	
	8 A	3.9 am	250	
	23 B	3.28 am	250	
	16 E	3.45 am	250)	
	8 A	4.5 am	250)	
	23 B	4.40 am	250)	Only if visibility low
	23 B	4.55 am	250)	
Tuesday 28/29th May 1918.	17 A	10.5 pm	250	
	17 A	11.0 pm	250	
	10 C	12.15 am	250	
	24 B }	12.55 am	(125	
	~~17 A~~ }	1.0 am	(125	
	15 A	2.30 am	250	
	10 C	3.15 am	250	
	24 B	3.45 am	250)	
	15 A	4.0 am	250)	Only if visibility low
	15 A	4.35 am	250)	

X A 4

NIGHT.	TARGET.	TIME	ROUNDS PER GUN.	REMARKS.
Wednesday. 29/30th May 1918.	10 A.	10.30 pm.	250	
	10 A.	(10.50 pm	125	
		(10.53 pm	125	
	10 B.	3.0 am	250	
	8 B.	3.27 am	250	
	16 B.	3.44 am	250)	
	16 B.	4.30 am	250)	Only if visibility low
	17 B.	4.47 am	250)	

21/5/18.

J Harington
Bt.Lieut-Colonel,
Commanding 46th Battn.M.G. Corps.

S E C R E T.   Copy No 16

46th BATTALION MACHINE GUN CORPS ORDER No. 34.

Reference 1/20,000 GORRE and VIEILLE CHAPELLE.

1. 'C' Company and 'C' Company Headquarters will relieve 'A' Company and 'A' Company Headquarters in the line in the GORRE Section on the night 23/24th May 1918.

2. 'A' Company and 'A' Company Headquarters thus relieved will move into reserve at the Transport lines, and will take over accommodation vacated by 'C' Company.

3. Any further details, also guides etc., will be arranged direct between Os.C. Companies and Groups concerned.

4. Completion of this relief will be wired to Battalion Headquarters by the code word "SIXTH".

5. Completion of this relief will also be notified to the General Officer Commanding Brigade in the GORRE Section.

6. Immediately the above relief is completed Major W.T.Boughey will take over the Command of No 1 Group from Major H.R.Nurse, M.C.

7. When this relief is completed guns will be distributed as follows:-

   No 1 Group, (Major W.T.Boughey) 16 (sixteen) guns 'C' Company
   4 (four) guns 'D' Company
   Total 20 (Twenty) guns.

   No 2 Group, (Major N.P.Bailey) 16 (sixteen) guns 'B' Company
   12 (twelve) guns 'D' Company
   Total 28 (Twenty eight) guns.

   In Divisional Reserve and situated at Battalion Transport lines
   16 (sixteen) guns of 'A' Company.

8. The O.C. 'A' Company will arrange for preliminary reconnaissance of the reserve positions to take place before this relief commences, and in communication direct with the O.C.'C' Company, who will hand over to the O.C.'A' Company all the necessary documents, correspondence, and details of any work in hand.

9. Acknowledge.

Issued at 7.0 a.m.

22/5/1918.

Capt & Adjt,
46th Battn.M.G. Corps.

Distribution:-

1. A.Coy.
2. B.Coy
3. C.Coy
4. D.Coy
5. T.O.
6. Q.M.
7. Signals.
8. 46th Division.
9. 3rd Bn.M.G. Corps.
10. 55th Bn. M.G.Corps
11. 137th Inf;Bde.
12. 138th Inf;Bde.
13. 139th Inf;Bde.
14. File.
15.)
16.) War Diary.

S E C R E T. Copy No 9

46th BATTALION MACHINE GUN CORPS AMENDMENT ORDER No.29 A.

Reference 1/20,000 GORRE and VIEILLE CHAPELLE.

The following amendments will be made to Order No 29 issued 7/5/18.

1. Delete para.4 and substitute :-
   Para.4. A. The Company in reserve less one sub-section will move to an assembly position about E.23.b. at LAUNDRY POST.
   B. All other animals will be harnessed but not hooked in, and all other Transport wagons will be loaded.

2. Delete paras. 5 & 6 and substitute :-
   Battery positions at the following places will be reconnoitred with a view to occupation in the event of the situation demanding it.
   A. Dock Battery, F.7.c.8.5., 4 (Four) guns, 60 (Sixty) boxes S.A.A.
   B. BETHUNE Locality Battery F.13.c.3.4., 4 (Four) guns, No S.A.A.
   C. LE QUESNOY EAST, F.8.b.15.10, 2 (two) guns)
   F.8.b.4.2 2 (two) guns) 60 boxes S.A.A.
   D. LE QUESNOY WEST, ~~[illegible]~~)
   F.8.c.38.50) 2 (two) guns) 60 (Sixty)
   F.8.d.1.5. 1 (one) gun) boxes S.A.A.
   F.8.d.25.00 1 (one) gun)

3. One sub-section under an Officer will be attached to the O.C. Battalion of the Reserve Brigade detailed for holding the CANAL BRIDGE line. This sub-section is intended to cover crossings over the Canal, GORRE BRIDGE.
   The position for this sub-section to occupy is about 80 yards West of the Bridge, approximately F.3.c.30.45 in the hedge on the South bank of the Canal, and a sub-section will be ordered to proceed thereto when the reserves move.

4. Other Battery positions are being constructed at LAWE Battery W.29.b.55.00, and another at BRIDGEHEAD Battery E.6.a.70.30 (Four guns each Battery)

5. ACKNOWLEDGE.

Issued at 7.0 p.m.

[signature]

23/5/1918.

Capt & Adjt,
46th Battn.Machine Gun Corps.

Distribution:-
1. A.Coy,
2. B.Coy,
3. C.Coy,
4. D.Coy,
5. T.O.
6. Signals
7. Q.M.
8. File,
9.)
10.)War Diary.

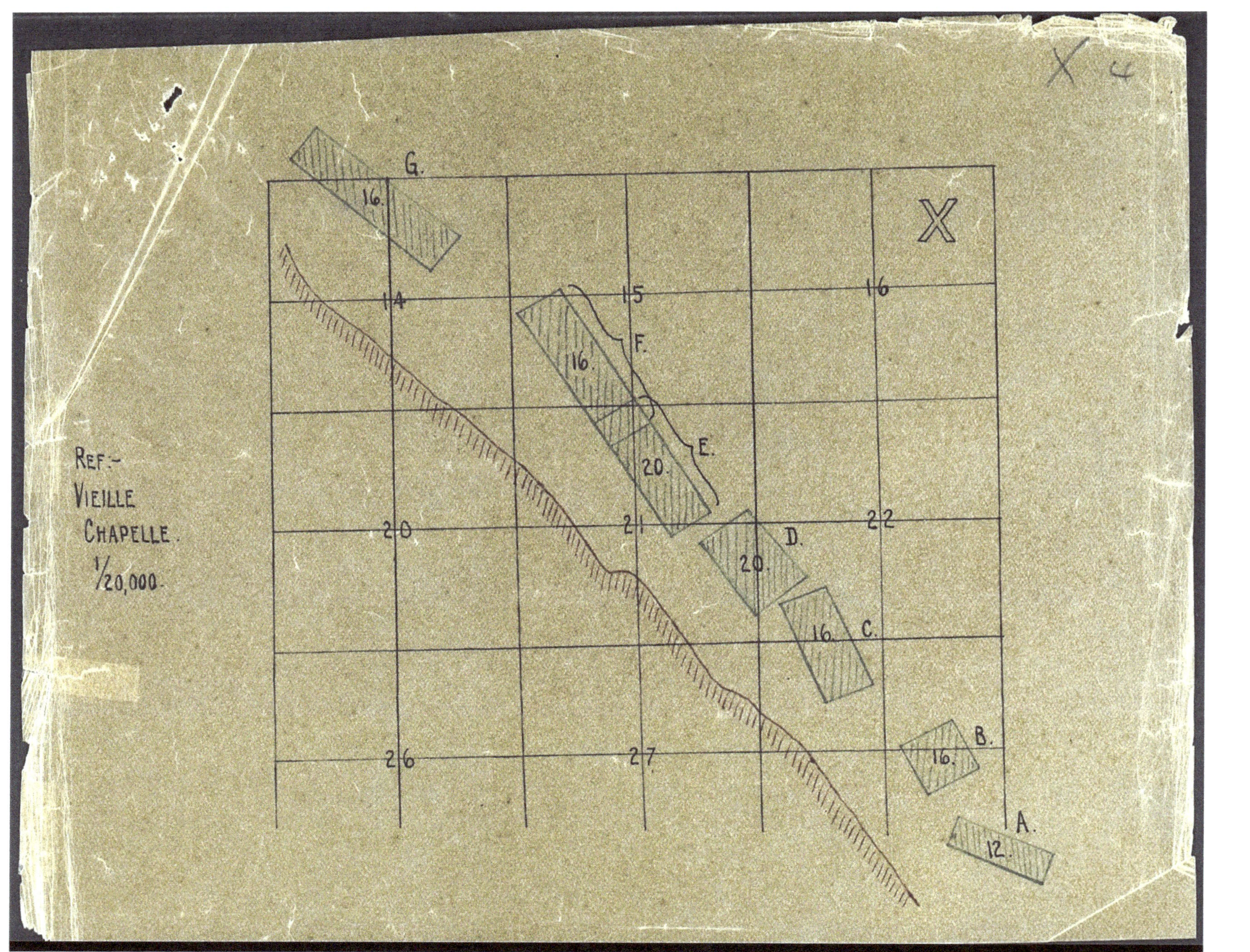
X
G.
16.
14
15
16
F.
16.
E.
20.
20
21
22
D.
20.
16.
C.
26
27
B.
16.
A.
12.
REF.-
VIEILLE
CHAPELLE.
1/20,000.

SECRET.

Machine Gun Concentration Shootsm, Week commencing Thursday May 30th.

NIGHT.	TARGET.	TIME.	ROUNDS per gun.
May 30/31.	8 A.	11-30 pm.	125
	8 A.	11-36 pm	125
	16 C.	12-0 mid.	250
	23 A.	12-45 am.	250
	24 C.	1-50 am.	250
	16 C.	2-2 am.	250
	24 C.	3-30 am.	250
June 1/2	8 B.	10-30 pm	250
	16 A.	11-0 pm	250
	23 B.	11-15 pm	125
	23 B.	11-18 pm	125
	17 C.	12-5 am	500
	16 D.	1-15 am	125
	16 D.	1-20 am	125
	17 C.	2-10 am	250
2/3	24 B.	10-45 pm	250
	24 A.	10-59 pm	250
	16 E.	11-20 pm	500
	24 B.	11-32 pm	250
	29 B.	12-15 am	250
	23 A.	1-0 am	250
	23 A.	1-50 am	250
	16 E.	2-0 am	250
3/4	15 A.	1-0 am	250
	16 C.	1-15 am	250
	17 B.	1-40 am	250
	16 C.	2-20 am	250
	15 A.	3-0 am	250
	19 A.	3-22 am	250
	16 C.	3-31 am	125
	16 C.	3-33 am	125
4/5	8 A.	10-35 pm	250
	8 A.	10-50 pm	250
	24 A.	12-1 am	125
	24 A.	12-2 am	125
	16 E.	1-0 am	250
	16 B.	1-20 am	500
5/6	8 B.	10-22 pm	250
	24 C.	10-38 pm	250
	19 C.	10-59 pm	250
	15 A.	11-20 pm	250
	10 B.	12-0 mid	250
	24 C.	12-50 am	250
	24 C.	1-30 am	250

Group Commanders will arrange additional concentrations on these targets should the early morning be very misty.

27/5/1918.

Major,
46th Battn.Machine Gun Corps.

A×

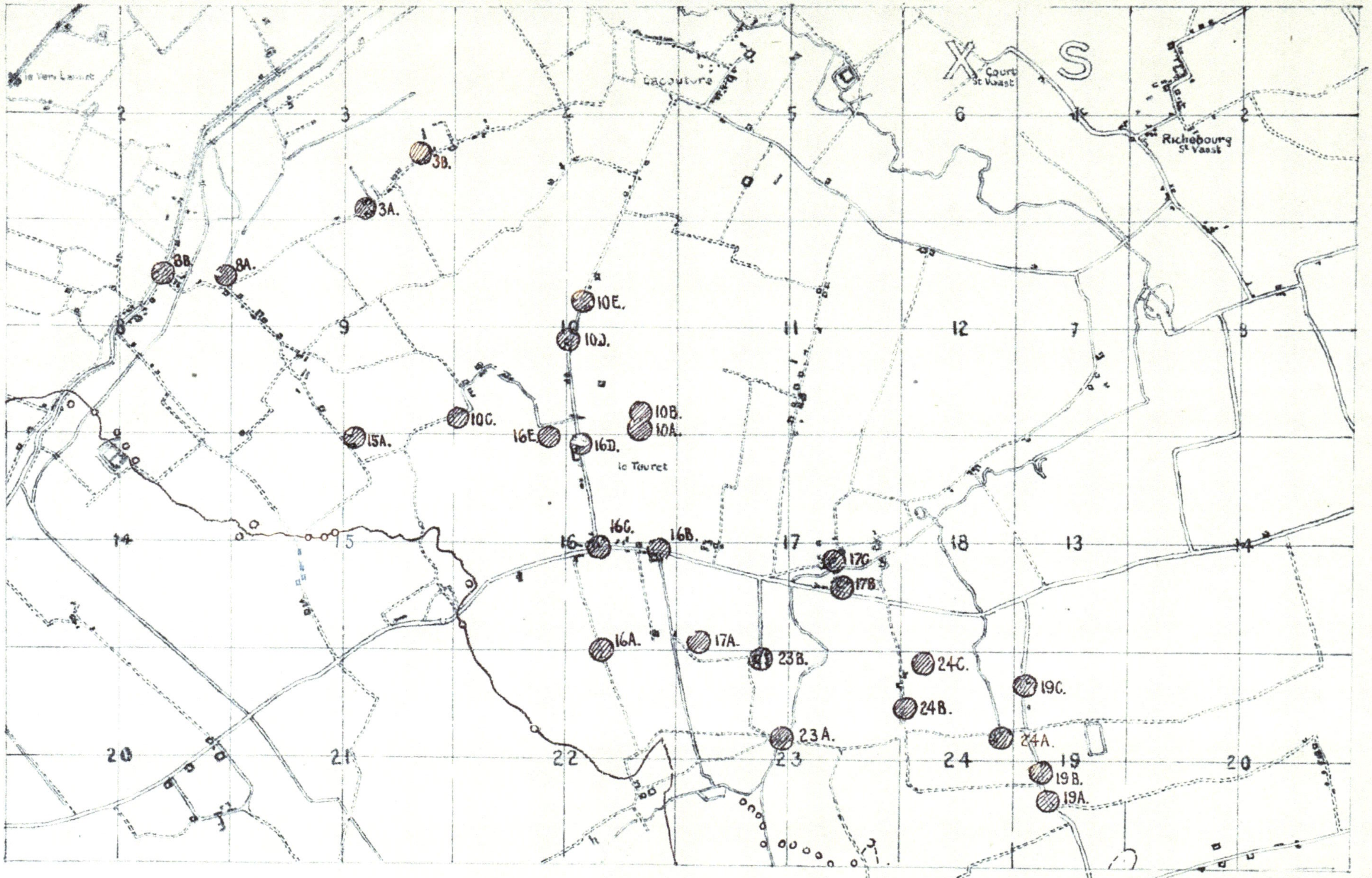
le Vert Lannot
Lacouture
X
S
Court St Vaast
Richebourg St Vaast
le Touret
3B.
3A.
8B.
8A.
10E.
10J.
10C.
15A.
16E.
16D.
10B.
10A.
16C.
16B.
16A.
17A.
23B.
17C.
17B.
24C.
24B.
23A.
24A.
19C.
19B.
19A.

1/20,000 VIEILLE CHAPELLE.

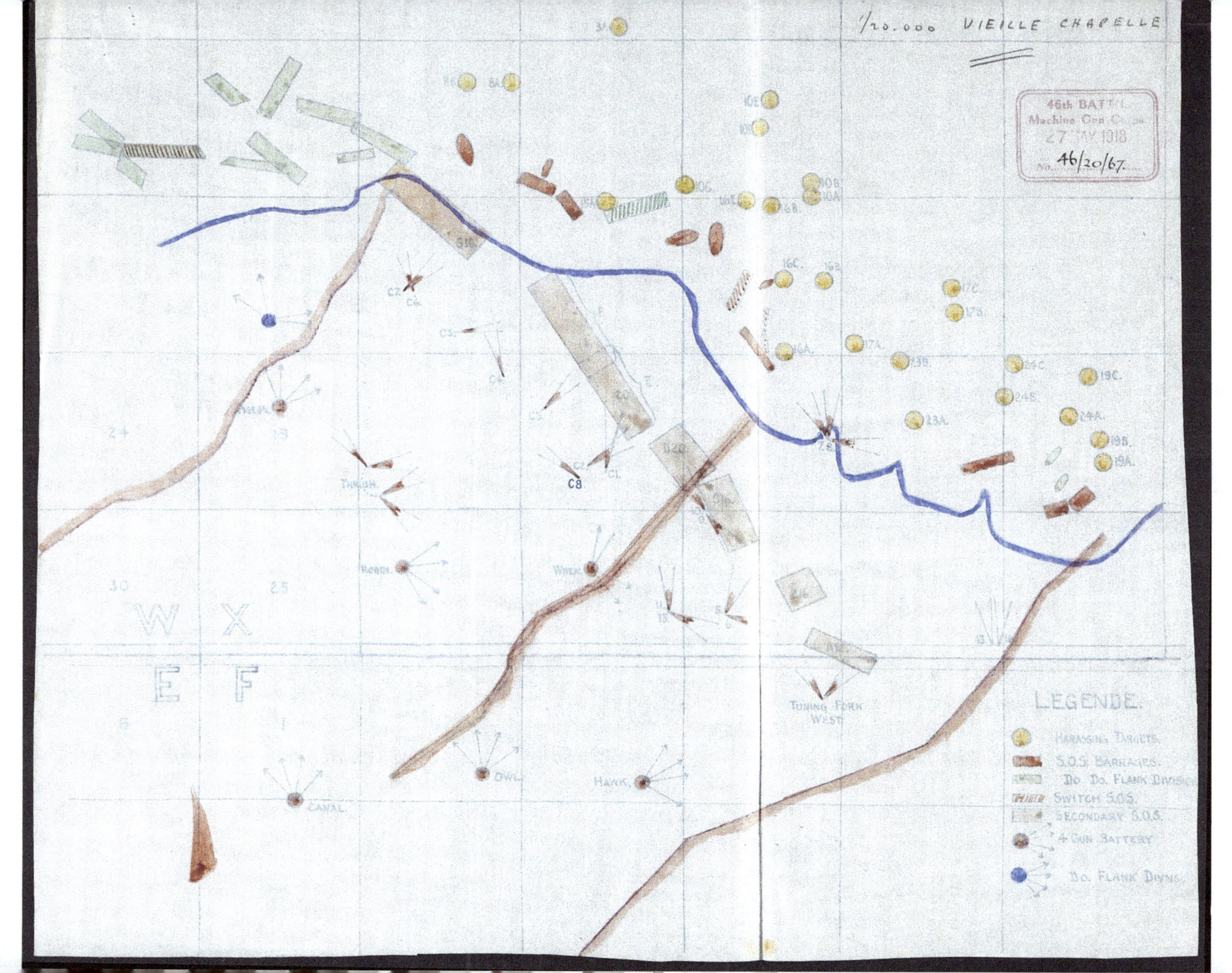

1/20.000 VIEILLE CHAPELLE
46th BATT'N. Machine Gun Corps
27 MAY 1918
No. 46/20/67.
LEGENDE.
HARASSING TARGETS.
S.O.S. BARRAGES.
Do. Do. FLANK DIVISION
SWITCH S.O.S.
SECONDARY S.O.S.
4 GUN BATTERY
Do. FLANK DIVN.
TUNING FORK WEST
THRUSH.
ROBIN.
WREN.
OWL.
HAWK.
CANAL.
C8
W X
E F

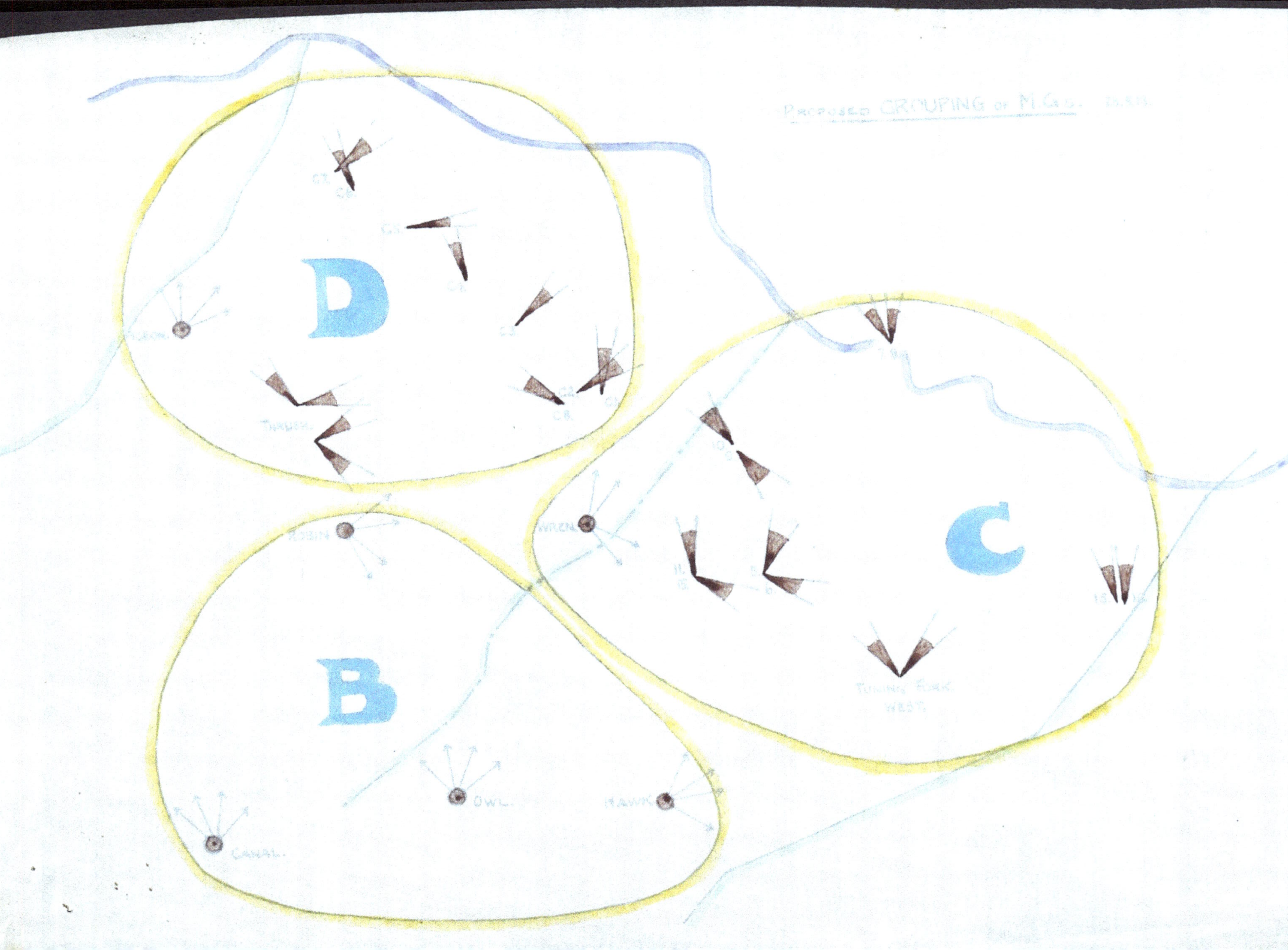

Proposed GROUPING of M.G.s.
D
C
B
THRUSH
ROBIN
WREN
OWL
HAWK
CANAL
TUNING FORK
WEST

SECRET & URGENT.

Copy No. 12

To:-

H.Q.46th Division,
H.Q.137th Inf:Bde.
" 138th Inf:Bde.
" 139th Inf:Bde.
O.C.'A' Coy,
O.C.'B' Coy.
O.C.'C' Coy,
O.C.'D' Coy,
O.C.No 1 Group,
O.C.No 2 Group,

46th BATTALION MACHINE GUN CORPS ORDER No.35.

Reference 1/20,000 GORRE and VIEILLE CHAPELLE.

1. In order to facilitate supervision by Company Commanders on the night 29/30th May 1918, the Machine Guns now in position will be reorganized as follows into Company Areas.

Rear Guns.	HAWK Battery OWL " CANAL " ROBIN "	B.Company.
Right forward guns.	13 16 7 8 9 10 5 6 TUNING FORK WEST. 11 15 WREN BATTERY.	C. Company.

WREN BATTERY will be thus transferred to No 1 Group.

Left Forward Guns.	C 1 C 2 C 3 C 4 C 5 C 6 C 7 C 8 THRUSH BATTERY PIGEON BATTERY.	D.Company.

A tracing showing these Groups is attached.

2. To obtain this arrangement, commencing at 9.0 p.m. 29th May 1918, under arrangements to be made between O.C. Companies concerned the following sections will exchange places :-
The Section of "C" Company now at HAWK Battery will change places with the section of "B" Company now at WREN Battery.
The two sections of "D" Company now at CANAL and OWL Batteries will change places with the two sections of "B" Company now at THRUSH and PIGEON Batteries.

3. This interchange will be so arranged that not more than one gun and team is absent from any one Battery at a time.

4. Completion of interchange will be wired to Battalion Headquarters by code word "BIRDS".

5. O.C. Companies will establish their Headquarters as follows :-

B. Company.	CHATEAU Le QUESNOY
C. Company	No 2 Sections Headquarters at approximately F.4.b.35.75.
D. Company	THRUSH Battery.

6. O.C."C" Company will be O.C. Right Forward Guns.
O.C."D" Company will be O.C. Left Forward Guns.
They will be in constant touch with the Infantry Battalion Commanders on right and left respectively, and will visit them daily.

O.C."B" Company will be O.C. Right Rear Guns and will be responsible for OWL and HAWK Batteries in every way. His Second-in-Command will be O.C.Left Rear Guns and will be responsible for the tactical handling of CANAL and ROBIN Batteries under orders of the Group Commander.
O.C."B" Company will be entirely responsible for the discipline etc., of the whole of his Company, including CANAL and ROBIN Batteries.

7. The Group Commanders, their duties and responsibilities will remain as before.

8. ACKNOWLEDGE.

Issued at 12 noon.

Blickens

29/5/1918.

Capt & Adjt,
46th Battn.Machine Gun Corps.

SECRET. Copy No. 16

46th BATTALION MACHINE GUN CORPS ORDER No.36.

Reference 1/20,000 GORRE and VIEILLE CHAPELLE.

1. 'A' Company will relieve 'B' Company in the line in the 'Rear Gun positions' on the night 30/31st May 1918.

2. 'B' Company and 'B' Company Headquarters thus relieved will move into reserve at the Transport lines and will take over accommodation vacated by 'A' Company, and as Sections arrive Transport lines they will come under two hours notice to move.

3. Any further details, also guides etc, will be arranged direct between O.C.'A' Company and O.C.Groups.

4. Completion of this relief will be wired to Battalion Headquarters by the code word "SEVENTH".

5. Completion of this relief will also be notified by Group Commanders to respective Brigade Commanders.

6. Immediately the above relief is completed the Commands of Groups and Companies will be allocated as follows :-

No 1 Group,	Major E.R.Nurse, M.C.
No 2 Group,	Major K.B.Wood, M.C.
O.C.Right Forward Guns,	Major W.T.Boughey.
O.C.Left Forward Guns,	Capt L.R.G.Heins.
O.C.Right Rear Guns,	Capt.R.Page.
O.C.Left Rear Guns,	An Officer of 'A' Company.
To Command 'A' Company	Capt.R.Page.
To Command 'C' Company	Major W.T.Boughey.
To Command 'D' Company	Capt.L.R.G.Heins.
Reserve Guns 'B' Company	Major N.P.Bailey.

7. All Trench and area stores, documents, maps, etc.,will be handed over,and receipts obtained.

8. The O.C.'B' Company will arrange for a preliminary reconnaisance of the reserve positions (see order 29 as amended by 29 A.) to take place before this relief commences,and in consultation direct with the O.C.'A' Company, who will hand over to the O.C.'B' Company all necessary documents, correspondence,etc.,regarding the reserve positions.

9. ACKNOWLEDGE.

Issued at [illegible]

[signature]
Capt & Adjt,
46th Battn.Machine Gun Corps.

29/5/1918.

Distribution :-

1. A.Coy.	9. 3rd Bn.M.G.Corps.
2. B.Coy.	10. 55th Bn.M.G.Corps.
3. C.Coy.	11. 137th Infantry Bde.
4. D.Coy.	12. 138th Infantry Bde.
5. T.O.	13. 139th Infantry Bde.
6. Q.M.	14. File.
7. Signals.	15.)
8. 46th Division.	16.)War Diary.

SECRET.

Copy No 16

46th BATTALION MACHINE GUN CORPS ORDER No.36 A.

The following amendment will be made to para.6 of 46th Battalion Machine Gun Corps Order No 36 dated 29th May, 1918.

1. To Command No 1 Group, for Major E.R.Nurse, M.C., substitute Major W.T.Boughey.

2. O.C.Right Forward Guns, for Major W.T.Boughey substitute Capt D.Harvey.

3. O.C.'C' Coy, for Major W.T.Boughey substitute Capt D.Harvey.

30/5/18.

[signature]
Capt & Adjt,
46th Battn.Machine Gun Corps.

Distribution:-
1.A.Coy.
2.B.Coy.
3.C.Coy
4.D.Coy.
5. T.O.
6. Q.M.
7. Signals.
8. 46th Division.
9. 3rd Bn.M.G.Corps.
10. 55th Bn.M.G.Corps.
11. 137th Inf:Bde.
12. 138th Inf:Bde.
13. 139th Inf:Bde.
14. File.
15.)
16.)War Diary.

46 Bn. M.G. Corps
Vol 4

On His Majesty's Service.

Confidential

D A G

3rd Echelon

****

W A R   D I A R Y.

46th BATTALION MACHINE GUN CORPS.

JUNE 1918.

****

Instructions regarding War Diaries and Intelligence Summaries are contained in F. S. Regs., Part II. and the Staff Manual respectively. Title pages will be prepared in manuscript.

WAR DIARY

or

~~INTELLIGENCE SUMMARY~~

(Erase heading not required.)

JUNE 1918.

46th BATTALION MACHINE GUN CORPS.

No 1.

Army Form C. 2118.

Place	Date	Hour	Summary of Events and Information	Remarks and references to Appendices
			1/20,000 VIEILLE CHAPELLE 1/20,000 GORRE.	
GORRE & ESSARS SECTIONS. N.LA-BASSEE CANAL.	1st.		Machine Guns fired 15,500 rounds harassing fire vide programme 'A' " " " 3,500 " at E.A. 3 O.Rs.returned Base Depot Medically unfit. 1 O.R. evacuated sick. 1 O.R. wounded at duty.	'A'
	2nd.		Machine Guns fired 20,500 rounds harassing fire in accordance with programme. " " " 550 " at E.A. Lieut.G.D.Hamilton wounded in action, and gassed. 2 O.Rs. wounded (gas) 1 O.R. wounded at duty. 10 O.Rs. rejoined after evacuation. 4 O.Rs. to Divisional Signalling Course.	
	3rd.		M.Gs.fired 19,000 rounds harassing fire vide programme. " " 300 " at E.A. 2 O.Rs. evacuated sick. Capt.M.Douglas joined from Base Depot.	
	4th.	7.0 pm.	Order No 37 issued(copy attached)	Order No 37
		7.0 pm.	M.G. harassing programme for week commencing June 6th, 1918 issued (copy attached,marked 'B') M.Gs. fired 17,000 rounds harassing fire vide programme. 1 O.R. evacuated sick, 1 O.R. returned to Base Depot. Major K.B.Wood to 2nd Bn.M.G.Corps. 1 O.R.to 2nd Bn.M.G.Corps, Batman to Major K.B.Wood, M.C. 2 O.Rs.returned after Evacuation.	'B'
	5th.		M.Gs.fired 14,500 rounds harassing fire vide programme. 3 O.Rs. evacuated sick. 1 O.R. returned after evacuation.	
	6th.		M.Gs. fired 12,000 rounds harassing fire vide programme. 3 O.Rs. evacuated.(sick) 1 O.R. rejoined after evacuation.	
	7th.		M.Gs.fired 13,750 rounds during hostile raid. " " 11,250 " harassing fire vide programme. 1 O.R. wounded. 18 O.Rs. reinforcements. 3 O.Rs. returned after evacuation.	
	8th.		M.Gs. fired 18,500 rounds harassing fire vide programme. 2 O.Rs.evacuated sick 2 O.Rs. returned after evacuation. 9 O.Rs. wounded in action.	

A5834 Wt. W4973/M687 750,000 8/16 D. D. & L. Ltd. Forms/C.2118/13.

Instructions regarding War Diaries and Intelligence Summaries are contained in F. S. Regs., Part II. and the Staff Manual respectively. Title pages will be prepared in manuscript.

WAR DIARY

~~INTELLIGENCE SUMMARY~~

(Erase heading not required.)

JUNE 1918.

Army Form C. 2118.

46th BATTALION MACHINE GUN CORPS

No 2.

Place	Date	Hour	Summary of Events and Information	Remarks and references to Appendices
			1/20,000 VIEILLE CHAPELLE. 1/20,000 GORRE.	
GORRE & ESSARS SECTIONS N.LA-BASSEE CANAL.	9th.	12.55 a.m.	Enemy plane dropped 2 bombs in front of WREN Battery in X.27.a. M.G.Defence Scheme issued (copy attached) M.Gs fired 10,750 rounds harassing fire vide programme. 1 O.R. evacuated sick. 10 O.Rs. wounded (Gas).	'C'
	10th.	6.30 p.m.	Order No 38 issued (copy attached.) M.Gs. fired 11,250 rounds harassing fire vide programme. " " 16,450 in connection with raid. " " 2,000 rounds at Low flying E.A. 2 O.Rs. evacuated sick. 5 O.Rs. returned after evacuation.	Order No.38
	11th.		8,625 rounds were fired by M.Gs. vide programme. Programme of harassing concentration shoots issued, for week ending June 19th, 1918. (copy attached) 22 O.Rs. reinforcements. Lieut C.H.Hargrave reinforcement. Lieut.C.W.Pugh reinforcement.	'D'
	12th.		M.Gs. fired 9,500 rounds harassing fire vide programme. 1 O.R. to Base Depot unfit. 1 O.R. returned after evacuation.	
	13th		M.Gs. fired 14,000 rounds harassing fire vide programme. Order No 39 issued (copy attached) 2 O.Rs. evacuated sick. 1 O.R. reinforcement. Major H.S.Windeler, reinforcement. Capt C.V.Rigby, M.C. reinforcement. 2/Lieut.W.G.Oncken reinforcement.	O.No.39.
	14th.		M.Gs.fired 32,000 rounds in conjunction with operation carried out by 3rd Division. " " 4,000 rounds as per programme. 1 O.R. evacuated sick. 1 O.R. returned after evacuation.	
	15th.		M.Gs. fired 11,750 rounds harassing fir vide programme. 3 O.Rs. evacuated sick 1 O.R. killed in action. 1 O.R. returned after evacuation.	
	16th.	7.pm.	Order No 40 issued (copy attached) Letter No 46/12/241 issued (copy attached marked E.) 11,700 rounds were fired by M.Gs. vide programme. 760 " " " " " at E.A..	O.No.40 'E'

A5834 Wt. W4973/M687 750,000 8/16 D. D. & L. Ltd. Forms/C.2118/13.

Instructions regarding War Diaries and Intelligence Summaries are contained in F. S. Regs., Part II. and the Staff Manual respectively. Title pages will be prepared in manuscript.

WAR DIARY

~~or~~

~~INTELLIGENCE SUMMARY.~~

(Erase heading not required.)

JUNE 1918.

Army Form C. 2118.

46th BATTALION MACHINE GUN CORPS

No 3.

Place	Date	Hour	VIEILLE CHAPELLE 1/20,000 GORRE 1/20,000 Summary of Events and Information	Remarks and references to Appendices
GORRE & ESSARS SECTIONS N.LA+ BASSEE CANAL.	17th.		Revised appendix to M.G Counter preparation Scheme issued under 46/12/250 (copy attached marked 'F') M.Gs.fired 8,500 rounds harassing fire vide programme.	'F'
		4.45 am.	1 Low Flying E.A. driven down in its own lines in X.7.c. 3 O.Rs. evacuated sick 1 O.R. returned after evacuation.	
	18th.		M.Gs fired 6,950 rounds harassing fire during special operation. " " 27,500 " " " vide programme. A fire was started in X.28.b., also in LE TOURET. 1 O.R. wounded (Gas) 1 O.R. evacuated sick. Major E.R.Nurse, M.C. To M.G.T.C. Grantham.	
	19th		16,750 rounds were fired by M.Gs. vide harassing fire programme. 1 O.R. to Cadet School U.K. 1 O.R. evacuated sick.	
	20th.		M.Gs. fired 900 rounds at E.A. during the day. Major N.P.Bailey to Base Depot as Instructor. 2 O.Rs. wounded. 4 O.Rs evacuated sick.	
	21st.		Machine Gun harassing programme for week commencing June 20/21st issued (copy attached marked 'G') Machine Gun concentration shoots issued (copy attached marked 'H')	'G' 'H'
		7.0 pm.	Order No 41 issued (copy attached) Also Map H.X issued M.Gs. fired 24,500 rounds harassing fire vide programme. Demonstration of Counter attack Signal by aeroplane. 1 O.R. wounded. 2 O.Rs. evacuated sick. Lieut.O.B.Tompkins to M.G.T.C.,Grantham. Lieut.C.G.Larking reinforcement.	O.No 41 Map H.X.
	22nd.		11,000 rounds fired by M.Gs. in support of raid. 21,750 " " " " vide harassing fire programme. An explosion in LAMOTTE at F.1.b. 1 O.R. evacuated sick. 1 O.R. wounded.	
	23rd.		M.Gs. fired 29,750 rounds harassing fire vide programme. " " 200 " at E.A. A fire seen at about X.16 .d. 90.90 1 O.R. evacuated sick.	
	24th.		M.Gs. fired 22,000 rounds harassing fire vide programme. " " 550 " at E.A..	

A5834 Wt. W4973/M687 750,000 8/16 D. D. & L. Ltd. Forms/C.2118/13.

Instructions regarding War Diaries and Intelligence Summaries are contained in F. S. Regs., Part II. and the Staff Manual respectively. Title pages will be prepared in manuscript.

JUNE 1918

Army Form C. 2118.

WAR DIARY

or

~~INTELLIGENCE SUMMARY~~. 46th BATTALION MACHINE GUN CORPS.

(Erase heading not required.)

No 4.

Place	Date	Hour	Summary of Events and Information	Remarks and references to Appendices
			1/20,000 VIEILLE CHAPELLE 1/20,000 GORRE.	
GORRE & ESSARS SECTIONS	25th.		M.Gs. fired 16,000 rounds harassing fire vide programme. " " 850 " at E.A. A fire was started at Left Forward Section H.Q. in Garden (X.14.c.65.40) by hostile shelling. Small dump destroyed. 2/Lieut.G.F.Renwick To 39th Stationary Hospital sick.	
N.LA-BASSEE CANAL.	26th.		M.Gs. fired 23,250 rounds harassing fire vide programme. " " 2,100 " at E.A. A number of bombs dropped on BETHUNE. 3 O.Rs. wounded. 17 O.Rs. reinforcements. Programme of Machine Gun Harassing Shoots for week commencing 27/28th June issued (copy attached marked 'J')	'J'
	27th.		3 O.Rs. returned after evacuation. 8,800 rounds fired by M.Gs. vide harassing fire programme. 1,450 " " " " at E.A.	
		8.50 p.m.	E.A. approached our lines firing green lights. Order No 42 issued (Copy attached)	O.No.42.
	28th.		1 O.R. returned after evacuation. M.Gs. fired 25,750 rounds harassing fire vide programme. " " 4,300 " at E.A. Order No 43 issued (copy attached)	O.No.43.
	29th.		1 O.R. evacuated sick. 27 O.Rs. reinforcements. M.Gs. fired 22,250 ~~har~~ rounds harassing fire vide programme. " " 2,150 " at E.A. Hostile aircraft dropped bombs on front line. Fires also were observed ablaze in his lines during the night.	
	30th.		M.Gs. fired 19,250 rounds harassing fire vide programme. " " 4,250 " at E.A..	
		5.45 pm.	E.A. very low over CANAL Battery firing its M.G., at same time dropping white parachute lights which was the signal for artillery fire. The farm at LAMOTTE receiving attention from 4.2's and gas almost immediately after.	
		10.0 am.	Battalion Headquarters moved from GOSNAY to BOIS DE MONTAGNE E.27.b.10.40	

John Harington Bt.Lieut-Colonel,
Commanding 46th Battn.Machine Gun Corps.

A5834 Wt. W4973/M687 750,000 8/16 D. D. & L. Ltd. Forms/C.2118/13.

Headquarters,
IX. Corps.
=*=*=*=*=*=*=*=*=

46th Battn. M. G. Corps. No. 46/2/18.
****

Herewith original War Diary for May 1919 for the Battalion under my Command.

T.E. Hyde Lieut & Adj
for Major,
Commanding 46th Battn. M. G.Corps.

1/6/19.

SECRET. Copy No 16

46th BATTALION MACHINE GUN CORPS ORDER No.37.

Reference 1/20,000 GORRE and VIEILLE CHAPELLE.

1. 'B' Company will relieve 'D' Company in the line in the 'Forward Gun positions' in the ESSARS Section on the night 5/6th June 1918.

2. 'D' Company and 'D' Company Headquarters thus relieved will move into reserve at the Transport lines and will take over accommodation vacated by 'B' Company, and as Sections arrive Transport lines they will come under two hours notice to move.

3. Any further details, also guides etc, will be arranged direct between O.C.'B' Company and O.C. Groups.

4. Completion of this relief will be wired to Battalion Headquarters by the code word "~~[illegible]~~"."CORONA".

5. Completion of this relief will also be notified by O.C.No 2 Group to the Brigade Commander whose front his guns are covering.

6. Immediately the above relief is completed Major H.P.Bailey will take over the Command of No 2 Group from Capt.L.R.G.Heins.

7. Capt.H.Witty will Command 'B' Company.
Capt.H.Witty will be O.C. ~~[illegible]~~ Forward Guns.

8. All Trench and area stores, documents, maps, etc, will be handed over, and receipts obtained.

9. The O.C.'D' Company will arrange for a preliminary reconnaisance of the reserve positions (see Order 29 as amended by 29 A.) to take place before this relief commences, and in consultation direct with the O.C.'B' Company, who will hand over to the O.C.'D' Company all necessary documents, correspondence, etc., regarding the reserve positions.

10. ACKNOWLEDGE.

Issued at :- 7.0 PM

[signature]

4/6/1918.

Capt & Adjt,
46th Battn.Machine Gun Corps.

Distribution :-
1. A.Coy
2. B.Coy
3. C.Coy
4. D.Coy
5. T.O.
6. Q.M.
7. Signals.
8. 46th Division.
9. 3rd Bn.M.G.Corps.
10. 55th Bn.M.G.Corps.
11. 137th Infantry Bde.
12. 138th Infantry Bde.
13. 139th Infantry Bde.
14. File.
15.)
16.)War Diary.

War Diary!

S E C R E T.

H.Q. 46th Division.
C.R.A.,46th Division.
55th Bn.M.G.Corps.
3rd Bn.M.G.Corps.
137th Inf:Bde.
138th Inf:Bde.
139th Inf:Bde.
O.C.No 1 Group
O.C.No 2 Group.

****

Herewith Programme of Harassing Concentration Shoots for week ending June 12th, 1918.

4/6/1918.

Major,
46th Battn.Machine Gun Corps.

SECRET.

Machine Gun Concentration Shoots, Week commencing Thursday June 6th,1918.

NIGHT.	TARGET.	TIME.	ROUNDS per gun.	REMARKS.
June 6/7th.	8 A.	10.45 pm.	250	
	16 C.	(11.2 pm.	250	
		(11.5 pm.	125	
		(11.7 pm.	125	
	10 A.	12.0 mid:	250	
	17 C.	1.32. am.	250	
		2.15 am.	250	
	24 B.	3.15 am.	250	
7/8th.	24 A.	12.35 am.	250	
	10 C.	1.2 am.	250	
	10 A.	1.15 am.	250	
	8 A.	(1.39 am.	250	
		(1.41 am.	250	
	16 E.	2.20 am.	250	
8/9th.	8 B.	10.30 pm.	250	
	16 D.	(10.58 pm.	250	
		(11.6 pm.	250	
	23 B.	12.0 mid.	250	
	16 C.	12.30 am.	250	
	15 A.	1.30 am.	250	
	10 D.	1.42 am.	250	
	16 B.	2.35 am.	250	Group Commanders will arrange additional concentrations on these targets should early morning be misty.
	10 B.	3.30 am.	250	
9/10th.		(10.50 pm.	125	
	16 C.	(10.55 pm.	125	
		(11.00 pm.	250	
	17 C.	11.30 pm.	250	
	19 C.	12.50 am.	250	
	24 B.	2.00 am.	250	
	23 A.	3.20 am.	250	
	24 C.	3.45 am.	250	
10/11th.	10 A.	11.00 pm.	250	
	15 A.	11.22 pm.	250	
	16 C.	11.30 pm.	250	
	24 A.	11.58 pm.	250	
	23 B.	2.00 am.	250	
	19 B.	2.15 am.	250	
	17 B.	3.10 am.	250	
	10 D.	3.35 am.	250	
11/12th.	15 A.	10.35 pm.	250	
	17 B.	(10.50 pm.	125	
		(10.55 pm.	125	
	23 B.	11.10 pm.	250	
	24 B.	11.50 pm.	250	
	24 C.	12.00 mid.	250	
12/13th.	24 A.	11.30 pm.	250	
	17 A.	12.00 mid.	250	
	8 A.	12.15 am.	250	
	10 A.	1.15 am.	250	
	13 B.	1.35 am.	250	
		(2.30 am.	250	
	16 D.	(2.35 am.	125	
		(2.37 am.	125	

4/6/1918.

Major,
46th Battn.Machine Gun Corps.

To:-
O.C. No 1 Group, Q.M.
" No 2 " Signals.
" 'A' Coy, File (3)
" 'B' " War Diary (2). (2)
" 'C' "
" 'D' "
T.O.

****

1. Herewith copy No 14 of Machine Gun Defence Scheme containing papers:-

Part I Page 1, 2, & 3.
" I Schedule 'A'
" II, III, IV, V, VI, VII, VIII, IX, X.

Also marked (M.G.D.S. Map I) shewing the positions named in Part I schedule 'A', routes, location of Dumps and bridges on the Canal etc.

2. The following certificates will be rendered to reach Battalion Headquarters by 9.0 a.m. each Tuesday commencing Tuesday June 11th 1918.

A. By O.C. No 1 Group, that in accordance with para XI Part I the positions, S.A.A., and notice boards for positions named in sub-para A of above are correct.

B. By O.C. No 2 Group, that in accordance with para. XI Part I the positions, S.A.A., and notice boards for positions named in sub-para B. of above are correct.

3. The O.C., Reserve Company will render a certificate to reach Battalion Headquarters by 9.0 p.m. the day following relief :-

A. That all the reserve positions named in Part I, Schedule 'A', the assembly point, and all routes thereto have been fully reconnoitred by his Company

B. That each of the positions named in Part I, para XI, sub-para 'C' and the S.A.A. and notice boards are correct.

4. Addressees to acknowledge receipt by signing and returning the form issued below.

9/6 .....1918.

Blake
Capt & Adjt,
46th Battn. M.G. Corps.

RECEIVED from the Headquarters, 46th Battalion Machine Gun Corps copy No of Machine Gun Defence Scheme dated 1918, and also copy of Map

................1918. ....

....

SECRET.

46th BATTALION MACHINE GUN CORPS.

MACHINE GUN DEFENCE SCHEME.

Machine Gun Arrangements.

1. The machine gun defence of the divisional sector is organized into two groups, corresponding with the brigade sections, each being commanded by a Group Commander.

2. Each Group of machine guns consists of guns under two categories :-
   (a) Forward guns.
   (b) Rear guns.

   The Reserve guns are controlled by the O.C.,Machine Gun Battalion.

3. In each group officers are appointed as O.C.,Forward guns and O.C.,Rear guns.

4. Forward guns.

   (a) Forward guns are, whenever possible sited in pairs also batteries, and are allotted to definite battle positions to form a screen of fire between the Front and Reserve Lines in the event of a penetration of the Front line. These tasks are carried out by direct fire.

   (b) In addition to the role described in the preceding paragraph, S.O.S. lines, to supplement the artillery barrage in case of raids or minor attacks, are arranged whenever practicable to cover selected positions of the front, as close as possible to our front line. These tasks are carried out by direct or indirect fire.

   (c) The lines of fire will be tested by firing on them by night under arrangements made with the infantry. The fire, if possible, should be observed from that position of the front line it is intended to cover. O.C., Forward guns will inform Infantry Battalion Commanders concerned when it is proposed to carry out a test. The Infantry Company Commander on whose front the S.O.S. line is laid should accompany O.C.,Forward guns so as to satisfy himself where the fire is directed and from what direction it comes.

   (d) Directors or other devices must be provided for each gun to assist machine gun sentries in recognizing the S.O.S. signal on the company front they are covering. These directors will be fixed a few yards from the gun and be laid on the S.O.S. signal stations of the company the machine gun is to cover.

   (e) Group Commanders will make themselves acquainted with all infantry posts in the front line as alterations in these posts may demand alteration in the S.O.S. lines.

   (f) It is of the utmost importance that all Forward guns should be warned of patrols. The Forward Machine Gun Officer is responsible for the communication of this information to his Group Commander for transmission to neighbouring groups.

   (g) Forward guns will open on their S.O.S. lines in the event of heavy shelling of the front they are covering.

Batteries.

5. The machine guns which are organized in batteries are sited to perform the following tasks :-

(a) To form a screen of fire between the reserve and the Newcastle Lines, in the event of the former being penetrated.

(b) To provide an indirect S.O.S. barrage co-ordinated with the artillery, to disorganize an enemy attack by engaging it at the outset.

(c) To engage targets of opportunity in the event of a hostile penetration by direct or indirect fire.

(d) Special orders have been issued to O.C., guns concerned with regard to method of carrying out tasks (a), (b) and (c).

Reserve Guns.

6. Certain gun positions are designed for occupation if necessary by guns in Divisional reserve or by those of a reinforcing unit. The positions of these guns in the divisional area are shown on Schedule 'A'.

Reserve guns are sited in batteries with as long a field of fire as possible, in order to disorganize an enemy advance by controlled and concentrated fire.

7. As there are not sufficient guns available to put down a barrage in front of the whole Liverpool Line, the area immediately in front of it has been divided into seven zones lettered 'A' to 'G', as shown on the tracing issued under 46/12/147dated 21/5/1918 which letter will now be attached to this scheme. (issued only to Groups)

The batteries now in position can bring fire to bear on any zone with the number of guns indicated thereon, upon receipt of orders to do so. The order for the S.O.S. lines to be brought back will normally be issued to O.C., ~~Rear~~ guns concerned by group commanders in consultation with the Infantry Brigadiers concerned.

Safety clearance is allowed over the whole length of the Liverpool Line.

8. Stores and equipment at gun positions. Every machine gun position will be provided with the following :-

(a) A notice board giving the number and the map co-ordinate of the position in the case of Forward guns, and the name of the battery and co-ordinate of the left hand gun in the case of Rear and Reserve positions.

(b) An order board defining clearly the action of the gun numbers on S.O.S., and in case of a bombardment of the front line: also orders regarding change from S.O.S. to direct lines.

(c) A range card showing S.O.S. line and direct line, each being clearly marked for direction and elevation.

(d) A night firing lamp per gun (these will be provided later for forward guns).

9. Ammunition. The following reserve of ammunition will be maintained ;-

(a) At all occupied positions :-

15 boxes S.A.A.)
16 belt boxes.) per gun.
8 belts in S.A.A. boxes.)

(b) 30 boxes S.A.A. at each of the following unoccupied reserve positions :-

Le Quesnoy E.Battery.
Bridgehead Battery.
Lawe Battery.
Le Quesnoy W.Battery.
Dock Battery.

(c) 100 boxes S.A.A. at each of the following positions as a reserve for the Laundry-Annequin Line ;-

Pry Battery.
Laundry Post.

(d) Range Cards will be prepared by the Reserve Company for each of the positions named in Part I, schedule 'A' and these will be handed over to the Company moving into reserve when reliefs take place.

10. To ensure guns firing when and where required, all duties must be carefully rehearsed as a drill. Hours for this drill will be laid down in the daily programme for each battery or gun positions.

11. The Officers named below will be responsible :-

(i) That the unoccupied reserve positions as stated are correct, in good order and correctly camouflaged.

(2) For the maintenance of all ammunition stocked in positions stated.

(3) For the inspection and maintenance of notice boards as stated.

A. The O.C. No 1 Group for positions :-

Le Quesnoy East, 2 pairs guns, 15 boxes S.A.A. at each gun position.
Le Quesnoy West, 1 pair guns, 15 boxes S.A.A. at each gun position.
2 single guns, 15 boxes S.A.A. at each gun position.
Bethune Locality Battery, 4 guns, 30 boxes S.A.A.

B. The O.C.No 2 Group for positions :-

Lawe Battery, 4 guns, 30 boxes S.A.A.

Bridgehead Battery, 4 guns, 60 boxes S.A.A.

C. The O.C. Reserve Company for positions :-

Dock Battery, 4 guns, 20 boxes S.A.A.

Fork Battery 4 guns, Nil.

Pry Battery, 4 guns, 100 boxes S.A.A.

Laundry Post East Battery, 4 guns)
) 100 boxes S.A.A.
Laundry Post West Battery, 4 guns)

Gerre Sheet 1/20,000

PART I. Schedule 'A'.

Machine gun positions from Bethune - Canal Bridgehead Line to Laundry - Annequin Line. (inclusive).

Name.	Co-ordinate.	Whether occupied.	No of guns.	Nature of emplacem't.	Ammunition.	Remarks.
1. Bethune - Canal Bridgehead Line.						
Le Quesnoy E. By.	F.8.b.15.10	No	2	Open.)	60 boxes S.A.A.	Dug-out accommodation for teams under construction.
" " "	F.8.d.4.2.	No	2	Open.)		
Bridgehead By.	E.6.a.7.3.	No	4	Open.	60,000 rds.S.A.A.	No cover for teams.
Lawe Battery.	W.29.b.55.00	No.	4	Open.	" " "	" " " "
2. Bouvry - Cambrin Line.						
Le Quesnoy W. By.	F.8.c.83.50	No.	2)	Open.	60,000 rds, S.A.A.	Cover for teams.
" " "	F.8.d.1.5.	No.	1)			
" " "	F.8.d.25.00	No.	1)			
Dock Battery.	F.7.c.8.5.	No.	4	Open.	" " "	Accommodation for teams under construction.
3. Bethune Retrenchment.						
Bethune Locality.	F.13.c.3.4.	No.	4	Open	Nil.	No cover for teams.
4. Laundry - Annequin Line.						
Fork Battery.	E.24.d.4.4.	No.	4	Open.	Nil	No cover for teams.
Laundry Post E.	E.25.d.50.85	No.	4	Open.)	100,000 rds: S.A.A. in the Laundry.)	No cover.
Laundry Post W.	E.25.c.3.9.	No.	4	Open.)		
Pry Battery.	E.18.c.9.4.	No.	4	Open.	100,000 rds: S.A.A.	Dug-out accommodation for teams.

PART II.

Divisional and Brigade Boundaries.

1. The 46th Division (H.Q. - GOSNAY) holds the Left Divisional front of the I Corps. The 55th Division is on the right and the 3rd Division (XIII Corps) on the left.

2. The Southern boundary of the Divisional Sector is.-

S 25 b 30.80 - X 30 a 5.0 - X 30 c 0.1 - F 5 d 9.8 - F 10 a 00.55 - F 14 c 8.0 - K 5 a 8.6 - K 4 b 5.6 - E 28 d 0.5 - J 6 c 9.0 - J 12 central - J 11 d 0.2 - J 21 b 9.9 - J 20 d 5.4.

The Northern Boundary of the Divisional Sector is.-

Canal de la Lawe from Pont Tournant (X 8 c 4.1) to bend at W 29 d 5.9 (inclusive to XIII Corps) - thence along track to bridge at E 5 a 6.6 (inclusive to XIII Corps) - thence along stream to bend in road at E 4 d 8.2 - thence to road junction E 10 a 3.5 - thence along southern bank of La Brette River to E 19 c 2.2 - thence to D 24 d 9.4 - D 29 a 10.25 - D 28 d 2.3 - J 4.a 4.6 - J 2 c 8.7 - J 7 a 6.4.

3. The dividing line between the Sections is :-

X 22 a 9.2 - X 27 central - X 27 c 2.8 - thence along road to F 3 b 4.1 - F 2 c 4.3.

PART III.

Defensive Line.

1. The Divisional Sector extends from S 25 b 3.8 to X 8 c 5.3 and is divided into two sections :-

Gorre Section from S 25 b 3.8 to X 22 a 8.2.
Essars Section from X 22 a 8.2 to X 8 c 5.3.

2. The Defensive systems in the Divisional Area are :-

(i) Front System.
(ii) Intermediate System, comprising the Canal-Bridgehead and Bethune Line and the Beuvry-Cambrin Line.
(iii) Second Line System - Laundry Annequin Line.
(iv) Third Line System - Lillers-Houchin Line.

The term 'Battle Zone' is given to the area between the main line of resistance and the Lillers-Houchin Line exclusive. The Lillers-Houchin Line forms the front line of the Rear Zone.
The various systems are described in subsequent paragraphs.

3. Important tactical features in the area are :-

(i) The Beuvry-Bethune Ridge and Le Quesnoy Spur.
(ii) Gorre Wood.

4. Defensive Flanks. In the event of the enemy penetrating the front of the divisions on our flanks, brigades will be prepared to form defensive flanks as follows :-

Right Brigade.- Tuning Fork Line from about F 5 c to Loisne Central Post (X 22 d).

Left Brigade.- The Line of the canal de la Lawe.

Locality Stores.

Location.	Map reference.	S.A.A. boxes.	Iron rations.	Petrol Tins.	Remarks.
Bethune Locality.	F.13,c.7.9.	250	3,000	100	
Canal Bridgehead Line.	F.8.c.6,2. F.9.b.2.9.	45 35			
Canal Dock Locality.	E.6.c.9.5. E.6.d.6.0.	25 25			
Essars Locality.	W.30.d.5.7.	150 (also 50 boxes No. 23 Rifle Grenades)	1,000	200	
Gorre.	Chateau F.3.b.5.5. Brewery F.3.c.45.50	50 –	700 200	150 30	
Quarry Post.)) Laundry Post.)	E.22.d. and E.23.a. & c. E.23.b. & d.	–	–	–	N.B. M.G. ammunition is stored at – Pry Battery. ... 100 boxes. Laundry Post. ... E.23.b. & d. ... 100 boxes.

There are also 1,200 iron rations stored at certain R.A. battery positions.
Details of stores at machine gun emplacements are shown in PART IV, Section I.

PART V.

Prisoners of War Cage.

1. The Prisoners of War Cage is at E.25.b.4.9.

PART VI.

S.O.S. Signals.

1. S.O.S.Signal. (a) The S.O.S.Signal is a rifle gronade fired from the rifle bursting into three lights, one over the other; the colours of the S.O.S.are :-

11th Division	-	Green over	Green Over	Green.
1st :	-	do	do	do
46th :	-	~~do~~ RED	~~do~~ RED	~~do~~ RED
55th :	-	Red over	Green over	Red.

The XIII Corps front is Red over Red over Red.

PART VII.

Location of S.O.S. Positions.

Gorre Section - (Right Brigade).

Right Sub-section.

F 3 c 60.50
X 29 d 90.25.
X 28 d 85.15.
F 5 a 1.1.

Left Sub-section.

X 28 a 45.80.
X 29 a 05.80.
X 25 c 40.20.
X 25 c 83.10.
X 22 d 30.25.
X 22 d 80.70.
X 28 a 10.15.
X 27 d 90.40.

Support Battalion.

F 3 c 2.2.
F 4 c 40.00
F 4 a 60.15.
F 3 d 45.50.
F 8 b 90.90.

Essars Section - (Left Brigade).

Right Sub-section.

X 20 d 8.4.
X 21 d 15.10
X 22 a 7.2.
X 16 c 20.05.
X 16 c 10.75.
X 15 b 20.05.
X 27 a 8.8.
X 15 c 9.2.
X 20 b 70.05

Left Sub-section.

X 20 a 1.6.
X 20 b 3.6.
X 15 c 75.99.
X 15 a 3.1.
X 14 b 1.7.
X 8 c 9.0.
X 8 c 6.3.
X 14 c 2.9.
X 20 c 25.95.

PART VIII.

Action in case of attack.

1. One Company of the Battalion is held in Divisional Reserve.

2. This reserve Company may be employed in :-

(a) The reinforcement of either the Gorre or the Essars Sections.

(b) The reinforcement of the troops holding the Canal Dock Locality and the defences of the Bridgehead about E.3.a.

(c) A counter attack, if the enemy succeeds in crossing the La Bassee Canal, either in the direction of Le Quesnoy or Bethune from the area about the Bethune Locality.

(d) The occupation of the Beuvry - Cambrin Line as far as the line of the Bethune Retrenchment.

(e) The possibility of supporting the flank divisions has also to be considered and the routes into their respective areas should be reconnoitred.

3. In the event of warning being received by Battalion Headquarters indicating an attack on the Divisional, or neighbouring Divisions, fronts, Battalion Headquarters will issue the order "Move Reserves" On receipt of this message the following action will be taken :-

(a) One sub section (2 guns) of the Reserve Company under an officer will at once proceed to occupy the Le Quesnoy East 2 guns position at F.8.b.15.10.
The O.C.No 1 Group will detail a guide to be permanently available to guide this sub section and who would meet the personnel on road junction at about F.14.a.40.70.

(b) The reserve Company)less 1 sub-section) will move to the assembly point at the Laundry about E.23.d.10.90.

(c) On reaching the assembly point the Headquarters of the Company will be marked by a flag or lamp so that it can be easily found.

(d) The Signalling officer would establish communication with the assembly point and Battalion Headquarters.
The wire is already laid.
Alternate communications will also be arranged.

(e) All other animals will be harnessed up but not hooked in and all transport wagons will be loaded.

4. All the positions named in Part I schedule 'A' will be reconnoitred and routes thereto by the Officers and N.C.O's of the Reserve Company with a view to their occupation in the event of the situation demanding it.

5. The Q.M. will hold in store 8 boxes of Iron Rations (sealed) and when the order "Move Reserves" is issued these rations will be issued to the Reserve Company, and will be taken 1 box with each sub-section. These are only for consumption in case of absolute necessity.

PART II.

Instructions regarding warning in case of hostile gas attack.

1. In case of a cloud gas attack or hostile gas shelling Company or Group Commanders will inform Battalion Headquarters by 'priority' wire :-

A. For cloud gas the word 'GAS' followed by name of section and the part of the section, e.g. 'GAS' GORRE night.

B. For shell gas the word 'POISON' followed by the locality shelled e.g. 'POISON' F.8.b. (map reference or name of village etc to be given)

2. In case of a cloud gas attack the Battalion is responsible for warning :-

(a) Group and Companies in the line.

(b) All Signal Stations within the Battalion.

(c) The Transport details.

(d) The Quartermaster.

(e) The Reserve Company.

(f) Battalion Headquarters details and Battalion Headquarters Guard (if any).

(g) S.A.A. Section D.A.C. (Headquarters E.27.c.90.05)

(1) 125th Battery H.A.Transport (Headquarters E.27.c.5.8).

The information will be sent out to all the above by O.C. Signals by the quickest method as soon as a telegram is received stating that a cloud gas attack has been made without awaiting orders from Battalion Headquarters.

3. In order that all ranks should have practice in adjusting their masks rapidly daily drill is to take place throughout the Battalion. It is important that work should be carried out for short periods whilst wearing masks.

Respirators of soldiers in the line will be inspected daily.

PART X.

Bridges and roads in the Divisional area prepared for Demolition.

1. (i). The existing Bridges in the 46th Divisional Area over the La Bassee Canal and sideways are as follows :-

	Name.	Map Reference.	Type.	To take.	Responsibility for demolition.
1.		F 10 a 70.45.		Infantry in file.	C.R.E., 46th Division.
2.	Stafford	F 5 d 40.05.	Wood Strut.	M.T. & H.A.	: :
3.	Gorre	F 3 c 45.45.	Lift.	: : :	: :
4.	Pt. Tournant.	F 7 a 70.85.	Iron Swing.	: : :	: :
5.	Foresters.	E 5 d 5.1.	Iron girder fixed.	Heavy transport.	: :
6.	Pont Neuf.	E 5 c 9.7.	: : :	:	: :
7.		E 5 d 50.18.	: : :	M.T. & H.A.	: :
8.	London	E 5 a 6.5.	: : :	: : :	: :
9.		E 6 a 25.85	Wood draw.	: : :	: :

All the above bridges have been prepared for demolition in case of necessity.

(ii) In addition to the above, pontoon bridges are in position or ready to be swung at the following sites. C.R.E., 46th Division, is responsible for swinging these bridges.

	Name.	Map Reference.	To take.
10	Midland.	F 2 d 6.5.	Field Artillery.
11	Lincoln.	F 2 c 90.35.	Infantry in file.
12	Leicester.	F 2 c 35.25.	Field Artillery.
13	Barge.	F 1 c 95,00.	Infantry in file.
14	Artillery.	F 1 c 1.0.	Field Artillery.
15	Sherwood.	E 12 b 45.95	Infantry in file.
16	Jumbo.	W 29 d 6.6.	Infantry in file.

All the above bridges have been prepared for demolition in case of necessity.
C.R.E. 46th Division, will be responsible for demolition, except in the case of Jumbo Bridge, for which the Left Brigade are responsible.

PART X.

2. The following bridges and culverts exist North of the La Bassee Canal (exclusive).

Name.	Map Reference.	Type.	Responsibility for Demolition.
17. Bridges over	F 4 b 4.3.	Culvert.	C.R.E. 46th Division.
18. Loisne Stream.	X 28 a 1.3.	:	: :
19. Crossing Rue de Bois.	X 21 a 15.30	:	: :
20. Bridges over	F 4 b 2.6.	Wood footbridge.	: :
21. Loisne Stream.	X 28 c 6.6.	: :	: :
22.	X 28 c 5.7.	: :	: :
23.	X 28 c 4.9.	Wooden light railway bridge.	: :

All the above bridges have been prepared for demolition in case of necessity.

3. Road bridges over the railway at E 18 b 79.19 and E 18 d 51.68 are prepared for demolition. The C.R.E., 46th Division, is responsible for blowing these bridges in case of emergency.

The authority to demolish either or both of these bridges will be given in writing by G.O.C., Right Brigade, to the Officer i/c of demolition party.

In the event of operations, the Officer i/c demolitions should be kept advised as to the situation by the Right Brigade.

4. The following cross roads have been prepared for demolition :-

E 6 a 30.78; F 4 b 40.25; and culvert at X 21 a 1.3.

C.R.E., 46th Division, is responsible for the blowing of the charges.

5. Orders will be issued to C.R.E., for the demolition of any roads or bridges by Divisional H.Q. Failing the receipt of any orders, either to demolish or withdraw without destroying, the officer i/c is to be instructed to act on his own initiative and carry out the demolition at the last possible moment after consultation with the nearest commander on the spot.

No new charge will be prepared without reference to Divisional Headquarters.

SECRET.
M.G.D.S. MAP I. (TRACING)
W X
E F
BÉTHUNE
9.6.18
CAPT. & ADJUTANT.
LEGEND.
ALTERNATIVE ROUTE.
DEFENDED LOCALITIES.
MINE LOCALITY
E F
K L
T.

S E C R E T.

Copy No 15

46th BATTALION MACHINE GUN CORPS ORDER No.38.

1. 'D' Company will relieve 'C' Company in the line in the 'Forward Gun positions' in the GORRE Section on the night 11/12th June 1918.

2. 'C' Company and 'C' Company Headquarters thus relieved will move into reserve at the Transport lines and will take over accommodation vacated by 'D' Company, and as Sections arrive Transport lines they will come under two hours notice to move.

3. Any further details, also guides etc, will be arranged direct between O.C.'D' Company and O.C.Groups.

4. Completion of this relief will be wired to Battalion Headquarters by the code word "ORANGE".

5. Completion of this relief will also be notified by O.C.No 1 Group to the Brigade Commander whose front his guns are covering.

6. Immediately the above relief is completed Major E.R.Nurse, M.C., will take over the Command of No 1 Group from Major W.T.Boughey.

7. Capt.R.Page will Command 'A' Company
Capt.R.Page will be O.C.,Right Rear Guns
Lieut.F.A.K.Park will be O.C.,Left Rear Guns.
Capt.M.Douglas will be O.C. Right Forward Guns.
Capt.M.Douglas will Command 'D' Company.

8. All Trench and area stores, documents, maps, etc, will be handed over, and receipts obtained.

9. ACKNOWLEDGE.

Issued at :- 6.30pm

10/6/1918.

[signature]
Capt & Adjt,
46th Battn.Machine Gun Corps.

Distribution :-

1. A.Coy	9. 3rd Bn.M.G.Corps.
2. B.Coy	10. 55th Bn.M.G.Corps.
3. C.Coy	11. 137th Inf:Bde.
4. D.Coy	12. 138th : :
5. T.O.	13. 139th : :
6. Q.M.	14. File.
7. Signals.	15.)
8. 46th Division.	16.) War Diary.

S E C R E T.

H.Q.46th Division,
C.R.A., 46th Division.
55th Bn.M.G.Corps.
3rd Bn. M.G.Corps.
137th Inf:Bde.
138th " "
139th " "
O.C.No 1 Group,
O.C.No 2 "

Herewith Programme of Harassing Concentration Shoots for week ending 18th June, 1918.

10/6/1918.

Major,
46th Battn.M.G.Corps.

S E C R E T.

MACHINE GUN CONCENTRATION SHOOTS, Week Ending June 19th, 1918.

NIGHT.	TARGET.	TIME.	No. of ROUNDS.
June 13/14th.	8 A.	11.5 pm.	250
	16 C.	11.50 pm.	250
	19 C.	12.0 mid.	250
	16 C.	1.30 am.	250
	16 C.	1.38 am.	250
	24 A.	1.50 am.	250
	8 B.	2.2 am.	250
	16 C.	2.45 am.	250
	16 A.	3.0 am.	250
14/15th.	24 C.	10.45 pm.	250
	24 C.	10.48 pm.	250
	17 C.	11.0 pm.	250
	10 D.	11.35 pm.	250
	10 D.	11.45 pm.	250
	17 C.	12.30 am.	250
	24 B.	1.0 am.	250
	10 E.	2.55 am.	250
15/16th.	8 A.	10.56 pm.	250
	16 D.	12.0 mid.	250
	24 C.	1.20 am.	250
	16 C.	2.1 am.	250
	8 A.	2.22 am.	250
	16 B.	3.0 am.	250
16/17th.	17 C.	10.30 pm.	250
	16 D.	10.36 pm.	250
	16 B.	10.50 pm.	250
	16 D.	10.55 pm.	250
	8 B.	11.30 pm.	250
	24 C.	1.0 am.	250
	17 C.	2.45 am.	50
	17 C.	2.52 am.	200
17/18th.	10 A.	2.0 am.	250
	16 E.	2.15 am.	250
	19 A.	2.30 am.	250
	10 D.	2.35 am.	250
	23 E.	2.50 am.	250
18/19th.	10 B.	10.35 pm.	250
	10 C.	11.2 pm.	250
	10 C.	11.6 pm.	250
	10 C.	11.8 pm.	250
	16 E.	12.0 mid.	250
	24 B.	1.0 am.	250
	24 C.	1.20 am.	250
19/20th.	16 B.	10.50 pm.	250
	16 E.	10.59 pm.	250
	16 B.	11.20 pm.	250
	16 B.	11.30 pm.	250
	16 B.	1.0 am.	250
	16 B.	2.40 am.	250
	16 B.	2.56 am.	250

10/6/1918.

[signature]

Major,
46th Battn. Machine Gun Corps.

Order No. 39

SECRET.

O.C.,
No.2 Group — War diary. 1.

No. 1 Group (for information). — " " 2.

Reference Map. VIEILLE CHAPELLE 1/20000

1. The 3rd Division will advance its front on the night 14/15th. June to the line Q34d 4. 2 - FORD LANE - TURBEAUTE CT at W 12 a 0. 8. thence along the bank of this stream to W 12 c 1. 6, thence to W 18 b 5.8 where it will connect up with our present front line.
The operation will be carried out as a surprise, without a preliminary bombardment.

2. Sixty eight machine guns will be employed for barrage purposes or for shooting on selected localities.

3. Four guns of PIGEON Battery and two guns of THRUSH Battery will cooperate by firing on to areas A & C as detailed below.

BATTERY	NO. OF GUNS.	TARGET.	DURATION OF FIRE.	RATE OF FIRE	REMARKS.
PIGEON	1	AREA "A" W 12 d 05.65-15.65 15.75-05.75	From ZERO to 3.0 a.m.	From Zero to zero plus 40 mins. one belt per gun per FOUR min.	
PIGEON THRUSH	3 2	AREA "C" W 12 b 60.50-80.50 W 6 d 50.10 - W 12 b 10.90		From Zero plus 40' to Zero plus 60' one belt per gun per eight mins. From Zero plus 60' to 3.0 a.m. one belt per gun per TWENTY mins. S.O.S. INTENSE.	Localities will be searched on "S.O.S." call.

4. Battery Charts and Gun Charts will be completed by 12 noon 13th June 1918 and copies sent in to Battalion Headquarters by that time.

5. Zero hour will be notified later.
The signal for opening fire at zero hour will be the opening of the Field Artillery Barrage.

6. O.C. No. 2 Group will arrange for watches for each position to be synchronized with those of O.C. Right M.G. Group 3rd Division (whose headquarters are in BETHUNE) between 5 p.m. and 6 p.m. on 14th June 1918.

7. Arrangements will be made to immediately switch all guns on to their normal S.O.S. lines should the S.O.S. be sent up on the 46th Divisional Front whilst the above operation is in progress.

8. O.C. No. 2 Group will keep in constant touch with the O.C. Right Group 3rd Battn. M.G. Corps so that he can obtain all information promptly.

9. ACKNOWLEDGE.

Bt. Lieut. Col.,

13/6/18

Cmdg., 46th Battn. M.G. Corps

S E C R E T.   Copy No 15

46th BATTALION MACHINE GUN CORPS ORDER No.40.

Reference 1/20,000 GORRE and VIEILLE CHAPELLE.

1. 'C' Company will relieve 'A' Company in the line in the 'Rear Gun positions' in the GORRE & ESSARS Sections on the night 17/18th June,1918.

2. 'A' Company and 'A' Company Headquarters thus relieved will move into reserve at the Transport lines and will take over accommodation vacated by 'C' Company, and as Sections arrive Transport lines they will come under two hours notice to move.

3. Any further details, also guides etc, will be arranged direct between O.C.'C'Company and O.C.Groups.

4. All Trench and area stores, documents, maps, etc, will be handed over, and receipts obtained. A certificate that all positions have been taken over in a clean and satisfactory state will be rendered by O.C.''C'Company to reach Battalion Headquarters 2nd D.R. 18th June,1918.

5. Completion of this relief will be wired to Battalion Headquarters by the code word "HOUSE".

6. Completion of this relief will also be notified by O.C.No 1 Group and O.C.No 2 Group to the Brigade Commander whose front his guns are covering.

7. Immediately the above relief is completed Major W.T.Boughey will take over the Command of No 1 Group from Major H.C.Windeler.

8. ACKNOWLEDGE.

Issued at :- 7.0 P.M.

16/6/1918.

Blickens
Capt & Adjt,
46th Battn.Machine Gun Corps.

Distribution :-

1. A.Coy	9. 3rd Bn.M.G.Corps.
2. B.Coy	10. 55th Bn.M.G.Corps.
3. C.Coy	11. 137th Inf:Bde.
4. D.Coy	12. 138th : :
5. T.O.	13. 139th : :
6. Q.M.	14. File.
7. Signals.	15.)
8. 46th Division.	16.)War Diary.

E

S E C R E T.

To:-

O.C.No 1 Group,
" No 2 " (For information)
War Diary (2).

1. The right Battalion left Brigade propose to raid the orchard in X.16.c. central. (Sheet LOCON)

2. Proposed date of raid is to-morrow night 17/18th inst:

3. You will co-operate as follows :-

<u>During raid.</u>
Two guns to bring enfilade fire to bear on road from X.10.d.1.1. to X.16.b.2.5.

<u>AFTER raid.</u>
WREN Battery to maintain fire on alternative S.O.S.line X.16.c.6.5 to X.16.a.9.1. at intervals for the remainder of the night.

4. To find out when to fire, i.e. when the raid is over, O.C., WREN Battery will remain during the raid at Support Company Headquarters X.27.a.8.8. A telephone message will be sent there when raid is over.

5. O.C.No 1 Group will as soon as possibleget into touch with O.C.No 2 Group to obtain further details.

6. Zero hour will be communicated later.

7. ACKNOWLEDGE.

16/6/1918.

[signature]
Major,
46th Battn.Machine Gun Corps.

F

O.C.No 1 Group,
" No 2 "
War Diary (2)
O.C.'A' Coy,
" 'B' "
" 'C' "
" 'D' "
" 55th Bn.M.G.Corps.
" 3rd Bn.M.G.Corps.

SECRET

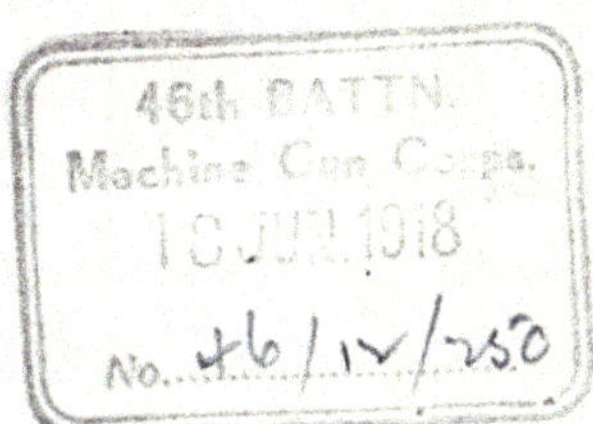

In reference to 46/12/213, herewith revised appendices to 46th Battalion Machine Gun Corps Counter Preparation Scheme.

Please destroy old copies.

ACKNOWLEDGE.

17/6/1918.

J Harington Bt.Lieut-Colonel,
Commanding 46th Battn.M.G.Corps.

MACHINE GUN COUNTER PREPARATION SCHEME.

APPENDIX "A"

TARGETS.	GUNS ABLE TO FIRE.																		BATTERIES ABLE TO FIRE.					
No.	C1.	C2.	C3.	C4.	C5.	C6.	C7.	C8.	5.	6.	TFW 1.	TFW 2.	9.	10.	13.	16.	11.	15.	THRUSH.	PIGEON.	WREN.	TOTAL.	DIRECTING GUNS.	REMARKS.
3C.	-	-	1	1	1	1	1	-	-	-	-	-	-	-	-	-	-	-	-	-	-	5	C 5.	
3D.	-	-	1	1	1	1	1	-	-	-	-	-	-	-	-	-	-	-	-	-	-	5	C 5.	
3G.	-	-	1	1	1	1	1	-	-	-	-	-	-	-	-	-	-	-	-	-	-	5	C 5.	
3H.	-	-	-	1	1	1	1	-	-	-	-	-	-	-	-	-	-	-	-	-	-	4	C 4.	
3J.	-	-	-	1	1	1	1	-	-	-	-	-	-	-	-	-	-	-	-	-	-	4	C 4.	
8C.	1	1	-	-	-	-	-	1	-	-	-	-	-	-	-	-	-	-	4	4	4	15	THRUSH.	
24D.	-	-	-	-	-	-	-	-	1	1	1	1	1	1	1	1	1	1	-	-	-	10	5.	

17/6/1918.

J Harrington

Bt.Lieut-Colonel,
Commanding 46th Battn.M.G.Corps.

APPENDIX "B"

TARGET.	TIME.	ROUNDS.
3 C.) 8 C.)	10.35 pm.	250
3 H.) 24 D.)	11.10 pm.	250
3 D.) 24 D.)	11.38 pm.	250
3 D.) 8 C.)	12.22 am.	250
3 J.) 24 D.)	12.50 am.	250
3 G.) 8 [illegible].) 24 D.)	1.15 am.	250
3 D.	1.41 am.	250
3 G.	2.00 am.	250
3 H.) 24 D.)	2.17 am.	250
3 J.) 24 D.)	2.29 am.	250
3 C.) 24 D.)	2.37 am.	250
3 J.) 8 C.)	3.5 am.	250
3 H.	3.14 am.	250
8 [illegible].) 24 D.)	3.20 am.	250
8 C.) 3 G.) 24 D.)	3.32 am.	250
3 C.) 24 D.)	3.45 am.	250
8 C.) 24 D.)	3.53 am.	250

APPENDIX "C"

AREA.	GUN.	TARGET.	REMARKS.
24 D.	13	X.24.a.60.40	Unchanged from 46/12/213 ~~24~~ of 9/6/18.
	16	X.24.a.60.40	
	TFW 1.	X.24.a.60.50	
	TFW 2.	X.24.a.60.50	
	5	X.24.a.60.40	
	6.	X.24.a.60.40	
	11.	X.24.a.60.50	
	15.	X.24.a.60.50	
	9.	X.24.a.65.35	
	10.	X.24.a.65.35	
3 C.	C 3.	X.3.c.42.10	Unchanged from 46/12/213 of 9/6/18.
	C 4.	X.3.c.42.22	
	C 5.	X.3.c.48.35	
	C 6.	X.3.c.48.35	
	C 7.	X.3.c.52.52	
3 D.	C 3.	X.3.c.81.80	This is different from 46/12/213 of 9/6/18.
	C 4.	X.3.c.72.77	
	C 5.	X.3.c.98.80	
	C 6.	X.3.c.99.79	
	C 7.	X.3.d.05.52	
3 G.	C 3.	X.3.c.45.68	New target.
	C 4.	X.3.c.40.80	
	C 5.	X.3.c.40.80	
	C 6.	X.3.c.35.94	
	C 7.	X.3.a.30.05	
3 H.	C 4.	X.3.a.35.20	New target.
	C 5.	X.3.a.35.20	
	C 6.	X.3.a.35.20	
	C 7.	X.3.a.35.20	
3 J.	C 4.	X.3.a.62.12	New target.
	C 5.	X.3.a.75.28	
	C 6.	X.3.a.85.40	
	C 7.	X.3.a.95.50	
8 C.	~~C 4.~~	~~X.8.d.91.50~~	New target
	C 8. (8)	X.9.c.04.51	
	C 2.	X.8.d.96.35	
	C 1.	X.8.d.96.35	
	THRUSH.	X.8.d.92.49	
	PIGEON.	X.8.d.97.34	
	WREN.	X.9.c.08.15	

17/6/1918.

J Harington

Bt.Lieut-Colonel,
Commanding 46th Battn.M.G.Corps.

TT

S E C R E T.

PROGRAMME OF MACHINE GUN CONCENTRATION SHOOTS

Week Ending June 27th, 1918.

21/6/1918

John Harrington Bt.Lieut-Colonel,
Commanding 48th Battn. M.G. Corps.

NIGHT.	TARGET.	TIME.	No.OF ROUNDS per gun.
June 20/21st.	NO FIRING.		
21/22nd.	17 A.	11.0 pm.	250
	8 A., 25 A.	11.30 pm.	250
	24 G., 9 D.	11.42 pm.	250
	13 C.	12.30 am.	250
	9 H., 19 C.	2.15 am.	250
	3 K., 23 C.	2.40 am.	250
22/23rd.	10 B.	11.20 pm.	250
	10 B.	11.30 pm.	250
	13 B.	11.53 pm.	250
	9 G., 24 E.	12.0 mid.	250
	9 F., 19 B.	12.40 am.	250
	23 B., 9 E.	12.59 am.	250
	3 A., 24 F.	1.31 am.	250
	24 A., 8 B.	2.30 am.	250
23/24th.	3 B., 25 D.	10.45 pm.	250
	9 J., 19 A.	11.0 pm.	250
	9 L., 24 B.	11.25 pm.	250
	10 C.	11.32 pm.	250
	13 D.	12.0 mid.	250
	17 D.	12.20 am.	250
	16 H.	1.0 am.	250
	10 G.	2.50 am.	250
	16 A.	3.0 am.	250
24/25th.	23 E., 9 K.	11.10 pm.	250
	24 C., 9 K.	11.15 pm.	250
	17 B.	11.20 pm.	250
	10 A.	11.29 pm.	250
	16 G.	12.0 mid.	250
	10 D.	12.5 am.	250
	17 C.	1.25 am.	250
	10 E.	1.30 am.	250
	15 A.	2.15 am.	250
25/26th.	10 H.	11.25 pm.	250
	16 E.	12.0 mid.	250
	16 G.	1.5 am.	250
	8 B., 25 E.	2.10 am.	250
26/27th.	19 B., 9 E.	11.39 pm.	250
	10 A.	12.5 am.	250
	9 J., 24 C.	1.0 am.	250
	23 C., 3 A.	1.10 am.	250
	8 B., 23 D.	2.15 am.	250
	19 C., 9 G.	2.30 am.	250
	16 C.	2.40 am.	250
	16 H.	2.45 am.	250

SECRET

H.Q.,46th Division.
C.R.A.,46th Division.
55th Bn.M.G.Corps.
3rd Bn. M.G.Corps.
137th Inf:Bde.
138th " "
139th " "
O.C.No 1 Group,
O.C.No 2 "
War Diary (2)
File.

G

Herewith programme of Harassing Concentration Shoots for week ending 27th June, 1918.

21/6/1918.

Major,
46th Battn.Machine Gun Corps.

S E C R E T.

H

Headquarters,
46th Division.
137th Inf:Bde.
138th " "
139th " "
55th Bn. M.G.Corps
3rd Bn. M.G.Corps.
O.C.No 1 Group,
O.C.No 2 Group,

Reference my 46/12/142 Machine Gun Concentration Shoots, herewith please find revised list of targets to take the place of those issued under above number, which should be destroyed.
ACKNOWLEDGE.

21/8/1918.

J Harington
Bt.Lieut-Colonel,
Commanding 46th Battn. M.G.Corps.

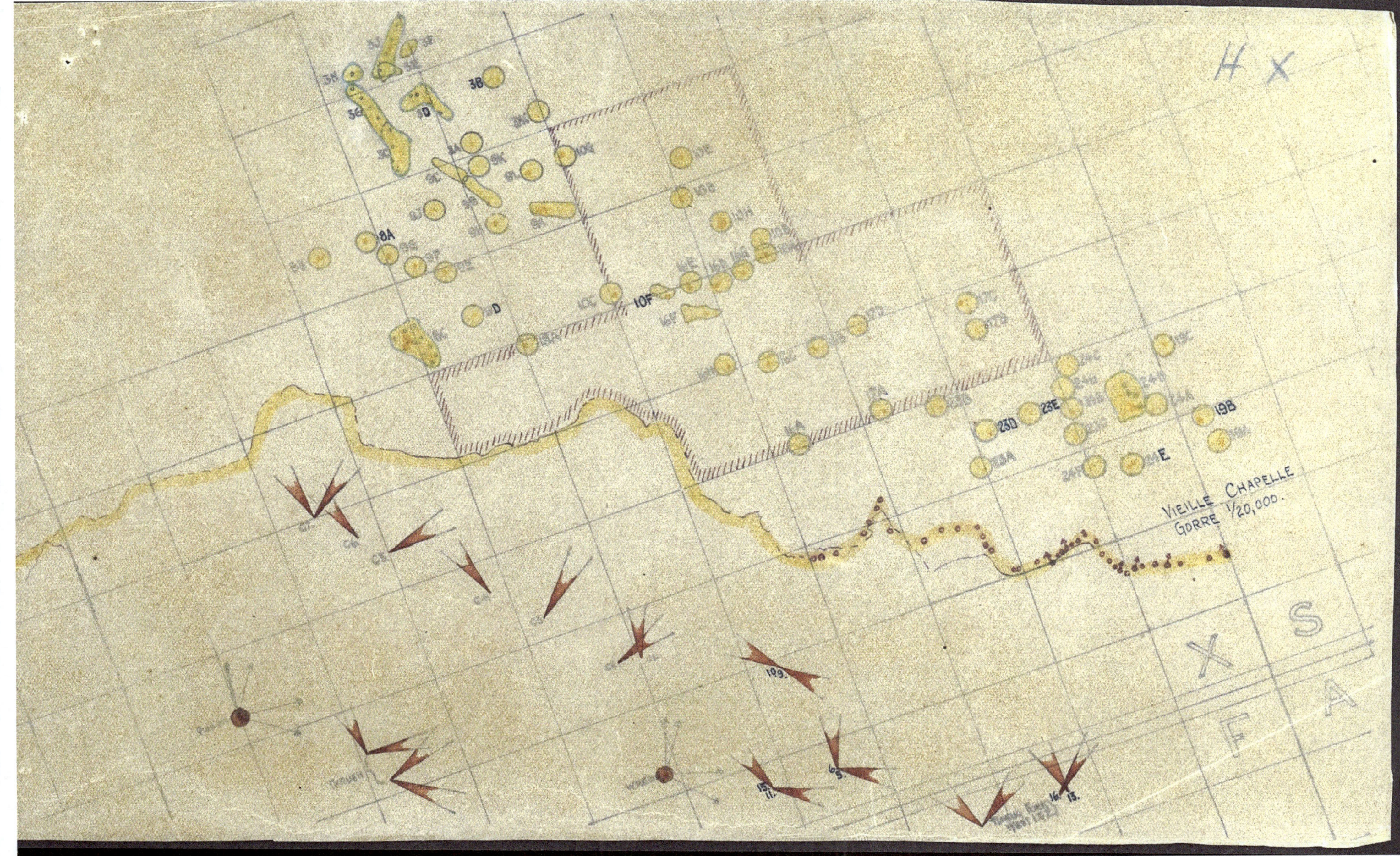

H X
3B
8A
D
10F
23D
23E
19B
E
VIELLE CHAPELLE
GORRE 1/20,000.
109.
S
X
A
F

H

COMBINED GROUPS.

No.	Map Ref.	C1.	C2.	C3.	C4.	C5.	C6.	C7.	C8.	5 &. 6	11 & . 15	15 & 16	Tuning Fork West	Thrush.	Pigeon.	Wren.	Hawk.	Directing Gun.	Total.
17.A.	X.17.c.19.09.	1	1	1	1	-	1	-	1	2	2	2	2	-	-	4	4	Wron.	22.
17.B.	X.17.d.43.52.	1	1	1	1	-	-	-	1	2	2	2	2	-	-	4	-	do	17.
17.C.	X.17.d.39.83.	1	1	1	1	-	-	-	1	2	2	2	2	-	-	4	-	do	17.
17.D.	X.17.a.25.00.	1	1	1	1	1	-	-	1	2	2	2	2	-	-	4	4	do	22.
15.A.	X.15.b.05.96.	-	-	-	-	-	1	-	-	-	-	-	-	4	4	4	-	do	13.
10.A.	X.10.d.65.02.	1	1	1	1	-	-	1	1	2	2	-	-	-	-	4	-	do	14.
10.B.	X.10.d.65.20.	1	1	1	1	-	1	-	1	2	2	-	-	-	-	4	-	do	14.
10.C.	X.10.c.05.15.	1	1	1	1	1	-	-	1	2	2	-	-	4	4	4	-	do	22.
10.D.	X.10.d.00.90.	1	1	1	1	-	1	-	1	-	-	-	-	-	-	-	-	C.S.	6.
10.E.	X.10.b.12.23.	1	1	1	1	-	-	1	1	-	-	-	-	-	-	-	-	C.S.	6.
10.G.	X.10.a.05.70.	1	1	1	1	-	1	-	1	-	-	-	-	-	-	-	-	C.S.	5.
10.H.	X.10.d.33.50.	1	1	1	1	1	-	-	1	2	-	-	-	-	-	4	-	Wren.	12.
16.A.	X.16.d.30.00.	-	-	1	1	-	-	1	-	2	2	2	2	-	-	4	4	do	19.
16.B.	X.16.d.80.90.	1	1	1	1	-	1	-	1	2	2	2	2	-	-	4	4	do	22.
16.C.	X.16.d.29.93.	1	1	1	1	1	-	-	1	2	2	2	2	-	-	4	4	do	22.
16.D.	X.16.b.12.90.	1	1	1	1	-	1	-	1	2	2	-	-	-	-	4	-	do	14.
16.E.	X.16.a.83.97.	1	1	1	1	-	-	1	1	2	2	-	-	-	-	4	-	do	14.
16.G.	X.16.a.35.95.	1	1	1	1	-	1	-	1	2	2	-	-	-	-	4	-	do	14.
16.H.	X.16.a.85.05.	1	1	-	-	1	-	-	-	2	2	2	2	-	-	4	4	do	19.

21/6/1918

John Harington Bt.Lieut-Colonel,
Commanding 4Sth Battn. M.G. Corps.

H

RIGHT GROUP.

Target.	Map Ref.	5 & 6.	11 & 15.	13 & 16.	Tuning Fork West.	Wren.	Hawk.	Directing Gun.	Total.
23.A.	X.23.a.95.20.	-	-	2	-	4	-	Wren.	6.
23.B.	X.23.a.75.92.	2	2	2	2	4	4	Hawk.	16.
23.C.	X.23.b.99.20.	2	2	2	2	-	4	do	12.
23.D.	X.23.b.14.55.	2	2	2	2	4	4	do	16.
23.E.	X.23.b.60.55.	2	2	2	2	4	4	do	16.
24.A.	X.24.a.86.22.	2	2	2	2	-	-	5.	8.
24.B.	X.24.a.03.47.	2	2	2	2	4	4	Hawk.	16.
24.C.	X.24.a.16.38.	2	2	2	2	-	4	do	12.
24.E.	X.24.c.40.70.	2	2	2	2	4	-	Wron.	12.
24.F.	X.24.c.03.80.	2	2	-	-	-	4	Hawk.	8.
24.G.	X.24.a.00.70.	2	2	2	2	4	4	do	16.
19.A.	S.19.d.30.63.	2	2	2	2	-	-	5.	8.
19.B.	S.19.d.24.92.	2	-	2	2	-	-	5.	6.
19.C.	S.19.b.08.70.	2	-	2	2	-	-	5.	6.

21/6/1918

John Harrington Bt.Liout-Colonel,
Commanding 46th Battn. M.G. Corps.

H

LEFT GROUP.

Target.	Map Ref.	C1.	C2.	C3.	C4.	C5.	C6.	C7.	C8.	Thrush.	Pigeon.	Directing Gun.	Total.
8.A.	X.8.b.92.43.	1	1	-	1	-	1	-	1	4	4	Thrush.	13.
8.B.	X.8.b.35.49.	1	1	-	1	1	-	1	-	4	4	do	13.
3.A.	X.3.d.20.10.	1	1	1	1	-	-	-	1	-	-	C.8.	5.
3.B.	X.3.d.70.35.	-	-	1	1	1	-	1	-	-	-	C.7.	4.
3.K.	X.3.d.96.20.	1	1	1	-	-	1	-	1	-	-	C.8.	5.
9.D.	X.9.c.62.41.	1	1	1	1	1	-	-	1	4	4	Thrush.	14.
9.E.	X.9.c.51.95.	1	1	1	1	-	1	-	1	4	4	do	14.
9.F.	X.9.a.25.08.	1	1	1	1	-	-	1	1	4	4	do	14.
9.G.	X.9.a.02.30.	1	1	1	1	-	-	D	1	4	4	do	14.
9.H.	X.9.b.18.22.	1	1	1	1	-	1	-	1	-	4	Pigeon.	10.
9.J.	X.9.a.35.59.	1	1	1	1	-	-	1	1	-	4	do	10.
9.K.	X.9.b.21.90.	1	1	1	1	-	1	-	1	-	-	C.8.	6.
9.L.	X.9.b.70.64.	1	1	1	1	1	-	-	1	-	-	C.8.	3.

21/6/1918

John Harington Bt.Lieut-Colonel,
Commanding 46th Battn. M.G. Corps.

S E C R E T.

Copy No. 18

46th BATTALION MACHINE GUN CORPS ORDER No.41.

Reference 1/20,000 GORRE and VIEILLE CHAPELLE.

1. 'A' Company will relieve 'B' Company in the line in the 'Forward Gun positions' in the ESSARS Section on the night 23/24th June, 1918.

2. 'B' Company and 'B' Company Headquarters thus relieved will move into reserve at the Transport lines and will take over accommodation vacated by 'A' Company, and as Sections arrive Transport lines they will come under two hours notice to move.

3. Any further details, also guides etc, will be arranged direct between O.C.'A' Company and O.C.Group.

4. All Trench and area stores, documents, special maps, aeroplane photographs and programmes of work in hand will be handed over and receipts obtained. A certificate that all positions have been taken over in a clean and satisfactory state will be rendered by O.C.'A' Company to reach Battalion Headquarters 1st D.R. 25th June,1918.
At No 2 Group Headquarters No 2 Group copy defence scheme, special maps, documents, aeroplane photographs etc will be handed over.

5. Completion of this relief will be wired to Battalion Headquarters by BAB code.

6. Completion of this relief will also be notified by O.C.No 2 Group to the Brigade Commander whose front his guns are covering.

7. Immediately the above relief is completed Major H.S.Windeler will take over the Command of No 2 Group from Major C.V.Rigby, M.C.

8. ACKNOWLEDGE.

Issued at :- 7.0 P.M.

21/6/1918.

R. Hickens.
Capt & Adjt,
46th Battn.Machine Gun Corps.

Distribution:-

1. A.Coy.	10. 55th Dn.M.G.Corps.
2. B.Coy.	11. 137th Inf: Bde.
3. C.Coy.	12. 138th : :
4. D.Coy.	13. 139th : :
5. T.O.	14. .No 1 Group,
6. Q.M.	15. No 2 Group.
7. Signals.	16. File.
8. 46th Division.	17.)
9. 3rd Dn.M.G.Corps.	18.)War Diary.

J

S E C R E T.

H.Q.,46th Division.
C.R.A.,46th Division.
O.C.,56th Bn.M.G.Corps.
O.C.,3rd Bn.M.G.Corps.
H.Q.,137th Inf.Bde.
H.Q.,138th : :
H.Q.,139th : :
O.C.No 1 Group
O.C.No 2 Group
War Diary (2)
File.

Copy

1. Herewith programme of Machine Gun Concentration and Area Shoots for week ending July 4th, 1918.

2. A new feature is the addition of Area Shoots in which the areas detailed are swept by either Traversing or Searching Fire.

3. ACKNOWLEDGE.

26/6/1918.

[signature]
Major,
46th Battn.Machine Gun Corps.

J

MACHINE GUN AREA SHOOTS.

AREA.	CORNERS OF AREA.	GUNS. Firing	TARGETS.	DIRECTING GUN.
		WREN.	From X.23.b.78.65. to X.24.c.10.66.	
	X.24.c.20.38.	01 & 2.	" X.23.b.78.65 to X.23.d.97.66.	
		03.	" X.17.d.95.10 - X.23.d.98.63.	
	X.23.d.70.70	05 & 6.	" X.23.b.75.25 - X.24.c.12.67.	
A.		11 &15.	" X.17.d.80.10 - X.24.a.25.42.	WREN.
	X.18.c.30.10	13 &16.	" X.23.c.73.08 - X.18.c.10.10	
		9 & 10	" X.23.b.80.94 - X.24.a.34.09	
	X.17.d.80.10	HAWK.	" X.23.b.78.40 - X.18.c.30.10	
		T.F.V.	" X.23.b.78.07 - X.24.a.39.95	
		01.	" X.16.c.70.95 - X.16.d.50.35	
		02.	" X.16.b.58.48 - X.17.c.05.99	
		03.	" X.16.b.36.50 - X.16.d.83.35	
	X.17.c.04.34.	08.	" X.16.b.05.50 - X.16.d.54.32	
		04.	" X.16.a.86.48 - X.16.d.28.32	
		05.	" X.16.b.55.48 - X.16.d.65.32	
	X.16.c.70.32.	06.	" X.16.b.80.48 - X.16.d.87.32	
B.		9 & 10	" X.16.a.70.48 - X.17.a.05.05	WREN.
		5 & 6	" X.16.c.75.95 - X.17.c.05.70	
	X.17.a.03.49.	11 &15	" X.16.a.70.25 - X.17.c.05.78	
		T.F.V.	" X.16.c.73.50 - X.17.c.05.52	
		HAWK.	" X.16.c.70.75 - X.17.c.05.52	
	X.16.a.70.50.	WREN.2 guns	" X.16.c.90.50 - X.16.b.65.50	
		WREN 2 guns	" X.16.d.10.32 - X.17.a.05.48	
		13 &16	From X.16.d.10.32 - X.16.b.99.49	
	X.17.a.19.79	WREN	" X.10.c.34.70 - X.17.a.16.99	
		01 & 2.	" X.10.c.64.55 - X.17.a.00.80	
	X.16.a.66.73	11 &15.	" X.10.c.65.37 - X.17.a.18.95	
C.		9 & 10.	" X.10.c.65.23 - X.17.a.18.78	WREN
	X.11.c.11.80	5 & 6	" X.16.c.65.95 - X.16.b.80.80	
		04.	" X.10.d.35.80 - X.16.b 99.79	
	X.10.c.62.80	05.	" X.10.d.75.80 - X.17.a.15.78	
		THRUSH.	" X. 8.b.56.42 - X. 9.c.75.85	
	X. 9.c.57.38.	PIGEON.	" X. 8.b.60.49 - X. 9.c.65.75	
D.	X. 8.b.56.42.	01 & 2.	" X. 9.a.00.08 - X. 9.a.50.12	THRUSH.
	X. 9.c.78.92.	03.	" X. 8.b.56.45 - X. 9.c.05.50	
	X. 8.b.78.70.	08.	" X. 8.b.85.20 - X. 9.a.40.22	

26th June, 1918.

John Harington Bt. Lieut-Colonel,
Commanding 46th Battn. M.G. Corps.

PROGRAMME OF MACHINE GUN CONCENTRATION & AREA SHOOTS, for week ending July 4th, 1918.

NIGHT.	TARGET.	TIME.	No. of ROUNDS PER GUN.	REMARKS.
June 27/28th.	15 A.	9.45 pm.	250	No gun will fire if it is not dark enough to obviate all possibility of the screen being seen.
	24 C.) 9 F.)	10.00 pm.	250	
	19 C.) 9 L.)	10.10 pm.	250	
	19 A.) 3 B.)	10.29 pm.	250	
	15 A.	10.35 pm.	50	
	15 A.	10.40 pm.	100	
	15 A.	10.50 pm.	100	
28/29th.	17 D.	9.55 pm.	250	
	23 B.) 9 J.)	10.10 pm.	250	
	AREA.B.	10.30 pm.	250	Slow traverse or V.S.
	19 B.) 9 F.)	10.45 pm.	250	
	10 D.	11.00 pm.	250	
	16 C.	1.00 am.	250	
	19 A.) 8 A.)	2.20 am.	250	
29/30th.	16 B.	9.45 pm.	250	
	23 D.) 5 A.)	9.55 pm.	250	
	AREA.C.	10.15 pm.	250	Slow traverse or V.S.
	10 G.	11.15 pm.	250	
	24 C.) 8 D.)	12.20 am.	250	
	AREA.C.	1.50 am.	250	
	17 D.	2.00 am.	250	
	19 A.) 9 H.)	2.15 am.	250	
	16 B.	2.35 am.	250	
June 30/ 1st July.	17 B.	9.35 pm.	50	
	17 B.	9.45 pm.	50	
	17 B.	9.50 pm.	50	
	17 B.	9.55 pm.	50	
	17 B.	10.00 pm.	50	
	AREA.D.	10.15 pm.	250	Slow traverse or V.S.
	10 C.	10.40 pm.	250	
	16 D.	10.50 pm.	250	
	23 B.) 3 K.)	2.00 am.	250	
	24 A.) 9 H.)	2.30 am.	250	
	23 D.) 3 K.)	2.45 am.	250	
July 1/2nd.	AREA.A.	10.10 pm.	350	Slow traverse or V.S.
	17 C.	10.30 pm.	50	
	17 C.	10.35 pm.	50	
	17 C.	10.37 pm.	50	
	10 E.	10.52 pm.	250	
	10 H.	1.2 am.	250	
	16 G.	1.20 am.	250	
	AREA.D.	2.00 am.	250	
	23 E.) 9 F.)	2.10 am.	250	
	19 B.) 9 F.)	2.20 am.	250	
	24 B.) 9 F.)	2.45 am.	250	
	24 G.) 9 F.)	2.55 am.	250	

NIGHT.	TARGET.	TIME.	No of ROUNDS PER GUN.	REMARKS.
July 2/3rd.	NO FIRING.			
3/4th.	AREA.B.	10.2 p.m.	250	
	9 K.) 19 B.)	10.20 p.m.	250	
	24 C.) 9 H.)	10.25 p.m.	250	
	9 D.) 25 B.)	10.45 p.m.	250	
	16 C.	12.00 mid.	250	
	17 A.	1.00 am.	250	
	17 A.	1.50 a.m.	250	
	10 A.	2.40 a.m.	250	
	10 B.	3.00 a.m.	250	

John Harington

[illegible]/[illegible]/1918.

Bt.Lieut-Colonel,
Commanding 48th Battn.M.G.Corps.

SECRET. Copy No....18....

46th BATTALION MACHINE GUN CORPS ORDER NO.42.

Reference 1/20,000 GORRE and VIEILLE CHAPELLE.

1. 'B' Company will relieve 'D' Company in the line in the 'Forward Gun positions' in the GORRE Section on the night 29/30th June,1918.

2. 'D' Company and 'D' Company Headquarters thus relieved will move into reserve at the Transport lines and will take over accommodation vacated by 'B' Company, and as Sections arrive at Transport lines they will come under two hours notice to move.

3. Any further details, also guides etc, will be arranged direct between O.C. 'B' Company and O.C.Group. I

4. All Trench and area stores, documents, special maps, aeroplane photographs and programmes of work in hand will be handed over and receipts obtained. A certificate that the positions taken over are in a clean and satisfactory state will be rendered by O.C. 'B' Company to reach Battalion Headquarters 1st D.R. 1st July 1918. ~~At No. 1 Group Headquarters No. 1 Group copy defence scheme, special maps, documents, aeroplane photographs etc will be handed over.~~

5. Completion of this relief will be wired to Battalion Headquarters by "B.A.B." code.

6. Completion of this relief will also be notified by O.C.No. 1. Group to the Brigade Commander whose front his guns are covering.

7. ACKNOWLEDGE.

Issued at 7.0. P.M.

27/6/1918.

Capt & Adjt.,
46th Battn.Machine Gun Corps.

Distribution :-
1. A. Coy.
2. B. Coy.
3. C. Coy.
4. D. Coy.
5. T.O.
6. Q.M.
7. Signals.
8. 46th Division.
9. 3rd Bn.M.G.Corps.
10. 55th Bn.M.G.Corps.
11. 137th. Inf: Bde.
12. 138th. Inf: Bde.
13. 139th. Inf: Bde.
14. No. 1 Group.
15. No. 2 Group.
16. File.
17.) War Diary.
18.)

S E C R E T   Copy No......20

46th BATTALION MACHINE GUN CORPS ORDER NO.45.

Reference sheet BETHUNE combined 1/40,000.

The Headquarters of this Battalion will close at GOSNAY at 9-0 a.m. 30th ~~July~~ JUNE and will open at BOIS DES MONTAGNES (E.27.b.00.40). at the same hour.

23/6/1918.

Issued at 7.0 PM

[illegible]
Capt & Adjt.,
46th Battn. M.G.Corps.

Distribution:-

1. 46th Division.	10. 55th.Bn.M.G.C.
2. 137th.Inf:Bde.	11. No.1 Group.
3. 138th. : :	12. No.2 :
4. 139th. : :	13. 'A' Coy,
5. C.R.A.	14. 'B' :
6. C.R.E.	15. 'C' :
7. D.A.D.O.S.	16. 'D' :
8. A.D.M.S.	17. Q. M.
9. 3rd.Bn.M.G.C.	18. T. O.

19, C.M.G.O. XIII Corps.
20. WAR DIARY (2 COPIES)
21. FILE

Vol 5

****

WAR DIARY

OF

46th BATTALION MACHINE GUN CORPS

JULY 1918.

****

Army Form C. 2118.

WAR DIARY

~~INTELLIGENCE SUMMARY~~ 46th BATTALION MACHINE GUN CORPS.

(Erase heading not required.)

No 1.

Instructions regarding War Diaries and Intelligence Summaries are contained in F. S. Regs., Part II. and the Staff Manual respectively. Title pages will be prepared in manuscript.

JULY 1918.

Place	Date	Hour	GORRE 1/20,000 VIEILLE CHAPELLE 1/20,000 Summary of Events and Information	Remarks and references to Appendices
GORRE & ESSARS SECTIONS.	1st.		M.Gs.fired 22,250 rounds harassing fire. M.Gs.fired 2,150 rounds at E.A. during the day. Enemy artillery reported rather more active than usual,although shelling was general rather than confined to particular localities. Hostile bombs were dropped in the vicinity of the front line. A dump was observed ablaze in enemy's lines. 1 O.R. evacuated sick. 11 O.Rs. reinforcements.	
	2nd.		M.Gs. fired 19,250 rounds harassing fire during night. 4,250 rounds fired at E.A. during the day. Artillery activity continues general. Hostile artillery active throughout the day. 10-30 p.m. dump observed to go up in enemy's lines.	
	3rd.		34,000 rounds harassing fire during night. 420 rounds fired on E.A. during day. Considerable activity amongst hostile machine guns. Intermittent gas shelling. Programme of area and concentration shoots week commencing 4/5th July issued. (copy attached marked 'A') Revised Appendices to Machine Gun Counter preparation Scheme issued (copy attached marked 'B') Programme of harassing targets issued (copy attached marked 'C') Letter re re-numbering of M.G. Positions issued (copy attached marked 'D'), also tracing marked 'DX' 2/Lieut.G.F.Thorpe to Base Depot for Medical Board. 3 O.Rs. evacuated sick.	'A' 'B' 'C' 'D' 'DX'
	4th.		M.Gs. did no harassing fire during the night,as it is desired to mislead hostile observation by having a quiet night for the safe conducting of reliefs. 2,700 rounds fired at E.A. during the day. Some hostile gas shelling on the front.	
		7-0 pm.	Order No 44 issued (copy attached) 1 O.R. wounded. 1 O.R. reinforcement.	Order No 44
	5th.		M.Gs. fired 19,000 rounds harassing fire during night. There was a renewal of hostile gas shelling, especially on GORRE locality. Lieut.F.A.L.Sloot and Lieut.R.N.Cornish reinforcements from Base Depot. 4 O.Rs. wounded. 4 O.Rs. reinforcements.	
	6th.		M.Gs. fired 21,000 harassing fire on area 'A' (see copy attached) Hostile messenger dog was captured near Canal F.l.d. with tin cannister attached to his neck containing messages, the purpose of which has been communicated. 2 enemy dumps seen to explode. 1 O.R. evacuated sick.	
	7th.		No harassing fire during the night. Hostile aircraft active. 2 O.Rs. wounded.	

A5834 Wt. W4973/M687 750,000 8/16 D. D. & L. Ltd. Forms/C.2118/13.

Army Form C. 2118.

WAR DIARY

~~INTELLIGENCE SUMMARY~~

Instructions regarding War Diaries and Intelligence Summaries are contained in F. S. Regs., Part II. and the Staff Manual respectively. Title pages will be prepared in manuscript.

JULY 1918. (Erase heading not required.) 46th BATTALION MACHINE GUN CORPS.

No 2

Place	Date	Hour	Summary of Events and Information GORRE 1/20,000 VIEILLE CHAPELLE 1/20,000	Remarks and references to Appendices
GORRE & ESSARS SECTIONS.	8th.		M.Gs. fired 29,000 harassing fire during the night. 2,500 rounds fired at E.A. during the day. Considerable hostile gas shelling on the front. Letter 46/12/313 issued (copy attached marked 'E') Programme of Area Concentration Shoots issued (copy attached marked 'F') (reference previous copy marked 'C') 2 O.Rs. evacuated sick. 1 O.Rs. reinforcement.	'E' 'F'
	9th.		M.Gs. fired 18,000 rounds harassing fire during the night. 900 rounds fired at E.A. during the day. 1 O.R. evacuated. 3 O.Rs. reinforcements.	
		1-0 pm.	Order No 45 issued (copy attached)	Order No 45
	10th.		M.Gs. fired 26,500 rounds harassing fire on Area 'C'. 818 rounds fired at E.A. during the day. I suggested that hostile batteries registered on ESSARS, and one of the machine gun batteries in X.19.b. Heavy shelling of GORRE during which GORRE BRIDGE received a direct hit, resulting in the detonation charge which in turn demolished central span. Letter 46/12/320 issued (copy attached marked 'G') Lieut.A.W.Briggs and 2/Lieut.S.A.Earl reinforcements from Base Depot. 2 O.Rs. evacuated sick 1 O.R. wounded.	'G'
	12th.		24,250 rounds fired by our machine guns during the night. 330 rounds fired at E.A.during the day. 2 O.Rs. evacuated sick. 1 O.R. reinforcement.	
	13th.		M.Gs. fired 25,250 rounds harassing fire during the night. Lieut.C.W.Pugh transferred to 38th Battn.Machine Gun Corps. 1 O.R. evacuated.	
	14th.		15,500 rounds harassing fire during the night. Hostile artillery quiet.	
	15th.		22,750 rounds harassing fire during the night. 2,140 rounds fired at E.A. during the day.	
		9-15 p.m.	1 E.A. crashed and 1 brought down out of control. 2 O.Rs. evacuated sick. 9 O.Rs.reinforcements.	
	16th.		M.Gs. fired 9,500 rounds harassing fire during the night. 1,580 rounds fired at E.A. during the day. Considerable hostile gas shelling during the day and night. 2 O.Rs returned to Base Depot (unfit).	
	17th.		M.Gs. fired 12,500 rounds harassing fire during the night. 4,650 rounds fired at E.A. during the day. Lieut.R.J.C.Shipley returned to 1/8th Sherwood Foresters for duty. Lt-Col.B.Mathew-Lannowe, D.S.O. 2nd Dragoon Guards attached to the Battalion. 1 O.R. evacuated sick. 4 O.Rs. wounded.	

A5834 Wt. W4973/M687 750,000 8/16 D. D. & L. Ltd. Forms/C.2118/13.

Army Form C. 2118.

WAR DIARY

or

~~INTELLIGENCE SUMMARY~~

(Erase heading not required.)

Instructions regarding War Diaries and Intelligence Summaries are contained in F. S. Regs., Part II. and the Staff Manual respectively. Title pages will be prepared in manuscript.

JULY 1918. 46th BATTALION MACHINE GUN CORPS

No 3

Place	Date	Hour	GORRE 1/20,000 VIEILLE CHAPELLE 1/20,000 Summary of Events and Information	Remarks and references to Appendices
GORRE & ESSARS SECTIONS.	18th.		M.Gs. fired 5,200 rounds at E.A. during the day. Letter 46/12/336 issued (copy attached marked 'H')	'H'
		5-0 pm.	Order No 46 issued (copy attached) 1 O.R. to Cadet School U.K. 1 O.R. evacuated sick.	Order No 46
	19th.		4,000 rounds fired in conjunction with minor operation by our infantry. 400 rounds fired during the day at E.A. 1 O.R. killed in action. 3 O.Rs. wounded. 4 O.Rs. reinforcements.	
	20th.		2,350 rounds fired at E.A. during the day. 1 O.R. killed in action. 5 O.Rs. reinforcements 2/Lieut.W.L.Smith to U.K. for transfer to the R.A.F.	
	21st.		300 rounds fired at E.A. during the day. Battalion Horse Show held (copy of programme attached marked 'J')	'J'
		12-0 noon.	Order No 47 issued (copy attached) 2 O.Rs. reinforcements.	Order No 47
	22nd.		650 rounds fired at E.A. during the day. 1 O.R. evacuated sick.	
	23rd.		500 rounds fired at E.A. during the day. 1 O.R. to Base Depot (unfit).	
	24th.		7,000 rounds harassing fire during the night. 100 rounds fired at E.A. during the day. Bt.Lieut-Colonel J.Harington, D.S.O. to Command 139th Infantry Brigade. Lieut-Colonel B.Mathew-Lannowe assumed Command of the Battalion. Lieut.S.A.Parkes and Lieut.N.MacVie. reinforcements from Base Depot. 1 O.R. killed in action. 2 O.Rs.reinforcements.	
	25th.		18,625 rounds fired in reply to S.O.S. on our front. 3,200 rounds harassing fire during the night. 2 O.Rs. reinforcements.	
	26th.		3,500 rounds harassing fire during the night. 1,000 rounds fired at E.A. during the day. Some considerable hostile gas shelling. Lieut.H.A.Spendlove, 1st Sherwoods attached for Transport duty. 1 O.R. evacuated. 1 O.R. reinforcement.	
	27th.		4,500 rounds harassing fire. 1,995 rounds fired at E.A. during the day.	
		12-0 noon.	Order No 48 issued (copy attached)	Order No 48.

A5834 Wt. W4973/M687 750,000 8/16 D. D. & L. Ltd. Forms/C.2118/13.

Army Form C. 2118.

WAR DIARY

~~or~~

~~INTELLIGENCE SUMMARY.~~ 46th BATTALION MACHINE GUN CORPS.

(*Erase heading not required.*)

Instructions regarding War Diaries and Intelligence Summaries are contained in F. S. Regs., Part II. and the Staff Manual respectively. Title pages will be prepared in manuscript.

JULY 1918.

No 4.

Place	Date	Hour	Summary of Events and Information GORRE 1/20,000 VIEILLE CHAPELLE 1/20,000	Remarks and references to Appendices
GORRE & ESSARS SECTIONS.	28th.		M.Gs. fired 4,000 rounds harassing fire during the night. 620 rounds fired at E.A. during the day. 1 O.R. wounded.	
	29th.		M.Gs. fired 9,000 rounds harassing fire during the night. 750 rounds were fired at E.A. during the day.	
	30th.		M.Gs. fired 10,500 rounds harassing fire during the night. 3250rounds fired at E.A. during the day. 1 hostile observation balloon and 1 hostile plane brought down by our planes during the day. 1 O.R. wounded. 1 O.R. evacuated. 1 O.R. reinforcement.	
	31st.		M.Gs. fired 8,200 rounds harassing fire during the night. 1,700 rounds fired at E.A. during the day. 1 O.R. evacuated. 1 O.R. reinforcement.	

B. Luxmoore.
Lieut-Colonel,
Commanding 46th Battn.Machine Gun Corps.

A5834 Wt. W4973/M687 750,000 8/16 D. D. & L. Ltd. Forms/C.2118/13.

S E C R E T.

H.Q.,46th Division.
C.R.A.,46th Division.
55th Bn.M.G.Corps.
3rd Bn.M.G.Corps.
137th Inf:Bde.
138th Inf:Bde
139th Inf:Bde.
O.C.No 1 Group,
" No 2 "
War Diary (2)
File.

A

Herewith programme of Area and Concentration Shoots for week ending 11th July, 1918.

3/7/1918.

Major,
46th Battn.Machine Gun Corps.

S E C R E T.

PROGRAMME OF MACHINE GUN AREA & CONCENTRATION SHOOTS
Week ending July 11th, 1918.

NIGHT.	TARGET.	TIME.	No. of ROUNDS PER GUN.	REMARKS.
July 4/5th.	AREA "A"	10.15 p.m. 10.29 p.m. 10.46 p.m. 11.00 p.m. 11.20 p.m. 11.23 pm. 12.00 mid. 2.2 a.m. 2.15 a.m.	250 250 250 250 125 125 250 250 250	No firing will be done if it is not dark enough to obviate all possibility of the screen being seen.
5/6th.	NO FIRING.			
6/7th.	AREA "B"	10.25 p.m. 10.30 p.m. 10.47 p.m. 11.3 p.m. 11.20 p.m. 11.22 p.m. 2.00 a.m. 2.20 a.m. 2.52 a.m. 3.00 a.m.	250 125 125 250 250 250 250 250 250 250	
7/8th.	17 A. 24 A.) 3 A.) 17 D. 24 C.) 3 K.) 9 H.) 19 A.) 17 A. 17 A.	10.20 p.m. 10.32 p.m. 10.47 p.m. 10.59 p.m. 11.25 p.m. 12.00 mid. 12.5 a.m.	250 250 250 250 250 250 250	
8/9th.	AREA "C"	10.35 p.m. 10.37 p.m. 10.50 p.m. 10.53 p.m. 10.59 p.m. 1.00 a.m. 1.5 a.m. 1.10 a.m. 1.30 a.m.	125 125 250 250 250 250 250 250 250	
9/10th.	17 B. 24 C.) 9 F.) 10 H. 23 B.) 8 A.) 10 C. 10 C. 15 A. 23 B.) 8 A.)	10.15 p.m. 10.30 p.m. 10.40 p.m. 11.20 p.m. 12.00 mid. 1.00 a.m. 2.5 a.m. 2.35 a.m.	250 250 250 250 250 250 250 250	

PROGRAMME OF MACHINE GUN AREA & CONCENTRATION SHOOTS continued.

NIGHT.	TARGETS	TIME.	No of ROUNDS PER GUN.	REMARKS.
July 10/11th.	17 C.	10.30 p.m.	250	
	23 D.) 9 L.)	11.2 p.m.	250	
	19 A.) 8 B.)	11.30 p.m.	250	
	17 C.	12.20 a.m.	250	
	24 G.) 3 B.)	1.00 a.m.	250	
	23 E.) 9 D)	1.30 a.m.	250	
	17 C.	2.00 a.m.	250	
	23 E.) 9 D.)	3.2 a.m.	250	

3rd July, 1917.

J Harington
Bt.Lieut-Colonel,
Commanding 46th Battn.M.G.Corps.

S E C R E T.

O.C.,55th Bn.M.G.Corps.
O.C.,3rd Bn.M.G.Corps.
O.C.No 1 Group,
O.C.No 2 Group,
O.C.'A' Coy,
O.C.'B' Coy,
O.C.'C' Coy,
O.C.'D' Coy,
War Diary (2)

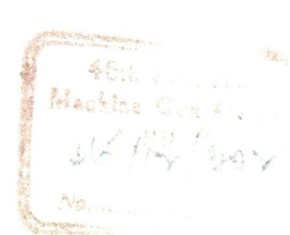

B

The Machine Guns of this Battalion in the line have been re-numbered. Herewith revised appendices to 46th Battalion Machine Gun Corps Counter preparation Scheme.

Please destroy old copies.

ACKNOWLEDGE.

J. Harington

3/7/1918.

Bt.Lieut-Colonel,
Commanding 46th Battn.M.G.Corps.

MACHINE GUN COUNTER PREPARATION SCHEME.

APPENDIX "A"

TARGETS.	GUNS ABLE TO FIRE.																		BATTERIES ABLE TO FIRE.					
No.	1.	2.	3.	4.	5.	6.	9.	10.	11.	12.	13.	14.	15.	16.	17.	18.	19.	20.	THRUSH.	PIGEON.	WREN.	TOTAL.	DIRECTING GUNS.	REMARKS.
3 C.	-	-	-	-	-	-	-	-	-	-	-	-	1	1	1	1	1	1	-	-	-	6	18	
3 D.	-	-	-	-	-	-	-	-	-	-	-	-	1	1	1	1	1	1	-	-	-	6	18	
3 G.	-	-	-	-	-	-	-	-	-	-	-	-	1	1	1	1	1	1	-	-	-	6	18	
3 H.	-	-	-	-	-	-	-	-	-	-	-	-	-	-	1	1	1	1	-	-	-	4	17	
3 J.	-	-	-	-	-	-	-	-	-	-	-	-	-	-	1	1	1	1	-	-	-	4	17	
8 C.	-	-	-	-	-	-	-	-	-	-	1	1	-	-	-	-	-	-	4	4	4	14	THRUSH.	
24 D.	1	1	1	1	1	1	1	1	1	1	-	-	-	-	-	-	-	-	-	-	-	10	5	

3rd July, 1918.

J Harington

Bt.Lieut-Colonel,

manding 46th Battn.M.G.Corps.

APPENDIX "B"

TARGET.	TIME.	ROUNDS.
3 C.) 8 C.)	10.35 pm.	250
3 H.) 24 D.)	11.10 pm.	250
3 D.) 24 D.)	11.38 pm.	250
3 D.) 8 C.)	12.22 am.	250
3 J.) 24 D.)	12.50 am.	250
3 G.) 8 C.) 24 D.)	1.15 am.	250
3 D.	1.41 am.	250
3 G.	2.00 am.	250
3 H.) 24 D.)	2.17 am.	250
3 J.) 24 D.)	2.29 am.	250
3 C.) 24 D.)	2.37 am.	250
3 J.) 8 C.)	3.5 am.	250
3 H.	3.14 am.	250
8 C.) 24 D.)	3.20 am.	250
8 C.) 3 G.) 24 D.)	3.32 am.	250
3 C.) 24 D.)	3.45 am.	250
8 C.) 24 D.)	3.53 am.	250

APPENDIX "C"

AREA.	GUN.	TARGET.	REMARKS.
24 D.	1	X.24.a.60.40	)
	2	X.24.a.60.40	)
	3	X.24.a.60.50	)
	4	X.24.a.60.50	)
	5	X.24.a.60.40	) Unchanged
	6	X.24.a.60.40	) from 46/12/213
	11	X.24.a.60.50	) of 9/6/18.
	12	X.24.a.60.50	)
	9	X.24.a.65.35	)
	10	X.24.a.65.35	)
3 C.	15 & 16.	X.3.c.42.10	)
	17	X.3.c.42.22	) Unchanged
	18	X.3.c.48.35	) from 43/12/213
	19	X.3.c.48.35	) of 9/3/18.
	20	X.3.c.52.52	)
3 D.	15 & 16.	X.3.c.81,80	)
	17	X.3.c.72.77	) This is
	18	X.3.c.98.80	) different from
	19	X.3.c.99.79	) 49/12/213 of
	20	X.3.d.05.52	) 9/3/18.
3 G.	15 & 16	X.3.c.45.68	)
	17	X.3.c.40.80	)
	18	X.3.c.40.80	) New target.
	19	X.3.c.55.94	)
	20	X.3.a.30.05	)
3 H.	17	X.3.a.35.20	)
	18	X.3.a.35.20	) New target.
	19	X.3.a.55.20	)
	20	X.3.a.35.20	)
3 J.	17	X.3.a.62.12	)
	18	X.3.a.75.28	) New target.
	19	X.3.a.85.40	)
	20	X.3.a.95.50	)
8 C.	15	X.9.c.04.51	)
	13	X.8.d.96.35	)
	14	X.8.d.93.35	) New target.
	THRUSH.	X.8.d.92.49	)
	PIGEON.	X.8.d.97.34	)
	WREN.	X.9.c.08.15	)

3rd July, 1918.

J. Harington Bt.Lieut-Colonel,
Commanding 46th Battn.M.G.Corps.

S E C R E T.

H.Q., 46th Division.
C.R.A. " "
137th Inf: Bde.
138th : :
139th : :
55th Bn.M.G.Corps.
3rd Bn.M.G.Corps.
No 1 Group,
No 2 Group,
War Diary (2)
File.

The Machine Guns of this Battalion in the line have been re-numbered. Reference 46/12/259 Machine Gun Concentration Shoots, herewith please find revised list of targets to take place of those issued under above number, which should be destroyed.

ACKNOWLEDGE.

3/7/1918.

J. Harington Bt. Lieut-Colonel,
Commanding 46th Battn.M.G.Corps.

LEFT GROUP.

Target.	Map Reference.	13	14	15	16	17	18	19	20	Thrush	Pigeon	Total	Directing Gun.
8.A.	X.8.b.92.48	1	1	-	1	1	-	1	-	4	4	13	THRUSH.
8.B.	X.8.b.35.49	1	-	-	1	1	1	-	1	4	4	13	do
3.A.	X.3.d.20.10	1	1	1	1	1	-	-	-	-	-	5	14
3.B.	X.3.d.70.65	-	-	1	-	1	1	-	1	-	-	4	20
3.K.	X.3.d.96.20	1	1	1	1	-	-	1	-	-	-	5	14
9.D.	X.9.c.62.41	1	1	1	1	1	1	-	-	4	4	14	THRUSH.
9.E.	X.9.c.51.95	1	1	1	1	1	-	1	-	4	4	14	do
9.F.	X.9.a.25.08	1	1	1	1	1	-	-	1	4	4	14	do
9.G.	X.9.a.02.30	1	1	1	1	1	-	-	-	4	4	13	do
9.H.	X.9.b.18.22	1	1	1	1	1	-	1	-	-	4	10	PIGEON.
9.J.	X.9.a.65.59	1	1	1	1	1	-	-	1	-	4	10	do
9.K.	X.9.b.21.90	1	1	1	1	1	-	1	-	-	-	6	14
9.L.	X.9.b.70.64	1	1	1	1	1	1	-	-	-	-	6	14

RIGHT GROUP.

Target.	Map Reference.	1 & 2.	3 & 4.	5 & 6.	11 & 12.	Wren.	Hawk.	Total.	Directing Gun.
23.A.	X.23.a.95.20	2	-	-	-	4	-	6	WREN.
23.B.	X.23.a.75.92	2	2	2	2	4	4	16	HAWK.
23.C.	X.23.b.99.20	2	2	2	2	-	4	12	do
23.D.	X.23.b.14.55	2	2	2	2	4	4	16	do
23.E.	X.23.b.60.55	2	2	2	2	4	4	16	do
24.A.	X.24.a.86.22	2	2	2	2	-	-	8	5
24.B.	X.24.a.03.47	2	2	2	2	4	4	16	HAWK
24.C.	X.24.a.16.88	2	2	2	2	-	4	12	do
24.E.	X.24.c.40.70	2	2	2	2	4	-	12	WREN.
24.F.	X.24.c.03.80	-	-	2	2	-	4	8	HAWK.
24.G.	X.24.a.00.70	2	2	2	2	4	4	16	do
19.A.	S.19.d.30.63	2	2	2	-	-	-	6	5
19.B.	S.19.d.24.92	2	2	2	-	-	-	6	5
19.C.	S.19.b.08.70	2	2	2	-	-	-	6	5

3rd July, 1918.

J. Harrington

Bt.Lieut-Colonel,
Commanding 46th Battn.M.G. Corps.

COMBINED GROUPS.

No.	Map Reference.	1 & 2	3 & 4	5 & 6	11 & 12	13	14	15	16	17	18	19	20	Thrush	Pigeon	Wren	Hawk	Total	Directing Gun.
17.A.	X.17.c.19.09	2	2	2	2	1	1	1	1	1	-	1	-	-	-	4	4	22	WREN.
17.B.	X.17.d.45.52	2	2	2	2	1	1	1	1	1	-	-	-	-	-	4	-	17	do
17.C.	X.17.d.39.85	2	2	2	2	1	1	1	1	1	-	-	-	-	-	4	-	17	do
17.D.	X.17.a.25.00	2	2	2	2	1	1	1	1	1	1	-	-	-	-	4	4	22	do
15.A.	X.15.b.05.96	-	-	-	-	-	-	-	-	-	-	1	-	4	4	4	-	13	do
10.A.	X.10.d.65.02	-	-	2	2	1	1	1	1	1	-	-	1	-	-	4	-	14	do
10.B.	X.10.d.65.20	-	-	2	2	1	1	1	1	1	-	1	-	-	-	4	-	14	do
10.C.	X.10.c.05.15	-	-	2	2	1	1	1	1	1	1	-	-	4	4	4	-	22	do
10.D.	X.10.d.00.90	-	-	-	-	1	1	1	1	1	-	1	-	-	-	-	-	6	14
10.E.	X.10.b.12.23	-	-	-	-	1	1	1	1	1	-	-	1	-	-	-	-	6	14
10.G.	X.10.a.05.70	-	-	-	-	1	1	1	1	1	-	1	-	-	-	-	-	6	14
10.H.	X.10.d.33.50	-	-	-	-	1	1	1	1	1	1	-	-	-	-	4	-	10	WREN
16.A.	X.16.d.30.00	2	2	2	2	-	-	1	1	1	-	-	1	-	-	4	4	20	do
16.B.	X.16.d.80.90	2	2	2	2	1	1	1	1	1	-	1	-	-	-	4	4	22	do
16.C.	X.16.d.29.95	2	2	2	2	1	1	1	1	1	1	-	-	-	-	4	4	22	do
16.D.	X.16.b.12.90	-	-	2	2	1	1	1	1	1	-	1	-	-	-	4	-	14	do
16.E.	X.16.a.83.97	-	-	2	2	1	1	1	1	1	-	-	1	-	-	4	-	14	do
16.G.	X.16.a.35.95	-	-	2	2	1	1	1	1	1	-	1	-	-	-	4	-	14	do
16.H.	X.16.a.85.05	2	2	2	2	-	-	-	-	-	1	-	-	-	-	4	4	17	do

3rd July, 1918.

J. Harington Bt. Lieut-Colonel,
Commanding 46th Battn. M.G. Corps.

S E C R E T.

H.Q.,46th Division.
C.R.A. "
137th Inf:Bde.
138th " "
139th " "
No 1 Group
No 2 Group
'A' Coy.
'B' "
'C' "
'D'Coy.
55th Battn.M.G.Corps.
3rd Battn.M.G.Corps.
War Diary (2)
File.

D

Herewith tracing showing ~~re-numbering~~ of Machine Guns of this Battalion in the line.

ACKNOWLEDGE.

3/7/1918.

J. Harington Bt.Lieut-Colonel,
Commanding 46th Battn.M.G.Corps.

S E C R E T.

H.Q.,46th Division.
C.R.A.,46th Division.
55th Bn.M.G.Corps.
3rd Bn. M.G.Corps.
137th Inf:Bde.
138th : :
139th : :
No 1 Group,
No 2 Group
'A'Coy
'B'Coy
'C'Coy
'D'Coy
War Diary (2)
C.M.G.O. XIII Corps.
****

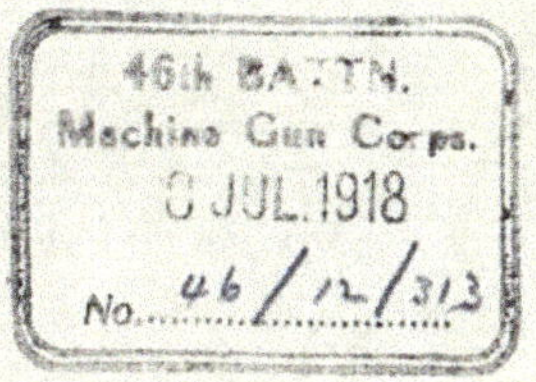

E

Reference my 46/12/279.

Machine Gun Area Shoots.

1. Herewith revised particulars of area shoots.

2. The procedure in firing same is as follows :-

At the times laid down in the weekly Harassing Programme, all guns are laid and ready to fire. The instant the directing guns are heard to fire all the guns detailed slowly traverse or search the lines assigned to them, the result being that the whole area is subjected to an intense concentration of traversing fire from various directions.

3. Small maps showing the areas are also attached and on them the sweep of each gun is shown by a red line.
In estimating the ground actually covered it should be borne in mind that the line should at least be 100 yards wide, but, for the sake of clearness is shown much less.

4. Directing Guns for Areas A, B, & C.,are WREN BATTERY and for D Area,THRUSH BATTERY.

5. Please acknowledge.

8th July,1918.

J Harrington Bt.Lieut-Colonel,
Commanding 46th Battn.M.G.Corps.

SECRET.

MACHINE GUN AREA SHOOT "A"

X.24.c.20.70 to X.23.d.70.70
to X.17.d.70.10 to X.18.c.20.10

GUN.	TARGET.
1.	X.23.b.70.17 to X.18.c.00.10
2.	X.23.b.70.34 to X.17.d.93.10
3.	X.23.b.70.15 to X.18.c.20.02
4.	X.23.d.70.89 to X.24.a.20.69
5.	X.24.a.20.69 to X.17.d.80.10
6.	X.24.a.20.82 to X.17.d.93.10
9.	X.24.a.20.00 to X.17.d.70.10
10.	X.24.a.20.20 to X.17.d.75.10
11.	X.23.d.70.95 to X.23.d.82.70
12.	X.23.b.70.13 to X.23.d.91.70
13.	X.23.d.95.70 to X.17.d.73.10
14.	X.24.c.07.70 to X.17.d.90.10
15.	X.23.d.83.70 to X.17.d.80.10
WREN 1.	X.24.c.20.70 to X.23.b.70.90
WREN 2.	X.23.b.70.77 to X.24.c.10.70
WREN 3.	X.23.b.70.60 to X.24.c.04.70
WREN 4.	X.23.b.70.43 to X.23.d.96.70
HAWK 1.	X.23.d.89.70 to X.24.c.20.96
HAWK 2.	X.23.d.72.70 to X.24.a.20.12
HAWK 3.	X.23.d.70.81 to X.24.a.20.29
HAWK 4.	X.23.d.70.99 to X.24.a.20.48

FROM RUE DU BOIS 1/10,000

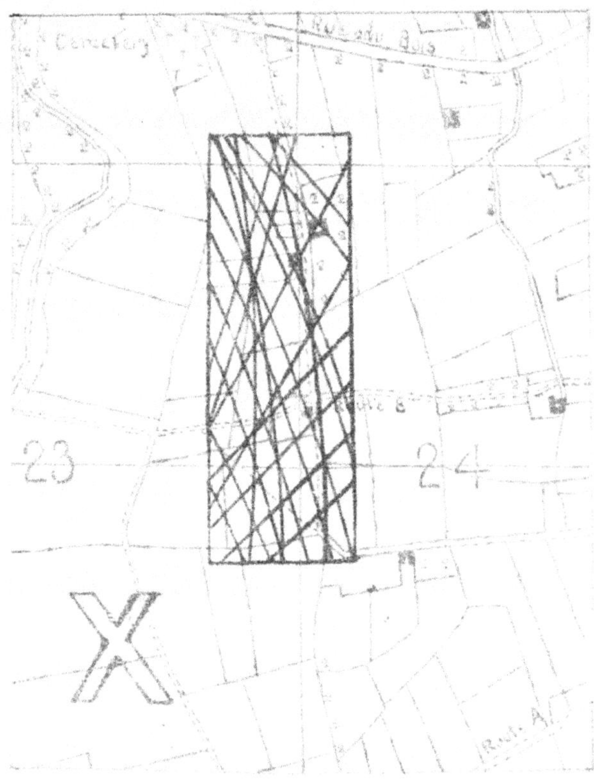

AREA "A".

SWEEP OF ONE GUN ————————

SECRET.

MACHINE GUN AREA SHOOT "B"

X.17.c.00.50 to X.16.c.70.50
to X.16.a.70.50 to X.17.a.00.50

GUN.	TARGET.
1.	X.16.c.70.53 to X.17.c.00.86
2.	X.16.c.83.50 to X.17.c.00.77
3.	X.16.c.70.87 to X.17.c.00.96
4.	X.16.c.70.77 to X.17.c.00.86
5.	X.16.a.70.16 to X.17.c.00.90
6.	X.16.a.70.09 to X.17.c.00.82
9.	X.16.a.95.50 to X.17.a.00.15
10.	X.16.a.70.45 to X.17.a.00.05
11.	X.16.a.70.37 to X.17.c.00.90
12.	X.16.a.70.30 to X.17.c.00.83
13.	X.16.b.53.50 to X.17.c.00.97
14.	X.16.b.43.50 to X.17.c.00.78
15.	X.16.b.17.50 to X.16.d.72.50
16.	X.16.b.03.50 to X.16.d.48.50
17.	X.16.a.70.50 to X.16.d.16.50
18.	X.16.b.42.50 to X.16.d.58.50
WREN 1.	X.16.c.70.58 to X.16.b.21.50
WREN 2.	X.16.c.75.50 to X.16.b.34.50
WREN 3.	X.16.d.27.50 to X.17.a.00.48
WREN 4.	X.16.d.32.50 to X.17.a.00.37
HAWK 1.	X.16.a.70.02 to X.17.c.00.78
HAWK 2.	X.16.c.70.96 to X.17.c.00.71
HAWK 3.	X.16.c.70.85 to X.17.c.00.60
HAWK 4.	X.16.c.70.70 to X.16.d.88.50

FROM RUE DU BOIS 1/10,000

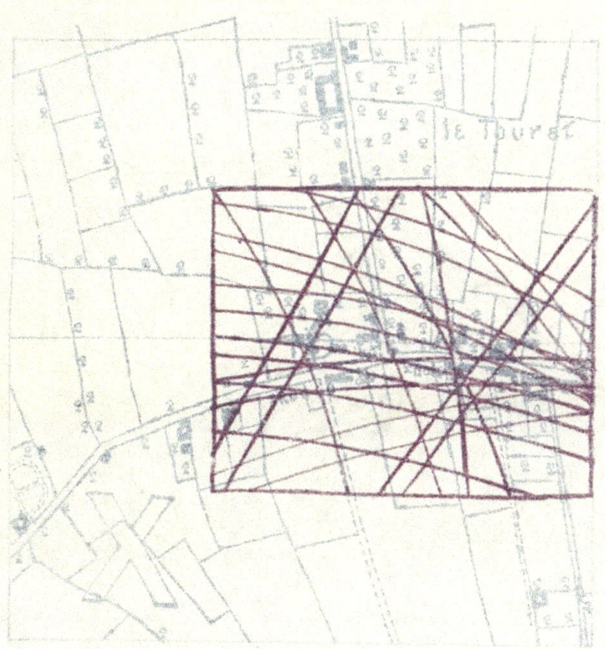

AREA "B."

SWEEP OF ONE GUN.

SECRET.

MACHINE GUN AREA SHOOT "C"

X.17.a.00.75 to X.11.c.00.80
to X.16.a.70.75 to X.10.c.70.80

GUN.	TARGET.
5.	X.16.a.70.92 to X.16.b.82.75
6.	X.16.a.70.87 to X.16.b.55.75
9.	X.10.d.48.80 to X.11.c.00.64
10.	X.10.c.70.80 to X.11.c.00.52
11.	X.10.c.70.12 to X.16.b.93.75
12.	X.10.c.70.05 to X.16.b.75.75
13.	X.10.c.98.80 to X.11.c.00.10
14.	X.10.d.32.80 to X.11.c.00.27
15.	X.16.a.96.75 to X.11.c.00.75
16.	X.16.a.70.75 to X.10.d.89.80
17.	X.10.c.76.80 to X.16.b.60.75
18.	X.10.d.42.80 to X.16.b.88.75
WREN 1.	X.10.c.70.57 to X.17.a.00.92
WREN 2.	X.10.c.70.46 to X.17.a.00.79
WREN 3.	X.10.c.70.33 to X.16.b.84.75
WREN 4.	X.10.c.70.22 to X.16.b.65.75

FROM RUE DU BOIS 1/10,000

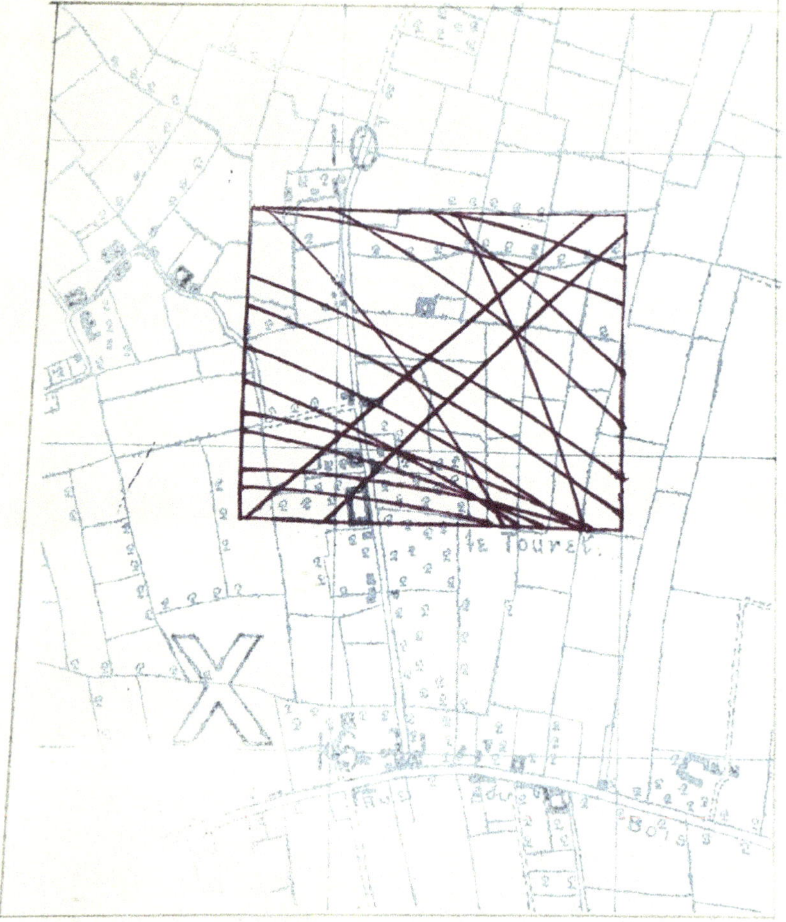

AREA "C."

SWEEP OF ONE GUN. ————

S E C R E T.

MACHINE GUN AREA SHOOT "D"

X.9.c.55.63 to X.8.b.79.71
to X.8.b.56.41 to X.9.c.78.92

GUN.	TARGET.
9.	X.9.a.05.49 to X.8.b.67.33
10.	X.9.a.33.29 to X.8.b.92.13
13.	X.9.a.03.52 to X.8.b.57.43
14.	X.9.a.33.28 to X.8.b.82.21
15.	X.8.b.96.09 to X.9.a.59.05
16.	X.8.b.72.29 to X.9.a.34.25
17.	X.9.c.14.96 to X.9.c.72.87
18.	X.8.b.91.13 to X.9.c.68.82
PIGEON 1.	X.9.c.70.83 to X.8.b.67.57
PIGEON 2.	X.9.c.73.85 to X.8.b.70.60
PIGEON 3.	X.9.c.76.89 to X.8.b.73.63
PIGEON 4.	X.9.c.77.92 to X.8.b.76.66
THRUSH 1.	X.9.c.60.70 to X.9.c.27.85
THRUSH 2.	X.9.c.64.76 to X.9.a.07.01
THRUSH 3.	X.9.c.78.92 to X.8.b.59.45
THRUSH 4.	X.9.c.74.89 to X.8.b.56.41

FROM MESPLAUX 1/10,000

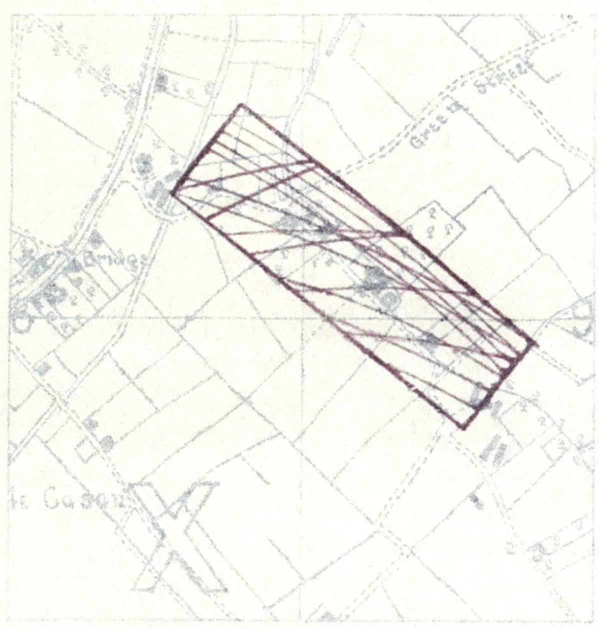

AREA "D"
SWEEP of ONE GUN. ————

S E C R E T. Copy No....18

46th BATTALION MACHINE GUN CORPS ORDER No.44.

Reference 1/20,000 GORRE and VIEILLE CHAPELLE.

1. 'D' Company will relieve 'C' Company in the line in the 'Rear Gun Positions' on the night 5/6th July, 1918.

2. 'C' Company and 'C' Company Headquarters thus relieved will move into reserve at the Transport lines and will take over accommodation vacated by 'D' Company, and as Sections arrive at Transport lines they will come under two hours notice to move.

3. Any further details, also guides etc, will be arranged direct between O.C.'D' Company and Os.C. Nos 1 & 2 Groups.

4. All Trench and area stores, documents, special maps, aeroplane photographs and programmes of work in hand will be handed over and receipts obtained. A certificate that the positions taken over are in a clean and satisfactory state will be rendered by O.C. 'D' Company to reach Battalion Headquarters 1st D.R. 7th July,1918.

5. As soon as the relief is completed Major M.Douglas will take over the Command of No 1 Group from Major W.T.Doughey.

6. At No.1 Group Headquarters No 1 Group copy defence scheme, special maps, documents, aeroplane photographs etc will be handed over.

7. Completion of this relief will be wired to Battalion Headquarters by "B.A.B." code.

8. Completion of this relief will also be notified by Os.C., Nos 1 & 2 Groups to the Brigade Commander whose front their guns are covering.

9. ACKNOWLEDGE.

Issued at 7.0 p.m.

R. Dickson
Capt & Adjt,
46th Battn.Machine Gun Corps.

4/7/1918.

Distribution :-

1. A. Coy	10. 55th Bn.M.G.Corps.
2. B. Coy	11. 137th Inf:Bde.
3. C. Coy	12. 138th Inf:Bde.
4. D. Coy	13. 139th Inf:Bde.
5. T.O.	14. No. 1 Group
6. Q.M.	15. No. 2 Group
7. Signals.	16. File.
8. 46th Division.	17.)
9. 3rd Bn.M.G.Corps.	18.)War Diary.

S E C R E T.

H.Q., 46th Division.
C.R.A., 46th Division.,
66th Bn. M.G.Corps.
3rd Bn. M.G.Corps.
137th Inf:Bde.
138th " "
139th " "
O.C.No 1 Group,
" No 2 "
War Diary (2)
File.

Herewith programme of Area and Concentration Shoots for week ending 13th July, 1918.

8/7/18.

[signature] Major,
46th Battn.Machine Gun Corps.

SECRET.

PROGRAMME OF MACHINE GUN AREA & CONCENTRATION SHOOTS.

Week Ending 18th July, 1918.

NIGHT.	TARGET.	TIME.	No. of ROUNDS PER GUN.	REMARKS.
July 11/12th.	NO FIRING.			
12/13th.	AREA D.	10.20 pm.	250	
		10.30 pm.	250	
		10.35 pm.	250	
		11.37 pm.	250	
		11.45 pm.	250	
		1.10 am.	125	
		1.20 am.	125	
		2.30 am.	250	
		3.00 am.	250	
13/14th.	17 A.	10.15 pm.	250	
	23 D.) 9 J.)	10.25 pm.	250	
	16 G.	11.00 pm.	250	
	24 A.) 3 B.)	1.00 am.	250	
	19 C.) 3 A.)	1.50 am.	250	
	10 C.	2.20 am.	250	No firing will be done if it is not dark enough to obviate all possibility of the screen being seen.
	9 J.	2.30 am.	250	
14/15th.	AREA A.	10.30 pm.	250	
		10.37 pm.	250	
		10.52 pm.	250	
		11.30 pm.	125	
		11.32 pm.	125	
		12.00 mid.	250	
		1.5 am.	250	
		1.7 am.	250	
		2.45 am.	125	
		2.50 am.	125	
15/16th.	10 G.	11.20 pm.	250	
	23 B.) 8 B.)	11.40 pm.	250	
	19 A.) 3 K.)	12.50 am.	250	
	17 B.	1.00 am.	250	
	23 E.) 9 G.)	2.15 am.	250	
	15 A.	3.00 am.	250	
	24 C.) 9 E.)	3.30 am.	250	
16/17th.	17 C.	10.20 pm.	250	
	16 A.	11.50 pm.	250	
	23 D.) 9 H.)	2.00 am.	250	
	9 K.) 19 B.)	2.10 am.	250	
	10 E.	2.25 am.	250	
	19 B.) 9 D.)	2.39 am.	250	
	17 D.	3.00 am.	250	
	9 L.) 23 D.)	3.7 am.	250	

Over.

PROGRAMME OF MACHINE GUN AREA & CONCENTRATION SHOOTS. continued.

NIGHT.	TARGET.	TIME.	No. of ROUNDS PER GUN.	REMARKS.
July 17/18th.	AREA B.	10.25 pm.	250	No firing will be done if it is not dark enough to obviate all possibility of the screen being seen.
		10.37 pm.	250	
		10.52 pm.	250	
		11.15 pm.	250	
		11.20 pm.	250	
		11.30 pm.	250	
		12.50 am.	250	
		1.39 am.	250	
		2.2 am.	250	
		3.5 am.	250	

8th July, 1918.

J Harington Bt. Lieut-Colonel,
Commanding 46th Battn. M.G. Corps.

S E C R E T.

H.Q.,46th Division.
C.R.A.46th Division.
O.C.,55th Bn.M.G.Corps.
O.C.,3rd Bn.M.G.Corps.
H.Q.,137th Inf:Bde.
H.Q.,138th Inf:Bde.
H.Q.,139th Inf:Bde.
O.C.No 1 Group,
O.C.No 2 Group,
War Diary (2)
File.

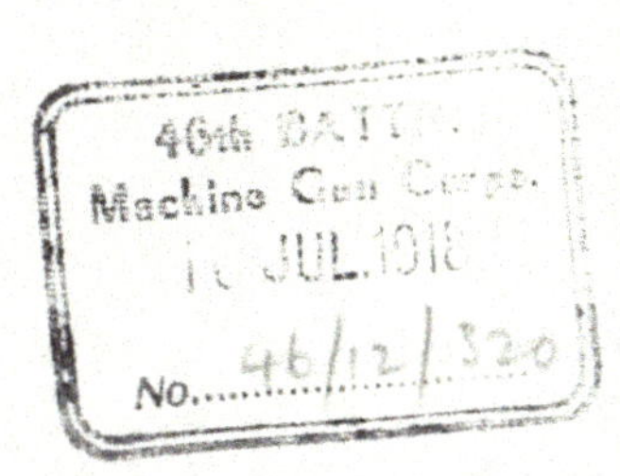

G

Reference 46/12/314.

1. As an enemy relief is anticipated on the night 11/12th July the programme laid down for the 16/17th will be fired then.

2. On the 16/17th there will be no firing.

3. Please acknowledge.

10/7/1918.

Bt.Lieut-Colonel,
Commanding 46th Battn.M.G.Corps.

S E C R E T .

H.Q. 46th Division.
C.R.A. 46th Division.
55th Bn. M.G.Corps.
3rd Bn. M.G.Corps.
137th Inf: Bde.
138th " "
139th " "
O.C. No. 1 Group.
" No. 2 Group.
War Diary (2)
File.

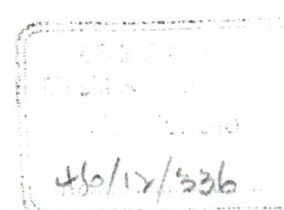

H

Ref. MACHINE GUN HARASSING FIRE.

1. Until further orders Group Commanders will arrange direct with the Brigade Commander concerned all details of indirect fire, targets, times and guns to be used.
2. No guns will fire from the LIVERPOOL LINE without reference to these Headquarters.
3. PLEASE ACKNOWLEDGE.

18/7/1918.

Harrington Bt. Lieut-Colonel,
Commanding 46th Battn. M.G.Corps.

S E C R E T.

Copy No...17..

46th BATTALION MACHINE GUN CORPS ORDER No.45.

Reference 1/20,000 GORRE and VIEILLE CHAPELLE.

1. 'C' Company will relieve 'A' Company in the line in the 'Left Forward Gun Positions' in the ESSARS Section on the night 11/12th July 1918.

2. 'A' Company and 'A' Company Headquarters thus relieved will move into reserve at the Transport lines and will take over accommodation vacated by 'C' Company, and as Sections arrive at Transport lines they will come under two hours notice to move.

3. Any further details, also guides etc, will be arranged direct between O.C.'C' Company and O.C.No 2 Group.

4. All Trench and area stores, documents, special maps, aeroplane photographs and programmes of work in hand will be handed over and receipts obtained. A certificate that the positions taken over are in a clean and satisfactory state will be rendered by O.C.'C' Company to reach Battalion Headquarters 1st D.R. 13th July, 1918.

5. As soon as the relief is completed Major W.T.Boughey will take over the Command of No 2 Group from Major H.S.Windeler.

6. At No.2 Group Headquarters No 2 Group copy defence scheme, special maps, documents, aeroplane photographs etc will be handed over.

7. Completion of this relief will be wired to Battalion Headquarters by "B.A.B." code.

8. Completion of this relief will also be notified by O.C.No 2 Group to the Brigade Commander whose front his guns are covering.

9. ACKNOWLEDGE.

Issued at 1.0 p.m.

R. Dickens

9/7/1918.

Capt & Adjt,
46th Battn.Machine Gun Corps.

Distribution:-

1. A. Coy.
2. B. Coy.
3. C. Coy.
4. D. Coy.
5. T.O.
6. Q.M.
7. Signals.
8. 46th Division.
9. 3rd Bn. M.G.Corps.
10. 55th Bn.M.G.Corps.
11. 137th Inf:Bde.
12. 138th Inf:Bde.
13. 139th Inf:Bde.
14. No 1 Group
15. No 2 Group.
16. File.
17.) War Diary.
18.)

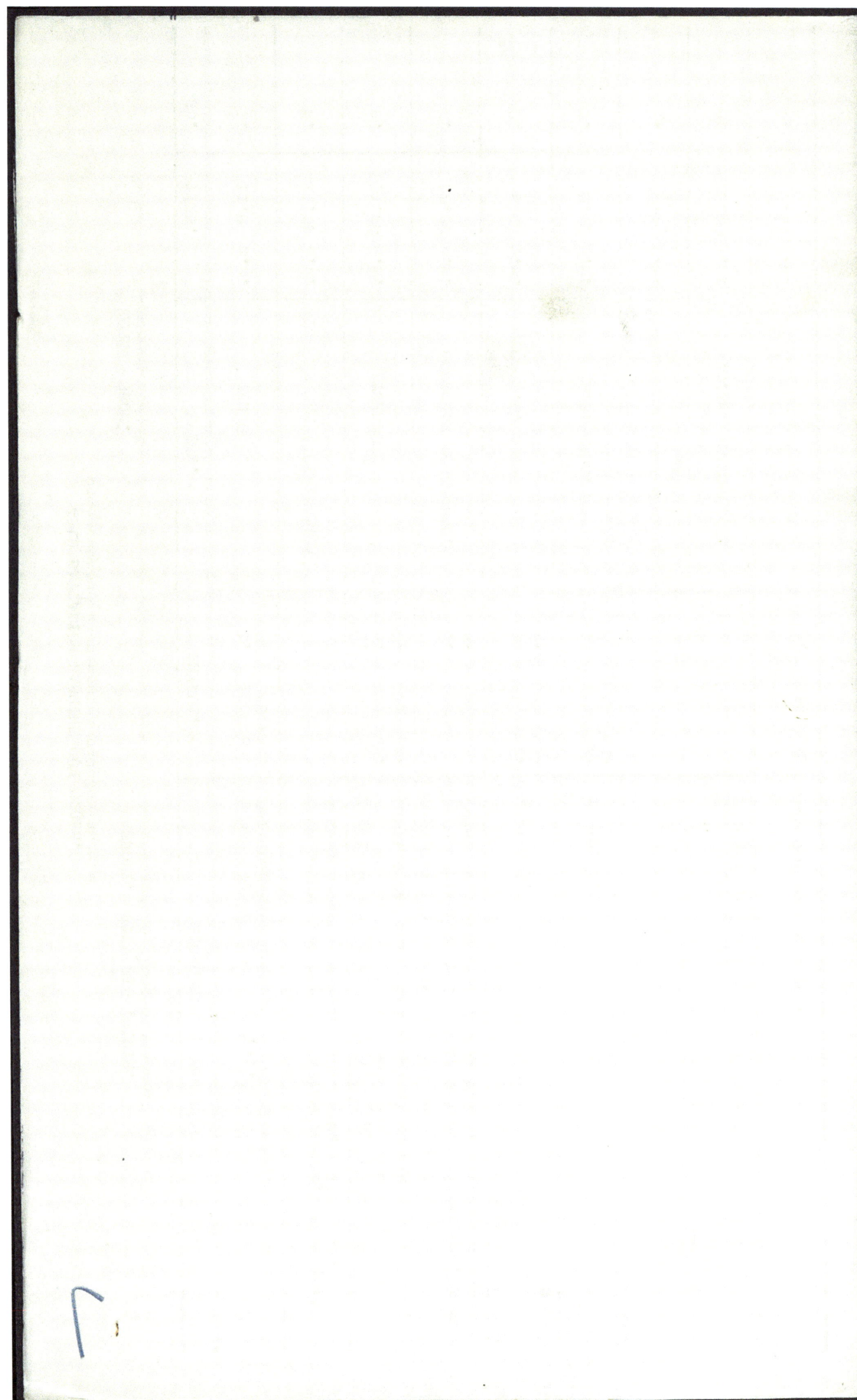

46th BATTALION MACHINE GUN CORPS.

HORSE SHOW.

SUNDAY, JULY 21st, 1918.

No.	TIME.	EVENT.	PRIZES.	REMARKS.
1.	11.0 a.m.	TURNOUT.	1. 100 Fcs. 2. 50 Fcs.	1 Gun Limber and 1 S.A.A. limber per Coy. Full Marching Order. Unloaded.
2.	11.30 a.m.	TUG OF WAR (First heat)		2 Teams Reserve Coy. 1 Team per Coy. Transport 1 Toam Reserve Details. 1 Team Battalion H.Q.
3.	11.50 a.m.	TURNOUT.	1. 30 Fcs. 2. 20 Fcs. 3. 10 Fcs.	1 Driver and pair. Full Marching Order. Limit 4 per Coy. and 1 Battalion H.Q.
4.	12.20 p.m.	OFFICERS CHARGERS.	1. 70% 2. 30%	Any Bridle or saddle.(Regulation) 5 Fcs.entrance fee. Drill Order. Ridden by Groom. Judged on turnout,manners, shape, action & riding.
5.	2.0 p.m.	L.D. HORSE.	1. 15 Fcs. 2. 10 Fcs.	STRIPPED.
6.	2.20 p.m.	L.D. MULE.	1. 15 Fcs. 2. 10 Fcs.	STRIPPED.
7.	2.35 p.m.	TUG OF WAR (2nd heat)		
8.	3.0 p.m.	N.C.Os. TURNOUT.	1. 70% 2. 30%	Full Marching Order Officers Chargers Barred. 5 Fcs.entrance fee.
9.	3.45 p.m.	OTHER RANKS JUMPING.	1. 20 Fcs. 2. 10 Fcs.	Ride one and lead one.

10.	4.15 p.m.	V.C. RACE.	1. 20 Fcs. 2. 10 Fcs.	Open to Battalion.
11.	4.30 p.m.	ALARM RACE.	1. 45 Fcs.	4 Horse or Mule Teams 1 per Coy & 1 Battalion H.Q.
12.	4.45 p.m.	MUSICAL CHAIRS.	1. 20 Fcs.	Open to Battalion.
13.	5.0 p.m.	FINAL. TUG OF WAR.	1. 100 Fcs. 2. 50 Fcs.	
14.	5.10 p.m.	WRESTLING ON MULES.	1. 80 Fcs.	2 Teams Reserve Coy. 1 Team per Coy. Transport 1 Team Battalion H.Q. 1 Team Reserve Details.
15.	5.30 p.m.	BENDING RACE.	1. 70% 2. 30%	Entrance fee 5 Fcs. Open to Officers of the Battalion.
16.	6.0 p.m.	OFFICERS JUMPING.	1. 70% 2. 30%	Entrance fee 5 Fcs. Open to 46th Division.
17.	6.45 p.m.	BAND RACE.	1. 20 Fcs. 2. 10 Fcs.	
18.	6.50 p.m.	N.C.Os' JUMPING.	1. 70% 2. 30%	Entrance fee 5 Fcs. Open to the Infantry of the 46th Division and the Battalion.
19.	7.20 p.m.	PRESENTATION OF PRIZES.		

NOTE :- No horse may be entered for more than 1 Jumping event. Tea on ground at 4.30 p.m.

=*=

S E C R E T. Copy No 18

46th BATTALION MACHINE GUN CORPS ORDER No 46.

Reference 1/20,000 GORRE and VIEILLE CHAPELLE.

1. 'A' Company will relieve 'B' Company in the line in the 'Right Forward Gun Positions' in the GORRE Section on the night 17/18th July 1918.

2. 'B' Company and 'B' Company Headquarters thus relieved will move into reserve at the Transport lines and will take over accommodation vacated by 'A' Company, and as Sections arrive at Transport lines they will come under two hours notice to move.

3. Any further details, also guides etc, will be arranged direct between O.C.'A'Company and O.C.No 1 Group.

4. All Trench and area stores, documents, special maps, aeroplane photographs and programmes of work in hand will be handed over and receipts obtained. A certificate that the positions taken over are in a clean and satisfactory state will be rendered by O.C.'A' Company to reach Battalion Headquarters 1st D.R. 19th July, 1918.

5. As soon as the relief is completed Major H.S.Windeler will take over the Command of No 1 Group from Major M.Douglas.

6. At No 1 Group Headquarters No 1 Group copy defence scheme, special maps, documents, aeroplane photographs etc will be handed over.

7. Completion of this relief will be wired to Battalion Headquarters by "B.A.B." code.

8. Completion of this relief will also be notified by O.C.No 1 Group to the Brigade Commander whose front his guns are covering.

9. ACKNOWLEDGE.

Issued at 5.0 p.m.

R. Dickson.

16/7/1918.

Capt & Adjt,
46th Battn.Machine Gun Corps.

Distribution :-

1. A. Coy.
2. B. Coy.
3. C. Coy.
4. D. Coy.
5. T.O.
6. Q.M.
7. Signals.
8. 46th Division.
9. 3rd Bn.M.G.Corps.
10. 55th Bn.M.G.Corps.
11. 137th Inf:Bde.
12. 138th Inf:Bde.
13. 139th Inf:Bde.
14. No 1 Group
15. No 2 Group
16. File.
17.)
18.)War Diary.

S E C R E T.

Copy No 17

46th BATTALION MACHINE GUN CORPS ORDER No.46.

Reference 1/20,000 GORRE and VIEILLE CHAPELLE.

1. 'D' Company will relieve 'C' Company in the line in the 'Left Forward Gun Positions' in the ESSARS Section on the night 29/30th July 1918.

2. 'C' Company and 'C' Company Headquarters thus relieved will move into reserve at the Transport lines and will take over accommodation vacated by 'D' Company, and as Sections arrive at Transport lines they will come under notice to move at two hours notice between the hours of 8-0 p.m. and 8-0 a.m. and six hours notice between the hours of 8-0 a.m. and 8-0 p.m.

3. Any further details, also guides etc, will be arranged direct between O.C.'C' Company and O.C.No 2 Group.

4. All Trench and area stores, documents, special maps, aeroplane photographs and programmes of work in hand will be handed over and receipts obtained. A certificate that the positions taken over are in a clean and satisfactory state will be rendered by O.C.'C' Company to reach Battalion Headquarters 1st D.R. 31st July, 1918.

5. As soon as the relief is completed Major M.Douglas will take over the Command of No 2 Group from Major W.T.Boughey.

6. At No 2 Group Headquarters No 2 Group copy Defence Scheme, special maps, documents, aeroplane photographs etc.,will be handed over.

7. Completion of this relief will be wired to Battalion Headquarters by "B.A.B." code.

8. Completion of this relief will also be notified by O.C. No 2 Group to the Brigade Commander whose front his guns are covering.

9. ACKNOWLEDGE.

Issued at 12-0 noon.

27/7/1918.

Capt & Adjt,
46th Battn.M.G.Corps.

Distribution:-

1. A.Coy.	10. 55th Bn.M.G.Corps.
2. B.Coy.	11. 137th Inf:Bde.
3. C.Coy.	12. 138th " "
4. D.Coy.	13. 139th " "
5. T.O.	14. No 1 Group
6. Q.M.	15. No 2 Group
7. Signals.	16. File.
8. 46th Division.	17.)
9. 3rd Bn. M.G.Corps.	18.)War Diary.

S E C R E T.

Copy No 18

46th BATTALION MACHINE GUN CORPS ORDER No. 47

Reference 1/20,000 GORRE and VIEILLE CHAPELLE.

1. 'B' Company will relieve 'D' Company in the line in the 'Rear Gun Positions' on the night 23/24th July 1918.

2. 'D' Company and 'D' Company Headquarters thus relieved will move into reserve at the Transport lines and will take over accommodation vacated by 'B' Company, and as Sections arrive at Transport lines they will come under notice to move at one hour's notice between the hours of 8-0 p.m. and 8-0 a.m. and four hours notice between the hours of 8-0 a.m. and 8-0 p.m.

3. Any further details, also guides etc, will be arranged direct between O.C.'B' Company and O.C.'D' Company.

4. All Trench and area stores, documents, special maps, aeroplane photographs and programmes of work in hand will be handed over and receipts obtained. A certificate that the positions taken over are in a clean and satisfactory state will be rendered by O.C.'B' Company to reach Battalion Headquarters 1st D.R. 25th July, 1918.

5. Completion of this relief will be wired to Battalion Headquarters by "B.A.B." code.

6. Completion of this relief will also be notified by O.C. No 1 and No 2 Groups to the Brigade Commanders whose front their guns are covering.

7. ACKNOWLEDGE.

Issued at :- 12 0 noon

21/7/1918.

[signature]
Capt & Adjt,
46th Battn. Machine Gun Corps.

Distribution :-

1. A.Coy
2. B.Coy.
3. C.Coy
4. D.Coy.
5. T.O.
6. Q.M.
7. Signals.
8. 46th Division.
9. 3rd Bn. M.G.Corps.
10. 55th Bn.M.G.Corps.
11. 137th Inf:Bde.
12. 138th Inf:Bde.
13. 139th Inf:Bde.
14. No 1 Group
15. No 2 Group
16. File.
17.) War Diary.
18.)

Vol 6

****

W A R   D I A R Y

OF

46th BATTALION MACHINE GUN CORPS.

AUGUST 1918.

****

Army Form C. 2118.

WAR DIARY

Instructions regarding War Diaries and Intelligence Summaries are contained in F. S. Regs., Part II. and the Staff Manual respectively. Title pages will be prepared in manuscript.

AUGUST 1918. 46th BATTALION MACHINE GUN CORPS

(Erase heading not required.)

Sheet No 1.

Place	Date	Hour	Summary of Events and Information GORRE 1/20,000 VIEILLE CHAPELLE 1/20,000	Remarks and references to Appendices
GORRE & ESSARS SECTIONS.	1st.		M.Gs.fired 8,750 rounds harassing fire on enemy's communications and tracks. M.Gs.fired 3,300 rounds at E.A.during the day. 3 O.Rs. wounded. MOIR PILLBOXES have been erected at the following localities,and were completed on date shown When these were erected by the Battalion this is stated,in other cases R.Es. carried out the work. 1 at X.20.c.21.28 (complete 23/7/18) and 1 at X.26.a.50.25 (complete 27/7/18).	
	2nd.		M.Gs. fired 4,750 rounds harassing fire during the night. 1,150 rounds during the day were fired at E.A. 1 O.R. Wounded. 1 O.R. reinforcement. 102400 Pte.W.Carlos awarded the M.M. for great courage and devotion to duty in maintaining a Machine Gun in action under heavy shell fire (XIII Corps R.O. No 1874).	
	3rd.		M.Gs. fired 7,450 rounds harassing fire during the night. 3,450 rounds during the day were fired at E.A. 1 O.R. evacuated (sick) 3 O.Rs. reinforcements	
		7 p.m.	Order No 49 issued (copy attached)	Order No 49
	4th.		M.Gs. fired 8,250 rounds harassing fire during the night. 2 O.Rs. Wounded.	
	5th.		M.Gs. fired 8,250 rounds harassing fire during the night. 2/Lieut.F.D.M.Harding (15th H.L.I.) attached to Battalion for Transport duties.	
	6th.		M.Gs. fired 4,000 rounds harassing fire during the night. 1 O.R. killed in action. 1 O.R. evacuated (sick).	
	7th.		M.Gs. fired 5,000 rounds harassing fire during the night. 1 O.R. reinforcement. 430 rounds during the day were fired at E.A. 4 Moir Pillboxes at F.19.a.10.80, F.19.a.20.95, E.24.b.9.5., E.24.b.85.85. Also at E.5.b.65.50 erected by R.E.	
	8th.		3,250 rounds harassing fire during the night. 2 O.R. reinforcements. Lieut.W.Ackland Reinforcement from Base Depot. Moir Pillbox at E.6.c.40.32, M.G.C.	
		7 p.m.	Order No 50 issued (copy attached) Letter 46/12/417 issued (copy attached marked 'A')	Order No 50. 'A'
	9th.		1,355 rounds fired at E.A. during the day. 2 O.Rs.Evacuated (sick) Lieut.C.H.Hargrave. To Base Depot for Medical Board.	
		7-30pm.	Orders 51 and 52 issued (copies attached)	Orders 51 & 52.

A5834 Wt. W4973/M687 750,000 8/16 D. D. & L. Ltd. Forms/C.2118/13.

Army Form C. 2118.

WAR DIARY

Instructions regarding War Diaries and Intelligence Summaries are contained in F. S. Regs., Part II. and the Staff Manual respectively. Title pages will be prepared in manuscript.

AUGUST 1918 46th BATTALION MACHINE GUN CORPS

(Erase heading not required.)

Sheet No 2.

Place	Date	Hour	Summary of Events and Information	Remarks and references to Appendices
			GORRE 1/20,000 VIEILLE CHAPELLE 1/20,000	
GORRE & ESSARS SECTIONS.	10th.		M.Gs.fired 6,000 rounds harassing fire during the night. 1 O.R. Evacuated (sick) 455 rounds fired at E.A. during the day. 5 O.Rs. Wounded (Gas) Letter 46/12/436 issued (copy attached marked 'B'. Pillbox at E.6.a.22.00. M.G.C..	'B'
	11th.		7,750 rounds harassing fire by M.Gs. during the night. 12 O.RS. Evacuated (sick). 380 rounds fired at E.A. during the day.	
	12th.		8,250 rounds harassing fire during the night. 1 O.R. Wounded. 1 O.R. Reinforcement. 3,950 rounds fired at E.A. during the day. 1 O.R. to U.K. for Course at Grantham. At XIII Corps Horse Show 'C' Company of this Battalion were first in M.G.Turnout, 'D' Company 1st in Best L.D.Horse,stripped (open), and 3rd in Mule Race. Administrative Instruction No 1 issued. (copy attached marked 'C') Letter 46/12/446 issued (copy attached marked 'D')	'C' 'D'
	13th.		M.Gs. fired 7,750 rounds harassing fire during the night. 1 O.R. reinforcement. Pillbox at F.2.a.02.79.	
	14th.		M.Gs. fired 14,750 rounds on enemy relief routes. 1 O.R. Evacuated (sick) 1 O.R. reinforcement. 1,590 rounds fired at E.A. during the day. 2/Lieut.T.S.Rees Reinforcement from Base Depot.	
		7 p.m.	Order No 53 issued (copy attached)	Order No 53.
	15th.		M.Gs. fired 10,250 rounds harassing fire during the night. 2,140 rounds fired at E.A. during the day. 2 O.Rs. Evacuated (sick).	
	16th.		M.Gs.fired 5,750 rounds harassing fire during the night. 2,455 rounds fired at E.A.during the day.	
	17th.		M.Gs. fired 10,250 rounds harassing fire during the night. 2 O.Rs. Evacuated (sick).	
	18th.		M.Gs. fired 8,250 rounds harassing fire during the night. 2 O.Rs. Reinforcements. Pillbox erected at X.19.c.21.45.	
	19th.		M.Gs. fired 12,000 rounds harassing fire during the night. 450 rounds fired at E.A. during the day.	

A5834 Wt. W4973/M687 750,000 8/16 D. D. & L. Ltd. Forms/C.2118/13.

Army Form C. 2118.

Instructions regarding War Diaries and Intelligence Summaries are contained in F. S. Regs., Part II. and the Staff Manual respectively. Title pages will be prepared in manuscript.

WAR DIARY

or

~~INTELLIGENCE SUMMARY.~~

(Erase heading not required.)

AUGUST 1918.

46th BATTALION MACHINE GUN CORPS

Sheet No 3.

Place	Date	Hour	GORRE 1/20,000 VIEILLE CHAPELLE 1/20,000 Summary of Events and Information	Remarks and references to Appendices
GORRE & ESSARS. SECTIONS.	20th.		M.Gs. fired 12,500 rounds harassing fire during the night. 1 O.R. Evacuated (sick). Pillboxes at following locations F.13.a.40.80, F.13.a.50.80, F.13.b.20.25, F.13.b.40.35. Erected by Corps. Letter 46/12/488 issued (copy attached marked 'E')	'E'
		7 pm.	Order 54 issued (copy attached)	Order No 54.
	21st.		M.Gs. fired 14,750 rounds harassing fire during the night. Order 54A issued (copy attached)	OrderNo 54A.
	22nd.		M.Gs. fired 7,500 rounds harassing fire during the night. 2 O.Rs. Evacuated (sick) 750 rounds fired at E.A. during the day. 11 O.Rs. reinforcements.	
	23rd.		Pillboxes at X.19.c.37.37, X.20.c.21.28, constructed by R.E.	
		1 p.m.	Order No 55 issued (copy attached).	Order No 55.
	24th.		M.Gs. fired 750 rounds at E.A. during the ~~six~~ day. 1 O.R. Evac:(sick) 1 O.R. Wounded.	
	25th.		Pillbox at F.1.b.97.47 Constructed by R.E. 1 O.R. Evacuated (sick) 1 O.R. Reinforcement.	
	26th.		Pillbox at X.26.a.45.25 Constructed by R.E. 1 O.R. Evacuated (sick) 1 O.R. Reinforcement. Lieut.E.B.Fletcher to U.K..	
		1 p.m.	Order No 56 issued (copy attached)	Order No 56.
	27th.		2 O.Rs. Evacuated (sick) 1 O.R. reinforcement.	
	28th		Nil.	
	29th.		M.Gs. fired 600 rounds at E.A. during the day. 1 O.R. Wounded. 1 O.R. reinforcement.	
	30th.		1 O.R. Wounded. 1 O.R. Reinforcement.	
	31st.		350 rounds fired at E.A. during the day. 1 O.R. reinforcement.	

Lieut-Colonel,
Commanding 46th Battn.Machine Gun Corps.

A5834 Wt. W4973/M687 750,000 8/16 D. D. & L. Ltd. Forms/C.2118/13.

S E C R E T.

Copy No 18

46th BATTALION MACHINE GUN CORPS ORDER No. 49.

Reference 1/20,000 GORRE and VIEILLE CHAPELLE.

1. 'C' Company will relieve 'A' Company in the line in the 'Right Forward Gun Positions' in the GORRE Section on the night 4/5th August 1918.

2. 'A' Company and 'A' Company Headquarters thus relieved will move into reserve at the Transport lines and will take over accommodation vacated by 'C' Company and as Sections arrive at Transport lines they will come under notice to move at two hours notice between the hours of 8-0 p.m. and 8-0 a.m. and six hours notice between the hours of 8-0 a.m. and 8-0 p.m.

3. Any further details, also guides etc, will be arranged direct between O.C.'C' Company and O.C.No 1 Group.

4. All Trench and area stores, charts & orders, documents, maps aeroplane photographs and programmes of work in hand will be handed over.
   A consolidated handing over certificate will be rondered to Battalion Headquarters.

5. As soon as the relief is completed Major C.V.Rigby, M.C. will take over the Command of No 1 Group from Major H.S.Windeler.

6. Major W.T.Boughey will be O.C. Right Forward Guns.
   Capt.H.Witty will be O.C.,Rear Guns.

7. Completion of this relief will be wired to Battalion Headquarters by "B.A.B. code.

8. Completion of this relief will also be notified by O.C. No 1 Group to the Brigade Commander whose front his guns are covering.

9. ACKNOWLEDGE.

Issued at 7-0 p.m.

R. Dicken

3/8/18.

Capt & Adjt,
46th Battn.Machine Gun Corps.

Distribution :-

1. A.Coy.
2. B.Coy.
3. C.Coy.
4. D.Coy.
5. T.O.
6. Q.M.
7. Signals.
8. 46th Division.
9. 3rd Bn.M.G.Corps.
10. 55th Bn.M.G.Corps.
11. 137th Inf:Bde.
12. 138th Inf:Bde.
13. 139th Inf:Bde.
14. No 1 Group,
15. No 2 Group.
16. File.
17.)
18.)War Diary.

S E C R E T.

Copy No 18

46th BATTALION MACHINE GUN CORPS ORDER No. 50.

1. 'A' Company will relieve 'B' Company in the line in the 'Rear Gun Positions' in the GORRE and ESSARS Sections on the night 10/11th August, 1918.

2. As soon as the relief is completed Major H.S.Windeler will take over the Command of No 1 Group from Major C.V.Rigby, M.C.

3. To be acknowledged by Companies and Groups.

Issued at 7-0 p.m.

8/8/1918.

R. Aitken.

Capt & Adjt,
46th Battn.Machine Gun Corps.

Distribution :-

1. A.Coy.
2. B.Coy.
3. C.Coy.
4. D.Coy.
5. T.O.
6. Q.M.
7. Signals.
8. 46th Division.
9. ~~2nd~~ 19 Bn.M.G.Corps.
10. 55th Bn. M.G.Corps.
11. 137th Inf:Bde.
12. 138th Inf:Bde.
13. 139th Inf:Bde.
14. No 1 Group
15. No 2 Group
16. File.
17.) War Diary.
18.) War Diary.

SECRET

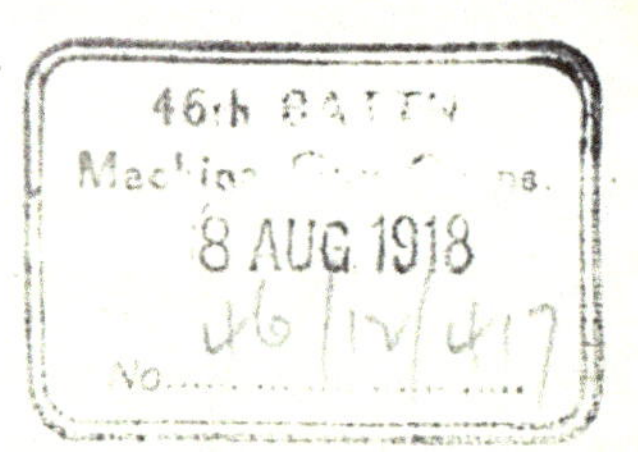

O.C. No 1 Group,
" No 2 "
" 'A' Coy,
" 'B' "
" 'C' "
" 'D' "
****

In order to reduce Operation Orders re reliefs the following 'Standing Order' will apply to all Company reliefs from this date whilst situated as at present.

1. The Company relieved will move into reserve at the Transport Lines and will take over the accommodation vacated by the relieving Company. An Officer or a N.C.O. will take over this accommodation beforehand.

2. Any further details, also guides etc, will be arranged direct between Companies or Groups concerned.

3. All Trench and area stores, charts & orders, documents, maps aeroplane photographs and programmes of work in hand will be handed over.
A consolidated handing over certificate will be rendered to Battalion Headquarters.

4. When a Group Commander is relieved the Group copy of Defence Scheme, all charts, orders, aeroplane photographs, maps, documents and Group file of correspondence etc will be handed over.

5. Completion of all reliefs, Group & Companies, will be notified to Battalion Headquarters by B.A.B. code stating time relief completed.

6. Completion of this relief will always be notified by O.C. Group to the Brigade Commander whose front his guns are covering.

7. The order issued would therefore be considerably reduced and would state at what notice reserves are held.

ACKNOWLEDGE.

8. Gun Commanders or Nol's of each of the relieving teams,also 1 N.C.O (Cpl or Sgt) each section will reach the position to be taken over at least 1 hour before sunset on the night of relief,i.e. when it is possible to visi the position in daylight.

8/8/1918.

Capt & Adjt,
46th Battn.M.G.Corps.

S E C R E T.

Copy No 15

46th BATTALION MACHINE GUN CORPS ORDER No.51.

Reference 1/40,000 BETHUNE COMBINED.

Battalion Headquarters will move from BOIS DES MONTAGNE to HESDIGNEUL CHATEAU E.25.d.45.65.

Move will be completed by 12-0 noon August 10th, 1918.

R. Dickens

Capt & Adjt,
46th Battn.Machine Gun Corps.

9/8/1918.

Distribution :-

1. 46th Division.
2. 137th Inf:Bde.
3. 138th Inf:Bde.
4. 139th Inf:Bde.
5. C.R.E.,46th Divn.
6. C.R.A.,46th Divn.
7. 19th Bn.M.G.Corps.
8. 55th Bn.M.G.Corps.
9. No 1 Group.
10. No 2 Group
11. A.Coy.
12. B.Coy.
13. C.Coy.
14. D.Coy.
15.)
16.)War Diary.
17. File.

S E C R E T.

Copy No 16.

46th BATTALION MACHINE GUN CORPS ORDER No. 52.

Maps. GORRE) 1/20,000
VIEILLE CHAPELLE.)

Instructions in the event of an enemy withdrawal.

1. Appreciation.
   (a) The possibilities of an enemy withdrawal from the ST.VENANT Salient are now a factor to be reckoned with.
   (b) Any withdrawal, either partial, or a complete withdrawal to his old system will pivot about the right of the 46th Division.
   It is probable therefore that a corresponding advance on our part will be slower and will be more strongly resisted than in the case of Divisions further North West.
   (c) The enemy is to be closely followed.

2. General Instructions.
   (a) Should the enemy be found to have retired the advance will be made by bounds under control of Divisional Headquarters.
   Divisional & Brigade Boundaries are shown on the attached tracing.
   (b) Brigades in the line will be responsible for reaching LINE A on attached map. The line is a general one and not intended to tie down Brigades if there is better ground a short distance forward or back.
   (c) Any advance beyond this line will be carried out by the Reserve Brigade.
   (d) The line occupied will be immediately consolidated in depth on the Post principle.
   (e) All men must be most strictly warned not to eat or drink any food etc left behind by the enemy.
   (f) The C.R.E. is arranging for one expert sapper to accompany patrols to examine dugouts etc for "Booby Traps".
   Men will not be allowed to enter these until they have been so examined.
   (g) The following bridges over the BEUVRY Brook are capable of taking Field Artillery :-
   F.4.b.3.3 - F.4.b.3.5 - X.28.a.1.3 - X.21.a.2.4 (under construction).

3. Machine Gun Instructions.
   (a) Should the Brigades in the line advance the following guns will be detailed by the Group Commanders to support them :-

Right Brigade	HAWK and OWL Batteries.
Left Brigade	PIGEON and THRUSH Batteries.

   When PIGEON Battery moves forward CANAL Battery will take its place as soon as possible.
   (b) When the Reserve Brigade moves forward of Line 'A' the Brigades in the line will receive orders from 46th Division to withdraw to their present positions. When this is done the guns of HAWK, OWL, THRUSH, PIGEON and CANAL Batteries will return to their normal Battery Positions.
   (c) The Machine Gun Company in Reserve will be attached to the Reserve Brigade and will come under the G.O.C. Reserve Brigade when it moves forward. The O.C.,Reserve Company will keep in constant touch with the G.O.C. Reserve Brigade and will carry out such reconnaissances as he may direct.
   (d) The Reserve Company will be held in readiness to move at two hours notice by night and four hours notice by day.
   (e) The present line of Retention will NOT for the moment be altered and in the event of an attack on the Reserve Brigade it will fall back,fighting,behind this line.
   (f) The Company Commanders concerned will ensure that the Batteries detailed are up to Fighting Strength and that everything is in readiness for an immediate move forward.

(g) Tho Group Commander will arrange for an adequate number of officers to remain with the guns remaining in the line.

Groups & Coys: to acknowledge.

Issued at 7-30 p.m.

B Licken

9/8/18.

Capt & Adjt,
46th Battn.Machine Gun Corps.

Distribution:-

1. No 1 Group.
2. No 2 Group.
3. A.Coy.
4. B.Coy.
5. C.Coy.
6. D.Coy.
7. Signals.
8. Q.M.
8. T.O.
10. 46th Division.
11. 137th Inf:Bde.
12. 138th Inf:Bde.
13. 139th Inf:Bde.
14. 19th Bn.M.G.Corps.
15. 55th Bn. M.G.Corps.
16. File.
17.)
18.)War Diary.

S E C R E T.

H.Q.,46th Division.
C.R.A.,46th Division.
H.Q., 137th Inf:Bde.
" 138th : :
" 139th : :
O.C.No 1 Group,
" No 2 "
" 'A' Coy.
" 'B' "
" 'C' "
" 'D' "
" 55th Bn. M.G.Corps.
" 19th Bn. M.G.Corps.
War Diary (2)
File.

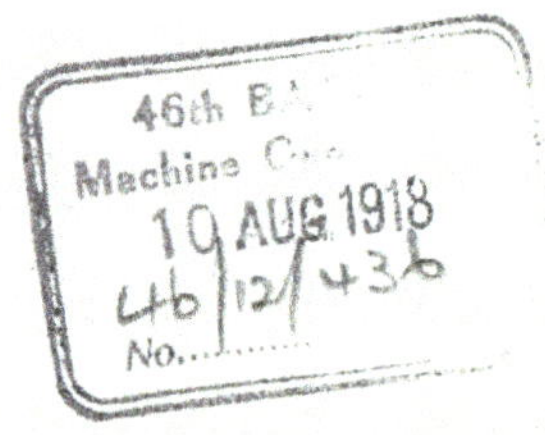

****

Machine Gun S.O.S. Lines.

1. Reference the tracing issued under my 46/10/106 of July 4th, I attach a further tracing showing alteration in S.O.S. Lines consequent upon advancement of our Front Line.

2. Acknowledge.

10/8/1918.

B.M. Lawrence.
Lieut-Colonel,
Commanding 46th Battn.M.G.Corps.

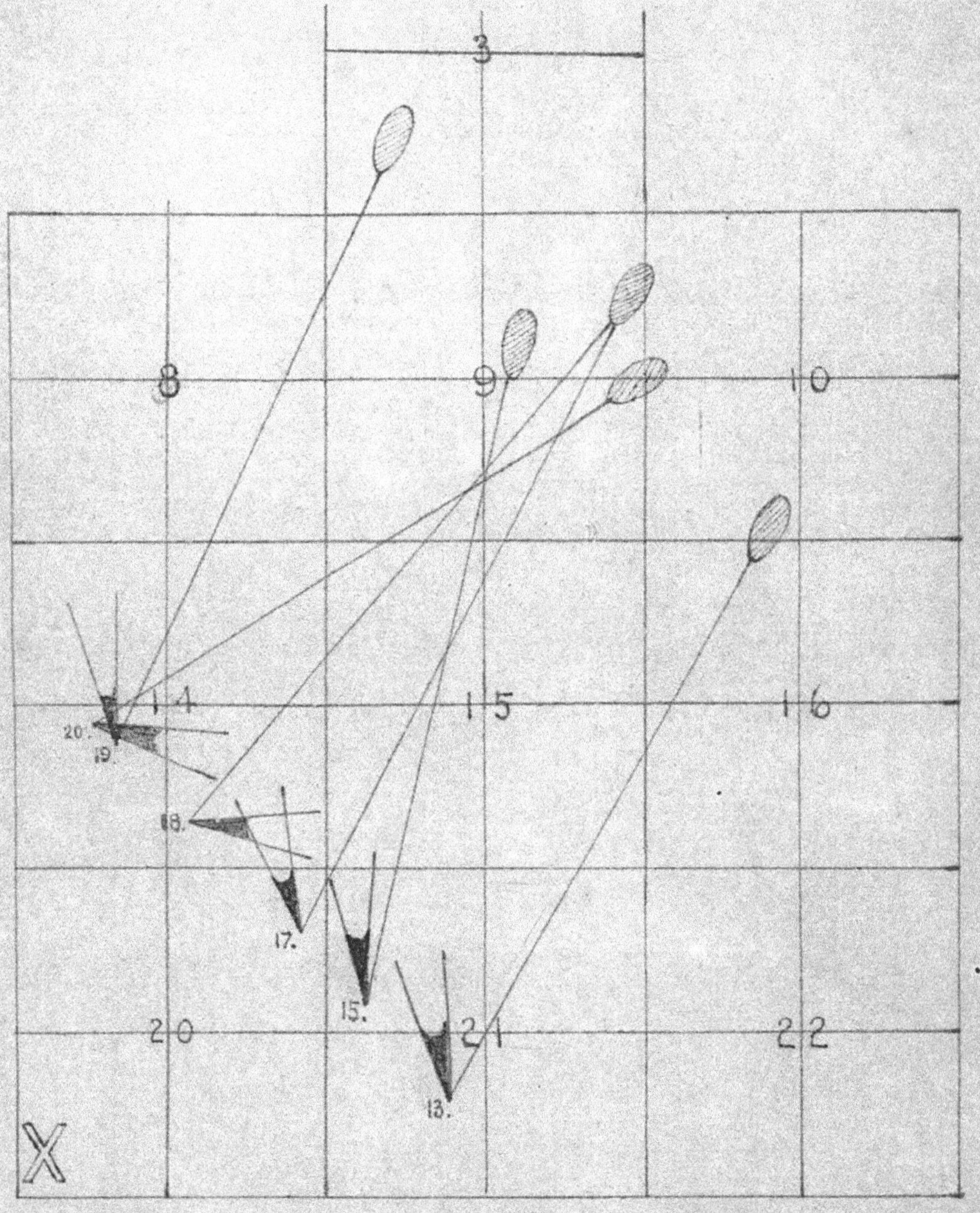

— 46th BTN. M.G.C. REVISED S.O.S. LINES. —

To be super-imposed upon VIEILLE CHAPELLE 1:20,000.

THRUSH and PIGEON Batteries do not fire on S.O.S.

S E C R E T.
****

ADMINISTRATIVE INSTRUCTION No. 1.

Arrangements for the collection of Stores in case of an advance.

1. In the event of a sudden move forward, only the transport allowed by regulations will be available.

2. Careful arrangements must therefore be made to ensure that useful stores are not lost, but are disposed of in such a manner that they will be available for use when required.

3. The Divisional Salvage Officer will be in charge of all this surplus kit etc, and his Headquarters will be at GOSNAY.

4. On the Scheme being brought into operation, Companies and the Q.M. will immediately collect at Q.M. Stores all the Stores that cannot be carried on the transport allowed. All Stores would be labelled.

5. Stores will be classified at the Unit Dumps by the Div:nl Salvage Officer in the following categories :-

(a) Ordnance Stores. (Braziers, Arms, Clothing etc.)
(b) Supplies. (Rations, Forage, Fuel etc.)
(c) R.E.Stores. (Barbed wire, picks, shovels, etc.)
(d) Medical Stores.
(e) Veterinary Stores.
(f) Ammunition, Grenades, Rockets, etc. (Careful arrangements being made for safety.

6. Stores actually in the trenches will be collected at suitable trench store dumps on forward routes for transport or light railways.

7. Trenches will not be dismantles of special stores, such as :- Loophole plates in position, until receipt of a definite order that this is to be done, but all moveable trench equipment is to be collected in trench store dumps.

8. One man (one of the Q.M. Storemen) would be left behind in charge of all this kit, which would then be dumped at PRIERE ST.PRY E.21.d.6.8.

This man would be rationed for 3 days and would subsequently be retained under arrangements to be made by the Divisional Salvage Officer.

ACKNOWLEDGE.

12/8/18.

Capt & Adjt,
46th Battn.Machine Gun Corps.

Distribution :-

'A' Coy.
'B' "
'C' "
'D' "
No 1 Group
No 2 "
M.O.
B.T.O.
Q.M.
Signals
T.O. 'A' Coy.
" 'B' "
" 'C' "
" 'D' "

S E C R E T.
****

H.Q.,46th Division.
C.R.A.,46th Division.
H.Q.,137th Inf:Bde.
" 138th : :
" 139th : :
O.C.No 1 Group,
" No 2 "
" 'A' Coy.
" 'B' "
" 'C' "
" 'D' "
" 55th Bn.M.G.Corps.
" 19th Bn.M.G.Corps.
War Diary (2)
File.
****

Machine Gun S.O.S. Lines.

Please make the following alteration to this office 46/12/430 :-

The S.O.S. target of No.20 gun is now X.9.a.93.97.

Rshikson Capt: &
Adjt. for
Lieut-Colonel,
Commanding 46th Battn.M.G.Corps.

12/8/1918.

S E C R E T. Copy No 18

46th BATTALION MACHINE GUN CORPS ORDER No.53.

Reference 1/20,000 GORRE & VIEILLE CHAPELLE.

1. 'B' Company will relieve 'D' Company in the line in the'Left Forward Gun Positions' in the ESSARS Section on the night 16/17th August, 1918.

2. As soon as the relief is completed Major C.V.Rigby, M.C. will take over the Command of No 2 Group from Major M.Douglas.

3. Capt.H.Witty will be O.C.,Left Forward Guns.

4. To be acknowledged by Companies and Groups.

Issued at 7-0 p.m.

14/8/18.

Capt & Adjt,
46th Battn.Machine Gun Corps.

Distribution:-

1. A.Coy.
2. B.Coy.
3. C.Coy.
4. D.Coy.
5. No 1 Group,
6. No 2 Group.
7. T.O.
8. Q.M.
9. Signals.
10. 46th Division.
11. 19th Bn.M.G.Corps.
12. 55th Bn.M.G.Corps.
13. 137th Inf:Bde.
14. 138th Inf:Bde.
15. 139th Inf:Bde.
16. File.
17.) War Diary.
18.)

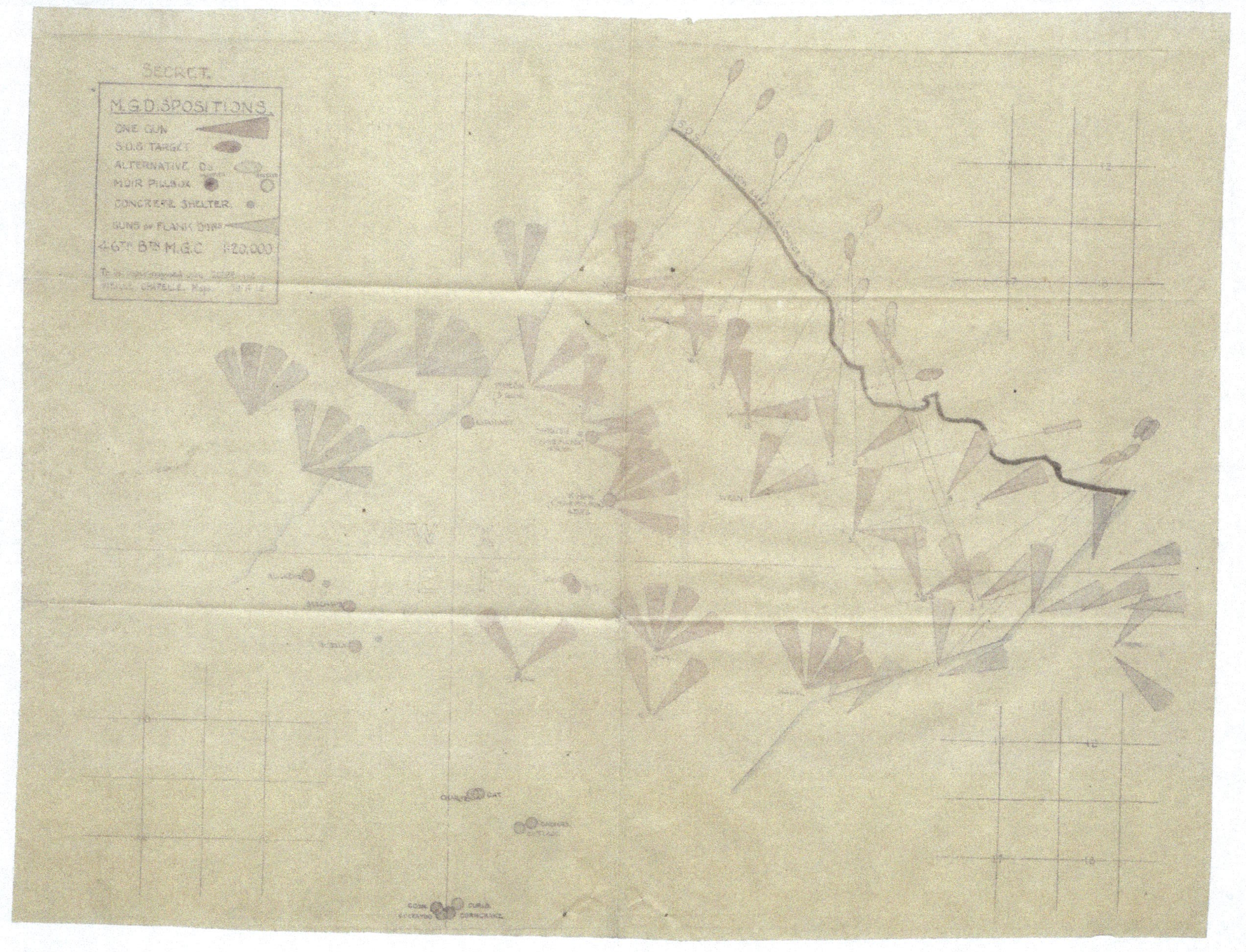
SECRET.
M.G.D.S POSITIONS.
ONE GUN
S.O.S TARGET
ALTERNATIVE Do
MOIR PILLBOX
CONCRETE SHELTER.
GUNS of FLANK DIVns
46TH Bn M.G.C 1:20,000

S E C R E T.
****

H.Q.,46th Division.
O.C.,19th Bn.M.G.Corps.
O.C.,55th Bn.M.G.Corps.
H.Q.,137th Inf:Bde.
H.Q.,138th : :
H.Q.,139th : :
C.R.A.,46th Division.
C.R.E.,46th Division.
O.C.No 1 Group,
" No 2 "
" 'A' Coy.
" 'B' "
" 'C' "
" 'D' "
War Diary (2)
File.
****

Machine Gun Dispositions.

1. The following Moir Pillboxes will be manned as soon as possible by guns taken from the positions indicatod.

2. Tho attached tracing shows the Machine Gun Dispositions and S.O.S. targets after the chango.

3.

Name of Pillbox.	Map Roference.	Gun to be taken from.
ESTAMINET.	X.19.c.21.45.	PIGEON Battery.
BEECHAMS.	E. 6.a.22.00	CANAL Battery.
BLICKENS.	E. 5.b.65.50	No 17 Position.
BUBBLY.	E. 6.c.40.32	CANAL Battery.
ECHO	F. 1.b.95.53	WREN Battery.
EVE.	F. 1.b.97.47	WREN Battery.

4. Please ACKNOWLEDGE.

20/8/1918.

[signature]
Lieut-Colonel,
Commanding 46th Battn.M.G.Corps.

SECRET. Copy No 18

46th BATTALION MACHINE GUN CORPS ORDER No.54.

Reference 1/20,000 GORRE & VIEILLE CHAPELLE.

1. 'D' Company will relieve 'C' Company in the line in the 'Right Forward Gun Positions' in the GORRE Section on the night 22/23rd August, 1918.

2. Major M.Douglas will be O.C.,Right Forward Guns.

3. Correspondence reference to 46th Battalion machine Gun Corps Order No 52 will be handed over to 'C' Company,and handing over certificate sent to this office.

4. To be acknowledged by Groups and Companies only.

Issued at 7-0 p.m.

20/8/1918.

R. Dickson
Capt & Adjt,
46th Battn.Machine Gun Corps.

Distribution :-

1. A.Coy.
2. B.Coy.
3. C.Coy.
4. D.Coy.
5. No 1 Group
6. No 2 Group.
7. T.O.
8. Q.M.
9. Signals.
10. 46th Division.
11. 19th Bn.M.G.Corps.
12. 55th Bn.M.G.Corps.
13. 137th Inf:Bde.
14. 138th Inf:Bde.
15. 139th Inf:Bde.
16. File.
17. }
18. } War Diary.

S E C R E T.
****

Copy No 18.

46th BATTALION MACHINE GUN CORPS ORDER No.54A.

Reference 46th Battalion Machine Gun Corps Order No 54.

Delete Para.2 of above Order and substitute :-

1. Immediately the above relief is completed Major M.Douglas will take over Command of No 1 Group from Major H.S.Windeler.

2. Capt.L.R.G.Heins will be O.C., Right Forward Guns.

21/8/1918.

Capt & Adjt,
46th Battn.Machine Gun Corps.

Distribution :-

1. A.Coy.	10. 46th Division.
2. B.Coy.	11. 19th Bn.M.G.Corps.
3. C.Coy.	12. 55th Bn.M.G.Corps.
4. D.Coy.	13. 137th Inf:Bde.
5. No 1 Group.	14. 138th Inf:Bde.
6. No 2 Group.	15. 139th Inf:Bde.
7. T.O.	16. File.
8. Q.M.	17.)
9. Signals.	18.)War Diary.

S E C R E T.
****

Copy No 17

46th BATTALION MACHINE GUN CORPS ORDER No.55.

Reference 1/20,000 GORRE & VIEILLE CHAPELLE.

1. 'D' Company will take over the following Guns from 'A' Company.

2 Guns ROUTE 'A' KEEP,	1 at X 23 d 70.10 1 at X 23 d 85.05	) From HAWK Battery
2 Guns LOISNE CENTRAL.	1 at X 22 b 90.10 1 at X 22 d 90.90	) From OWL Battery

2. 'A' Company will then take over from 'D' Company :-

   3 Guns WREN BATTERY X 27 a 90.30
   1 Gun EVE. F 1 b 97.47

3. Above to be completed by 3-0 a.m. 24/8/18.

4. This will leave all present Right Forward Guns with 'D' Company.

5. To be acknowledged by No 1 Group, 'A' and 'D' Companies.

Issued at 1-0 p.m.

23/8/1918.

Capt & Adjt,
46th Battn.Machine Gun Corps.

Distribution:-

1. A.Coy.
2. B.Coy.
3. C.Coy.
4. D.Coy.
5. No 1 Group.
6. No 2 Group
7. T.O.
8. Q.M.
9. Signals.
10. 46th Division.
11. 19th Bn.M.G.Corps.
12. 55th Bn.M.G.Corps.
13. 137th Inf:Bde.
14. 138th Inf:Bde.
15. 139th Inf:Bde.
16. File.
17.)
18.)War Diary.

SECRET.
****

Copy No 18

40th BATTALION MACHINE GUN CORPS ORDER No.56

Reference 1/20,000 GORRE & VIEILLE CHAPELLE.

1. 'C' Company will relieve 'A' Company in the line in the 'Rear Gun Positions' in the GORRE and ESSARS Sections on the night 28/29th August, 1918.

2. Major W.T.Boughey will be O.C., Rear Guns.

3. To be acknowledged by Groups and Companies only.

Issued at 1-0 p.m.

28/8/18.

R. [signature]

Capt & Adjt,
40th Battn. Machine Gun Corps.

Distribution:-

1. A.Coy.
2. B.Coy.
3. C.Coy.
4. D.Coy.
5. No 1 Group.
6. No 2 Group.
7. T.O.
8. Q.M.
9. Signals.
10. 40th Division.
11. 19th Bn.M.G.C.
12. 55th Bn.M.G.C.
13. 137th Inf:Bde.
14. 138th Inf:Bde.
15. 139th Inf:Bde.
16. File.
17. } War Diary.
18. }

****

W A R   D I A R Y.

46th BATTALION MACHINE GUN CORPS.

SEPTEMBER 1918.

****

Instructions regarding War Diaries and Intelligence Summaries are contained in F. S. Regs., Part II. and the Staff Manual respectively. Title pages will be prepared in manuscript.

WAR DIARY

Army Form C. 2118.

46th BATTALION MACHINE GUN CORPS.

SEPTEMBER 1918 ~~INTELLIGENCE SUMMARY.~~

(Erase heading not required.)

Sheet No 1.

Place	Date	Hour	36A.S.E. & 36.S.W. GORRE } 1/20,000 Summary of Events and Information AMIENS 1/100,000. ST.QUENTIN 1/100,000 62.B. 1/40,000	Remarks and references to Appendices
ESSARS & GORRE SECTION.	1st.		) The usual harassing fire was carried out on the enemy's tracks and roads.))	
	2nd.	1900	Order No 57 issued (copy attached) 2 O.Rs. evacuated (sick).	Order No 57.
	3rd.		Operation detailed in order No 57 was carried out successfully and guns moved forward in conformity with the Infantry advance.	
	4th.	2300	Harassing fire was carried out. 1 O.R. reinforcement. 3 Officers Posted. Order No 58 was issued (copy attached)	Order No 58.
HESDIGNEUL.	5th.		Relieved by 19th Battn.M.G.Corps. All Companies moved to HESDIGNEUL AERODROME for accommodation and training. 1 O.R. Wounded. 1 O.R. evacuated (sick). 1 O.R. reinforcement.	
	6th.		1 O.R. Evacuated (sick).	
	7th. 8th. 9th.		)After a long period in the line the battalion was re-equipped and carried out extensive)training on the range, and in the vicinity of the aerodrome.)6 O.Rs. Evacuated (sick) 3 O.Rs. Wounded in Action. 3 O.Rs. re-inforcements.)1 Officer Evacuated to Base (sick).	
	10th.		1 Officer to U.K. for transfer to R.A.F.	
LOZINGHEM.	11th.	1700	Moved from HESDIGNEUL to LOZINGHEM. 2 O.Rs. Evacuated (sick).	
	12th.	1630	Moved by road to LILLERS. Entrained at 0800 for HEILLY. Arrived HEILLY 1900. Marched by Road to BAISIEUX. 4 Officers Posted	
	13th. 14th. 15th.		) Tactical exercises were carried out by Companies in conjunction with Infantry Brigades under) Divisional arrangements. Field firing was also carried out on various ranges in the) neighbourhood.of BAISIEUX.) 1 O.R. to Base Depot 13/9/18. 1 O.R. reinforcement.	

D. D. & L., London, E.C.
(A8004) Wt W1771/M2031 750,000 5/17 Sch. 52 Forms/C2118/14

Army Form C. 2118.

WAR DIARY

46th BATTALION MACHINE GUN CORPS.

Instructions regarding War Diaries and Intelligence Summaries are contained in F. S. Regs., Part II. and the Staff Manual respectively. Title pages will be prepared in manuscript.

SEPTEMBER 1918.

(Erase heading not required.)

Sheet No 2.

Place	Date	Hour	Summary of Events and Information	Remarks and references to Appendices
			AMIENS 1/100,000. 62.B. 1/40,000 ST.QUENTIN 1/100,000	
BAISIEUX.	16th.		"D" and "A" Coy field firing on range. "C" Coy carried out scheme in conjunction with 139th Infantry Brigade. 1 O.R. transferred to R.Es. 1 O.R. reinforcement.	
	17th.		"B" Coy carried out tactical scheme in conjunction with 138th Infantry Brigade.	
	18th.		"C" Coy field firing on range. "D" Coy tactical scheme in conjunction with 137th Inf:Bde.	
	19th.	1600	"B" Coy field firing on range. Embussed at BAISIEUX (near CORBIE) for ESTREES. Arrived ESTREES 2330. 1 Officer to U.K. for transfer to R.A.F.	
ST.QUENTIN CANAL.	20th.		"A" Coy relieved Company of 1st Division in the line 20/21st. Order No 59 issued (copy attached)	1/20,000 62B.S.W. 62.B.N.W. 62.C.S.E. Order No 59
	21st.	1700	Order No 60 issued (copy attached)	Order No 60
	22nd.		"B", "C" & "D" Coys relieved the 4th Australian M.G.Battn. in the line. 10 O.Rs. reinforcements. 2 Officers Killed in Action. 1 Officer Posted.	
	23rd.	1500 1800	Battalion H.Q. and Transport moved from ESTREES to VRAIGNES. 1 O.R. Evacuated (sick). Order No 61 issued (copy attached) 3 O.Rs. Killed in Action. 4 O.Rs. Wounded in action. 1 O.R. Evacuated (sick).	Order No 61.
	24th.		Machine Guns co-operated in conjunction with 1st and 6th Divisions operations with barrage and in close support to Infantry. 2 Officers, wounded in action. 4 O.Rs. wounded in action. 6 O.Rs. Killed in action.	
	25th.		36 guns were employed in firing on barrage lines in support of the attacks detailed in Order No 61. 1 O.R. wounded in action. 4 O.Rs. Evacuated (sick).	

D. D. & L., London, E.C. (A8004) Wt W1771/M2031 750,000 5/17 Sch. 52 Forms/C2118/14

Army Form C. 2118.

WAR DIARY

Instructions regarding War Diaries and Intelligence Summaries are contained in F. S. Regs., Part II. and the Staff Manual respectively. Title pages will be prepared in manuscript.

SEPTEMBER 1918

46th BATTALION MACHINE GUN CORPS

~~INTELLIGENCE SUMMARY~~

(*Erase heading not required.*)

Sheet No 3.

Place	Date	Hour	Summary of Events and Information AMIENS 1/100,000 ST.QUENTIN 1/100,000 62.B. 1/40,000	Remarks and references to Appendices
	26th.		18 O.Rs. reinforcements 2 Officers Posted.	
		2330	Order No 62 issued (copy attached)	Order No 62.
	27th.		'A' & 'B' Companies were relieved by 1st Battn.M.G.Corps and moved to assembly positions as detailed in Order No 63 (copy attached) 2 O.Rs. wounded in action. 1 Officer posted.	Order No 63.
	28th.		Detailed arrangements as stated in Orders No 64A & 65 (copies attached) were carried out in preparation for a major operation against the HINDENBURG LINE & ST.QUENTIN CANAL Defences to be carried out by the 46th Division. Orders Nos 66, 67, 68 & 69 issued (copies attached) 2 O.Rs. wounded in action. 1 Officer wounded in action.	Orders 64A & 65. Orders 66, 67,68 & 69.
	29th.		Successful operation was carried out. (M.G. Details attached). 32 O.Rs. wounded in action. 1 O.R. killed in action. 1 Officer wounded in action.	
	30th.		2 O.Rs. Killed in Action. 4 O.Rs wounded in action.	

Allan R Th Darby Capt for Lieut-Colonel,
Commanding 46th Battn.Machine Gun Corps.

D. D. & L., London, E.C.
(A8004) Wt W1771/M2031 750,000 5/17 Sch. 52 Forms/C2118/14

S E C R E T.

Adjutant

Copy No______

46th BATTALION MACHINE GUN CORPS WARNING ORDER No 57.

Reference Maps 36a.S.E. & 36 S.W.) 1/20,000
GORRE.

1. FIRST OBJECTIVE. Orders have been received that, at a very early date, the 46th and 19th Divisions will attack and occupy such portions of the following line as are not already in our possession :-

L'EPINETTE EAST POST (S.19.a.) - River in S.8.a. and C. - RICHEBOURG ST.VAAST - CROIX BARBEE.

2. SECOND OBJECTIVE. Subsequently an operation will be carried out to establish the General Line ROUGE CROIX - PONT LOGY (M.34.c.) WINDY CORNER (S.9.a.6.9) - S.15.a.3.6 to SOUTHERN DIVISIONAL BOUNDARY, about S.27.a.5.5.

3. FIRST ATTACK. Group and Company Commanders will at once put in hand all preparations for supporting these attacks as follows :-
For the attack detailed in Para.I. by covering fire from as many guns as can be brought to bear upon the enemy's probable lines of approach to the objective, and, if required by the Brigade Commander concerned, by sending guns forward to assist in consolidation and defence of the objective.

4. SECOND ATTACK. For the attack detailed in Para.2, 'D' Company will be allotted to the right Brigade and will detail sections as under.
One Section for the immediate defence of the captured objective.
One Section as a mobile battery of opportunity, which will remain on the right flank, and will be always in readiness to protect it against counter attacks.
One Section for the provision of Barrage fire from about the first objective.
One Section as a Reserve.

B.Company will be allotted to the Left Brigade and will detail sections as under :-
One Section for the immediate defence of the captured objective.
One Section as a Battery of opportunity.
One Section for the provision of Barrage Fire from about the first objective.
One Section as a Reserve.

The Reserve Sections will be disposed where they can bring fire to bear over the heads of our own troops when they have reached the objective, and will be allotted areas to barrage.
The Batteries of opportunity will take advantage of every chance of inflicting loss on the enemy and will give close support by direct fire to the infantry during counter attacks. They will also engage low flying hostile aeroplanes and keep in close touch with infantry commander.

C.Company will be disposed as follows for the defence of the Line of Retention.
One Section in Nos.1, 2, 3 & 4 Positions.
One Section in Nos 5, 6, 9 & 10 Positions.
One Section in LOISNE CENTRAL & X.17.c.
One Section in X.17.a. and SLOANE SQUARE.

5. DETAILS. Orders for the rearrangement of guns in readiness for the attack will be issued later. In the meantime the officers concerned will make all possible reconnaissance of the ground, carefully avoiding unnecessary movement by day, and will make all preparations such as the provision of S.A.A. dumps well forward, the selection of battery positions, assembly areas and Battle Headquarters so that the above arrangements may be put into operation at very short notice.

As/

As far as possible the guns nearest the final positions will be chosen to move forward and ammunition etc should be taken up by pack or limber as far as possible the night before the attack.

6. DIAGRAM. A diagram showing the action of the machine guns and their approximate disposition after the objective has been consolidated is attached. This is not intended in any way to tie down Group and Company Commanders to the positions shown thereon, but is merely to show the general scheme upon which the machine guns will be employed.

7. ACKNOWLEDGE.

Issued at 7-0 pm.

2/9/1918.

[signature]

Major,
46th Battn.Machine Gun Corps.

Distribution:-

1. A. Coy.
2. B. Coy.
3. C. Coy.
4. D. Coy.
5. No.1 Group
6. No 2 Group
7. }War Diary.
8. }
9. File.
10. 46th Division.
11. 19th Bn.M.G.Corps.
12. 55th Bn.M.G.Corps.
13. 137th Inf:Bde.
14. 138th Inf:Bde.
15. 139th Inf:Bde.

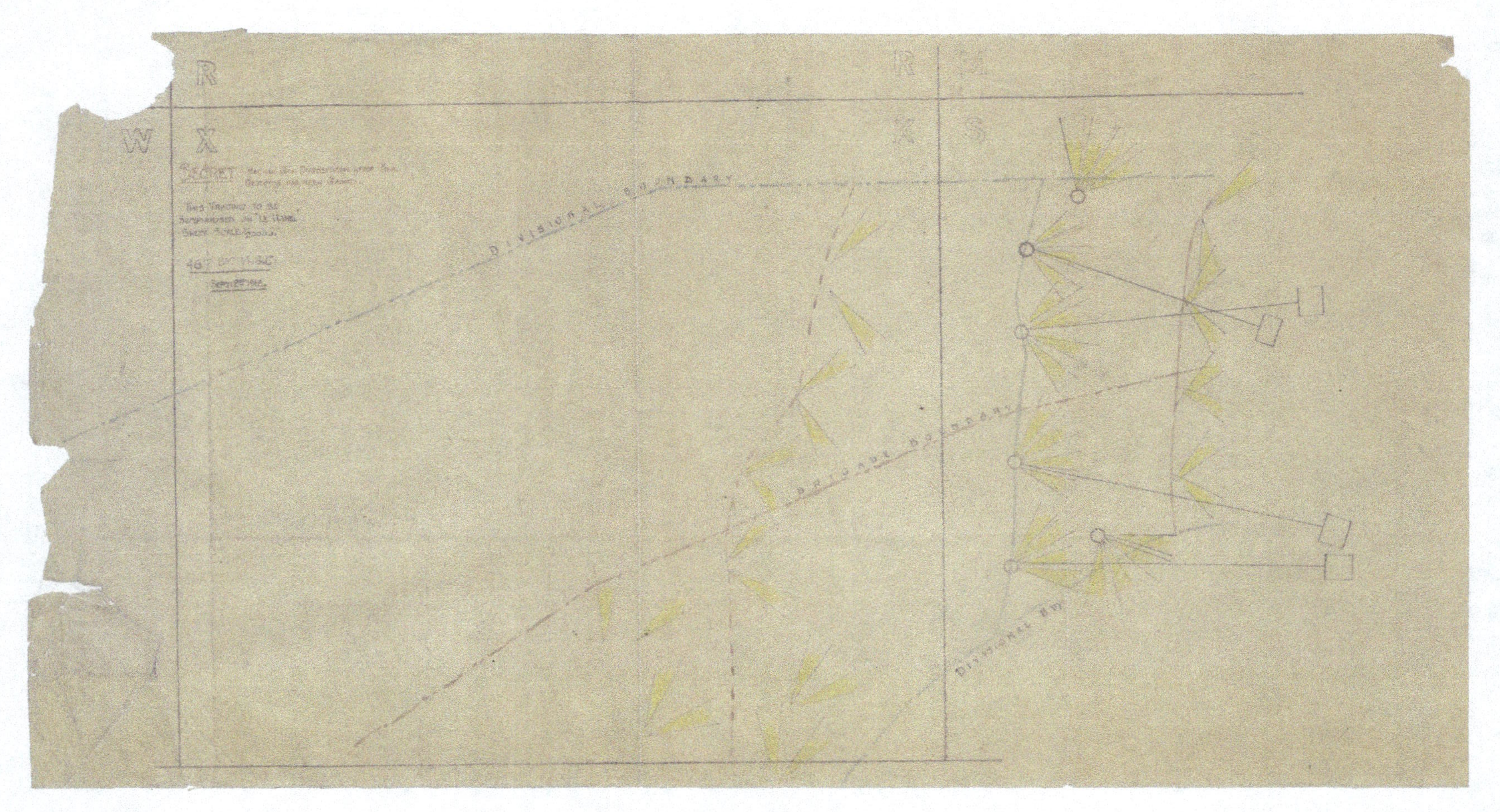
R
R
M
W
X
X
S
SECRET
DIVISIONAL BOUNDARY
BRIGADE BOUNDARY
DIVISIONAL BY

S E C R E T.
****

Copy No 16

46th BATTALION MACHINE GUN CORPS ORDER No. 58.

Reference 1/20,000 GORRE & VIEILLE CHAPELLE.

1. Companies in the line will be relieved by the 19th Battalion Machine Gun Corps to-morrow September 5th, 1918.

2. The following positions will be manned by relieving Battalion :-

In present line of Retention:- 4 guns CHAVATTES, 'B' Company.
4 guns L'EPPINETTE N. 'D' Company.
4 guns L'EPINETTE E. 'D' Company.

In Rear of above :- 2 guns in X.11.d. 'B' Company
2 guns in X.17.a. 'B' Company.
2 guns in X.16.d. 'C' Company.
2 guns in LOISNE Central, 'C' Company.
Nos 1, 2, 3 & 4 TUNING FORK & SWITCH 'C' Company.

Note. If Nos 1 & 2 have moved to ROUTE 'A' KEEP these 2 guns will be handed over at ROUTE 'A' KEEP.

3. No guns or gun equipment will be handed over.
From gun positions not being occupied by relieving Battalion water tins will be brought out.

4. Officers and necessary guides of 'B' & 'D' Companies (Forward guns) will be at Orchard RUE DES CHAVATTES S 7 d 9.8 at 10.0 a.m. to-morrow, and for 'B' and 'C' Companies (Rear guns) at X 5 d 6.2 junction of SLOANE SQUARE and KING GEORGE'S ROAD at same time.

5. When above reliefs are complete respective Group Commanders will issue orders for remainder of each 'B', 'C' and 'D' Companies to evacuate the positions now occupied by them and not taken over.
All evacuated positions will be left in a thoroughly clean condition.

6. Respective Companies are responsible that the Boxes of Iron Rations are returned to Q.M. to-morrow certain vide 46/9/50.

7 - All disposition maps, documents, defence schemes etc and programmes of work in hand will be handed over.

~~7~~. Consolidated handing over certificates for Nos 1 & 2 Groups and 'B', and 'D' Companies will be sent to Battalion Headquarters as soon as possible after relief. Section Officers will receive receipts that positions handed over are in a clean condition.

8. Groups and Companies will hand over a complete list of all dumps of S.A.A. etc in their areas and will send handing over list to Battalion Headquarters.

9. As relieved 'B', 'D' and 'C' Companies will proceed to Aerodrome, HESDIGNEUL which has been taken over. The Q.M. will allot accommodation on arrival. Blankets are there.

10. Signals will arrange for all instruments etc to be withdrawn as reliefs are completed under orders to be issued by Group Commanders.
Cpl.Blakkshaw, R.E. will be at No 1 Group.
Sgt.Shaw will be at No 2 Group.

11. Q.M. will arrange for water carts,cookers and Cooks of 'B', 'C' and 'D' Companies to move to HESDIGNEUL to-morrow morning.

12. 'A' Company, Q.M. and Transport will until further orders remain as at present situated.

Over/

13. Completion of reliefs will be wired to Battalion Headquarters by Commanders concerned by "B.A.B." code.

14. ACKNOWLEDGE.

Issued at 11.0 p.m.

4/9/1918.

Capt & Adjt,
46th Battn.Machine Gun Corps.

Distribution:-

1. A.Coy.	10. 46th Division.
2. B.Coy.	11. 19th Bn. M.G.Corps.
3. C.Coy.	12. 55th Bn. M.G.Corps.
4. D.Coy.	13. 137th Inf:Bde.
5. No 1 Group	14. 138th Inf:Bde.
6. No 2 Group	15. 139th Inf:Bde.
7. B.T.O.	16. File.
8. Q.M.	17.)
9. Sig[illegible]	18.)War Diary.

ADDENDA.

Reference para.2 of above order, the Line of Retention has now been amended to LACOUTURE, SLOANE SQUARE, LOISNE Central, TUNING FORK; and Groups and Companies will be prepared to meet wishes of the 19th Battalion Machine Gun Corps in case they require 12 guns in rear of this line. Rendez-vous for guides remain as in para.4.

S E C R E T.
****

Copy No 13

46th BATTALION MACHINE GUN CORPS ORDER No 59

Reference Maps 1/20,000, 62.B. S.W., 62.B. N.W., 62.C. S.E.

1. 'A' Company will take over 16 (sixteen) guns in the line in the Left Brigade (2nd Infantry Brigade) of the 1st Division on the night 20/21st September, 1918.

2. 139th Infantry Brigade are taking over Infantry dispositions as above.

3. Temporarily the 139th Brigade will come under the orders of the 1st Division.
Administrative arrangements will be made by this Division.

4. Various positions and Headquarters will be as follows :-

'A' Company H.Q.	R.17.c.90.20
4 guns No 1 section	M.2.c.0.4.
4 " " 2 "	M.8.a.
4 " " 3 "	M.14.a.0.2.
4 " " 4 "	M.1.b.95.85.

'A' Company Transport Lines R.21.b.8.8.
2 Fighting limbers of 'A' Company will be detached to R.18.d.8.3.

5. Ration Dumps :-

For 1, 2 & 4 Sections	R.6.c.
For 3 Section	M.13.d.0.4. This can be used in daylight.

6. Drinking water will require to be sent up under arrangements to be made by 'A' Company and under the supervision of the R.M.O.

7. 'A' Company will notify completion of relief by runner message.

[signature]

20/9/18.

Capt & Adjt,
46th Battn. M.G.Corps.

Distribution :-

1. 46th Division.
2. 137th Infantry Bde.
3. 138th : :
4. 139th : :
5. A.Company.
6. B.Company.
7. C.Company.
8. D.Company.
9. Q.M.
10. Signals.
11. M.O.
12.)
13.)War Diary.
14.)
15.)File.
16 1 Bttn: M.G. Corps

S E C R E T.   Copy No 13
****

46th BATTALION MACHINE GUN CORPS ORDER No 60.

Reference Maps 1/20,000, 62.B. SW; 62.B. NW; 62.C. SE.

Reference 46/12/580 to Companies only.

1. 'B', 'C' & 'D' Companies will relieve the 4th Australian M.G.Battalion on the night ~~21/22nd~~ 22/23 September,1918, as follows :-

'B' Company (Right) will relieve	8 guns 12th Company. 8 guns 13th Company.
D 'C' Company (Centre) will relieve	8 guns 4th Company. 8 guns 24th Company.
C 'D' Company (Left) will relieve	4 guns 4th Company 8 guns 12th Company. 4 guns 24th Company.

2. Tracing is attached shewing guns to be taken over and also positions that will be evacuated by the 4th Australian M.G.Battalion when above reliefs are completed.
(This tracing also shows the guns of 'A' Company in the 139th Brigade Sector).

3. 'B', 'C' & 'D' Companies will each take over 33 Petrol Tins. These have already been signed for and do not require replacing.

4. Company Commanders will make all further arrangements.

5. Advance parties have been sent forward this day.

6. Companies will notify completion of relief by ~~next runner message.~~

7. Company Headquarters will be as follows :- Code HRd Newcastle

'D' Company) 'C' Company)	L.34.a.30.80
'B' Company	for night 21st/22nd R.2.c.40.10 (Then about R.4.d. or R.10.b.)
('A' Company	at R.17.c.90.20).

Issued at 5.0 P.M.

R. [signature]
Capt & Adjt,
46th Battn.Machine Gun Corps.

Distribution.

1. 46th Division.
2. 1st Bn.M.G.Corps.
3. 4th Australian M.G.Battn.
4. 1st Australian M.G.Battn.
5. 137th Infantry Brigade.
6. 138th Infantry Brigade.
7. 139th Infantry Brigade.
8. 'A' Company.
9. B.Company.
10. C.Company.
11. D.Company.
12.)
13.)War Diary.
14.)
15.)File.
16.)

Identification Trace for use with Artillery Maps.

NOTE.—(1). These traces are intended to facilitate the communication of information as to the position of targets, which have been located on a squared map.

(2). The squares on this trace are 500 yards in length on the 1/10,000 scale, 1,000 yards in length on the 1/20,000 scale, and 2,000 yards in length on the 1/40,000 scale.

(3). The squares on the trace are fitted to the squares of the map showing the targets, which are then drawn on the trace. Sufficient letters and numbers must also be added to enable the recipient to place the trace in the correct position on his own map. A little detail may also be traced, but this is not essential. The name and scale of the map to which the trace refers must be always given. The trace can be used for the 1/10,000, 1/20,000, or 1/40,000 scale.

G.S.G.S. 3085.

Tracing taken from Sheet ....

of the 1 .... *map of* ....

Signature .... *Date* ....

S E C R E T. Copy No 17.
****

46th BATTALION MACHINE GUN CORPS ORDER No 61.

Ref: Maps 1/20,000

62.B. SW; 62.B.NW; 62.C.SE; 62.C.NE.

1. On the 24th September the 1st and 6th Divisions are attacking to the SOUTH of the 46th Division with a view to gaining certain high ground. The final objective of the LEFT Brigade of the 1st Division is shown in BLUE on the map issued to Companies this morning. The 46th Division is co-operating [by capturing] the village of PONTRUET & FORCANS Trench as far South as about M.10.b.5.3.

2. The 1st Division advancing at Zero under a creeping barrage captures 3 objectives :-

First YELLOW
Second GREEN
Third BLUE

Tanks and low flying aeroplanes will co-operate.

3. The attack by the 46th Division will be carried out by the 138th Infantry Brigade on the following lines :-

(a) Attacking Infantry:- The attack will be made by one Battalion from the NORTH; the use of the forming up line shown in RED on Map "A", being ensured by the establishment of Posts prior to the day of attack.

At Zero, two companies will advance from the RED line under a creeping barrage which will extend S.W. and N.E. from the PONTRUET - S. HELENE road to FORCANS Trench, both inclusive.

Those two companies will capture the area marked YELLOW on Map "A", and as rapidly as possible establish strong posts about M 10.a.8.2 and M 10 b 5.4.

They should not proceed WEST of the road from M 10 central to S. HELENE.

The other two Companies will follow and take up a position facing S.W. along the Road M 10 a 6.4 - M 3 d 9.2.

Meanwhile PONTRUET Trench, PALARIO Trench and BLOCKHOUSE will be kept under Artillery fire. This barrage will lift clear to the N.E. of FORCANS Trench at a time to be arranged by the G.O.C, 138th Infantry Brigade, the two companies waiting on the road will then rush in and mop up the village, paying special attention to PONTRUET and PALARIO Trenches and the BLOCKHOUSE.

In this way it is hoped that the whole enemy garrison will be either killed or captured.

(Note) The advanced companies must be warned to look out on all sides as they will have cut the enemy off and will be able to shoot him down or capture him as he retires.

The 139th Inf: Bde will, at Zero hour, occupy FOURMI Trench from M 3 c 8.6 to M 3 d 7.7; and on PONTRUET Trench being captured will m[op] up BEUX and LEDUC Trench and GALLICHET Alley joining hands with the 138th Inf: Bde in PONTRUET.

(b) Supporting Infantry:- The 137th Inf: Bde will move one Battalion to the position vacated by the attacking Battalion.

(c) Relieving Infantry:- The 139th Inf: Bde will relieve the 138th Inf: Bde as far NORTH as the Inter-Brigade boundary on Z/Z plus 1 night.

(d) Machine Gun Arrangements:- Eight guns will be moved forward for the close protection of the strong points M 10 central and M 10 b 5.4 (at least twp to each) and such other positions as may be considered necessary.

The O.C, 46th Bn, M.G.Corps, will further arrange,

(i) in conjunction with the Artillery, a creeping barrage up FORCANS Trench.

(ii) in conjunction with the 1st Division a roaming barrage in the Valley M 10 c and d.

(iii) a roaming barrage in the valley M 4 a, d and M 11 a.

(c) Artillery Plan:- The C.R.A. will arrange for the following artillery bombardments and barrages :-

(i) On Y day, a bombardment of suspected strong points and M.G. nests within and covering our objectives.

(ii) Standing heavy artillery barrages (including smoke) on the trench systems in M 11 d, c, M 11 a, M 11 b, M 5 d and c, M 4 b and BELLENGLISE Hill.

(iii) Counter battery work.

(iv) Creeping barrage for YELLOW objective to be arranged with the G.O.C, 138th Inf: Bde.
Guns to form a protective barrage 300 yards N.E. of FORCANS Trench as they complete their barrage role.

(v) A Bombardment of PONTRUET Village (especially BLOCKHOUSE, PONTRUET and PALARIO Trenches); from Zero until a time to be arranged between the C.R.A. and G.O.C, 138th Inf: Bde.
On this bombardment ceasing, the guns will be used to thicken the protective barrage N.E. of FORCANS Trench and E. of the grid between M 10 and 11.

(vi) A crash bombardment of Heavy Artillery on selected points in and around PONTRUET to start at Zero and end at Zero plus 3 minutes.

4. In detail the Machine gun co-operation will be as follows :-

Coy.	No of guns.	Approx:present position.	Move to Approximately.	Letters refer to Task tracing issued to Companies.	Time & rate.	Remarks.
A.	4	M.13.b.	--	Roaming barrage in "C" Valley M 10 c & d.from M 10 c.9.4. to M.10.d.5.5	Zero to + 14 Rapid.	
A.	4	M.7.b.	M.8.a.	"B" Creeping barrage up FORCANS TRENCH.	ZERO to + 14 Rapid.	Lifts ah shown on tracing.
A.	4	M.1.b.	M.8.a.			
A.	4	R.11.d.	M.15.a.	"D" Barrage on trench M.11.a. & b.in case of S.O.S.	S.O.S.	
B.	4	G.27.d.	--	"A" Roaming barrage in valley M.4.a., d, & M.11.a.	ZERO to + 26 Medium & on S.O.S.	Ample clearance must be allowed from post at M.10.b.5.4.
B.	4	M.2.c.	M.3.d.	Barrage PONTRUET	ZERO to + 10 Rapid.	
B.	4	M.1.b.	M.8.a.	"B"	ZERO to + 14 Rapid.	These guns come under O.C.'A'Coy.
C.	8	G.31 & 25	M.3.	To consolidate captured positions. 2 to approx M.10 central. 2 to approx M.10.b.5.4 2 to approx M.10.a.9.8 2 to approx M.4.a.1.3.	As soon as possible after positions have been captured.	

Coy.	No of guns.	Approx: present position.	Move to Approx-imately.	Letters refer to Task tracing issued to Companies.	Time & rate.	Remarks.
C.	4	L.30	G.31 & 25.	To take over positions vacated by guns moved forward from G.31 & 25.		

A tracing is issued to Companies showing above barrages.
Guns moving forward will be prepared to come into action at any moment in case of any unexpected situation and all detachments will keep a keen lookout for any opportunity of assisting the infantry or inflicting loss on the enemy.

5. On reaching the S.E. point of their objective (M.10.b.5.4) the 138th Infantry Brigade will send up the Success Signal (White over White over White) repeating it after five minutes.

6. O.C.Companies will synchronize watches at Brigade Headquarters and will ensure that each battery has the correct time. The actual moment of Zero will be indicated however by the commencement of the artillery barrage.

7. ZERO hour will be 5.00 a.m.

8. ACKNOWLEDGE.

Issued at 6.0 p.m.

23/9/18.

C.A.Wade
Major,
46th Battn.Machine Gun Corps.

Distribution.

1. 46th Division.
2. C.R.A.
3. C.M.G.O.
4. 1st Division.
5. 1st Bn.M.G.Corps.
6. 137th Inf:Bde.
7. 138th : :
8. 139th : :
~~10.~~ 9. A.Coy
10. B.Coy.
11. C.Coy.
12. D.Coy.
13. Signals.
14. M.O.
15. Q.M.
16.)
17)War Diary.
18. File.

S E C R E T.
******* ********

Copy No 14

46th BATTALION MACHINE GUN CORPS ORDER No 62.

Reference Sheets 62.C.NE. & SE; 62.B.NW & SW.

Reference 46/12/598 to Companies.

1. On the night 27/28th September, 1918, the 1st Battalion Machine Gun Corps will relieve the following guns in the line :-
   - 4 guns of 'A' Company at M 13 b 9.4.
   - 4 guns of 'A' Company at M 7 b 9.8.
   - 4 guns of 'B' Company at M 2 c 0.5.
   - 4 guns of 'B' Company at M 2 b 2.5.

2. The 8 (eight) guns of 'B' Company thus relieved will then relieve the following :-
   - 4 guns of 'A' Company at M 1 a.
   - 4 guns of 'C' Company at M 31 b & d.

3. The following guns will be withdrawn after stand down evening 27th September, 1918.
   - 4 guns of 'A' Company in M 9 c.
   - 4 guns of 'C' Company in M 3 b.
   - 4 guns of 'C' Company in G 25 b & d.
   - 4 guns of 'C' Company in G 27 d & G 33 b.

4. The O.C.'B' Company will arrange that his battery remaining in G 33 b. also protects the ground covered by the battery of 'C' Company being withdrawn from G 27 d & G 33 b.
   If necessary the arcs of fire of the battery will be altered.

5. 'A' Company and 'C' Company thus relieved will retire to vicinity of Company Headquarters and JEANCOURT respectively.
   'A' and 'C' Company H.Q. will remain as at present.

6. The O.C.'A' and 'B' Company will meet the Company Commanders of the 1st Battalion Machine Gun Corps concerned at 'A' Company H.Q. at 10.0 a.m. to-morrow September 27th and will arrange all further necessary details regarding this relief.

7. Disposition maps, programmes of work in hand etc etc will be handed over. Copy of handing over list will be sent to Battalion Headquarters.

8. Completion of these orders will be notified by 'C' and 'D' Companies by wire by the code word "NOMAD"

9. Companies and 1st Battalion M.G.Corps to acknowledge.

Issued at 11.30 p.m.

26/9/18.

[signature]
Capt & Adjt,
46th Battn.Machine Gun Corps.

Distribution.

1. 46th Division.
2. C.R.A.
3. 137th Infantry Bde.
4. 138th : :
5. 139th : :
6. * 1st Bn.M.G.Corps.
7. * 30th American Div:M.G.Battn.
8. C.M.G.O. IX Corps.
9. A.Coy.
10. B.Coy.
11. C.Coy.
12. D.Coy.
13. Signals.
14.)
15.)War Diary.
16.)
17.)File.

* Tracing attached showing approximate dispositions of guns of this Battalion as they will be after reliefs.

S E C R E T.   Copy No______
****

46th BATTALION MACHINE GUN CORPS ORDER No. 64.

Reference 1/20,000 OMISSY.

In continuation of previous orders to Companies.

1. Advanced Battalion Headquarters will be at R.8.b.6.5. (with Divisional Headquarters) and will be established by 10.0 p.m. September 28th. They will be marked by the Battalion flag.

2. The Battalion Forward Dump will be established at G.27.c.0.1. and will consist of :-

A. 500 Boxes M.G. Bundle Packed S.A.A. (already there).
B. About 200 German Belt boxes with filled belts.
C. About 200 belts filled.
D. About 50 Tins of Water (For Drinking or guns).
E. Two drums of oil.
F. Ten spare barrels.
G. Ten lock springs.
H. Ten fusee springs.
I. Three rolls of 4" x 2".
J. One positioning machine.
K. Two belt filling machines per Company previously tested and found suitable, and to be delivered at Dump by Transport Officers.
L. All spare belts not being taken into action with the guns will be dumped at this dump by Companies before M.N. Y/Z night.
M. Five rolls of each Green and Brown netting camouflage.

The R.S.M. will be i/c of this dump.

Note.

The Mobile reserve of S.A.A. on wheels will not be used except in case of emergency when Company Transport Officers must have this replenished direct from Divisional Bomb Store.

The D.A.C. Mounted Orderly will be at the Battalion Forward Dump as a guide to S.A.A. Section at K. 36.c.9.3.

3. An advanced Armourers shop will be established at the dump by 10.0 p.m September 28th. The Armourer Staff Sgt and Company Artificers will do duty there, and the Q.M. will have the necessary tools sent forward.

4. All wire cutters to establishment must be in possession of the respective gun numbers.

5. Companies will make their own arrangements re disposition of cookers and water carts. The Hot Food Containers should be useful.

The water at the dump for drinking must only be called for in case of emergency.

6. A second issue of rations (for 30th) will be made at 3.0 p.m. to-morrow September 28th. A full issue of rum will also be drawn for n half issue on each of the two following days.

7. Pack animals must be used as much as possible for ration and water carrying.

8. Companies will wire by 2.0 p.m. to-morrow the proposed location for their forward transport lines.

9. Company Transport Officers will each send two mounted orderlies (conversant with location of and route to their proposed forward transpor t lines) to report to the Battalion dump by 12.0 midnight 28/29th September so that orders for transport to move forward etc etc can quickly be passed.

Over/

10. The Signalling Officer will have the Battalion Forward dump connected by telephone to HUDSON'S POST.
HUDSON'S POST will be the report centre, and the Signalling Officer will be established there with three signallers and four H.Q. runners.
Four H.Q. runners will be at Battalion Forward dump which will be a relay post for Company runners. Beyond the forward dump visual or runner communications will be adopted under orders to be issued by the Signalling Officer. Signallers attached to Companies will be prepared to take visual into use at any time.

11. Particular attention is drawn to 46th Division Administrative Instruction No 2 para 3. Rations and 4 Water

12. Indents for absolute requirements in Ordnance Stores will be sent through relay post to Advanced Battalion Headquarters.

12A. 'C' Company on crossing the CANAL will send back to the Relay Post 2 Runners stating roughly the situation and their requirements.
'A' and 'D' Companies will do likewise.

13. When the attack has made progress the Battalion forward dump will be moved forward to about G.34.d.3.5 under arrangements to be made by the Battalion Transport Officer.
The order for this move will be given by the Second-in-Command.

14. When this dump moves forward the Relay Post will move with it.

15. When Company Headquarters have moved forward a runner will be sent to the Relay Post stating the situation and location of Company Headquarters.

16. A supply tank (if available) conveying S.A.A. will make a dump at about G.35.a.9.9 (LA BARAQUE).

x 17. Casualties during heavy fighting.
(a) A Company that has suffered more than six casualties will send in numbers at 6.30 a.m., 10.30 a.m. and 4.30 p.m. daily (but no estimated report is to be sent unless six more casualties have occurred in that Company since the previous wire).
(b) In all casualty wires officers will be shown separately as heretofore.
(c) Note. Accurate casualty wires will continue to be sent in as at present to reach Advanced Headquarters through Relay Post by 4.30 p.m. daily.

18. ACKNOWLEDGE within Battalion.

27/9/18.

(Sd) R.DICKENS, Capt & Adjt,
46th Battn.Machine Gun Corps.

Distribution.

1. 46th Division.	10. T.O.'B' Coy.
2. 137th Inf:Bde.	11. T.O.'C' "
3. 138th : :	12. T.O.'D' "
4. 139th " :	13. Q.M.
5. A.Coy.	14. Signals.
6. B.Coy.	15.)
7. C.Coy.	16.)War Diary.
8. D.Coy.	17)
9. T.O.'A' Coy.	18) File.

S E C R E T.
****

Copy No 12

46th BATTALION MACHINE GUN CORPS ORDER No.63.

Reference Sheets 62.C.NE. & SE; 62.B.NW & SW.

Action of Machine Guns in detail.

Reference 46/12/609 (to Companies only).

1. On Y/Z night the Companies will take up assembly positions in readiness for the attack as under :-

'A' Company about G.33.c.3.5.
'B' Company about G.32.b.3.2.
'C' Company about G.26.d.9.5.
'D' Company about G.20.c.8.2.

Guns occupying positions in the line will not vacate their present positions till midnight Y/Z. Battalion commanders concerned will be informed before guns are moved.

2. In moving to assembly positions the greatest care must be taken to ensure that companies do not get scattered, as considerable movement of infantry will be taking place.

3. 'A' & 'D' Companies will form batteries to put down a barrage from as soon as possible after Zero, according to Group Organization Orders issued separately to 'A' & 'D' Companies.

After firing the barrage the companies will, as soon as bridges are constructed, cross the CANAL and advance to approximately :-

'A' Company H 31 c 9.9, H 31 b 6.7, H 25 d 8.3, H 19 b 8.3.
'D' Company H 32 d 2.2, H 26 d 5.5, H 26 b 5.4, H 20 a 7.3.

One section in each of the above localities.

'C' Company will assemble at G 26 d 9.5 and as soon as possible after the infantry have captured the BROWN Line will proceed forward to positions somewhere in the area of G.35 c 9.5, G 30 c 3.4, G 29 b 9.8, G 23 a 9.2, One section in each locality. When the YELLOW Line has been taken these sections will be advanced if necessary so as to be able to cover the YELLOW LINE.

The task of the sections which advance will be to consolidate the captured territory, to assist the infantry in their advance, and to sieze every opportunity of inflicting loss on the enemy.

Section Commanders will handle their sections with the greatest boldness and determination and although localities are indicated which will afford good positions the actual placing of the guns will be left entirely to the "Officers" on the spot, who will dispose them according to the tactical situation and the needs of the infantry.

'B' Company will be in Reserve and will be ready to move forward with pack or limber to any part of the Divisional Area immediately on receipt of orders.

'B' Company will also assist 'A' & 'D' Company in belt filling and Ammunition Supply under arrangements to be made between O.C.'B' Coy and Major H.S.WINDELER.

4. Instructions re transport will be issued later but in the meantime Companies should select suitable places for assembling their transport where it may easily be communicated with and brought up as the battle develops.

5. Tracing to follow.

6. ACKNOWLEDGE.

27/9/1918.

[signature]
Capt & Adjt,
46th Battn.Machine Gun Corps.

Over/

Distribution.

1. 46th Division.
2. 137th Inf: Bde.
3. 138th " "
4. 139th " "
5. C.R.A.
6. A.Coy.
7. B.Coy.
8. C.Coy.
9. D.Coy.
10. Signals.

11.)
12.)War Diary.
13)

14) File.

S E C R E T.
****

Copy No 16

46th BATTALION MACHINE GUN CORPS ORDER No 65.

Reference 1/20,000 OMISSY.

In continuation of Order No 63.

1. O.C.'B' Company will detail six guns to protect the Left flank of the Division. A suitable position will be found in G.28.a. or G.28.b.
   These six guns will not fire in the barrage, but will be prepared to engage any target which presents itself and to smash up a counter attack should one be made from the area between the attacks of the 46th and American Divisions.

2. The Officers Commanding Batteries of 'A' and 'D' Companies will ensure the keenest possible lookout being kept for targets East of the CANAL. Should any be seen it will be engaged with direct fire, guns being diverted from barrage fire for the purpose - the number of guns employed being determined by the importance of the target offered.

3. Officers Commanding guns going forward to consolidate objectives will report their positions to the Brigade Commander concerned as soon as possible afterbthe guns are in position.
   O.Cs.Companies will keep Battalion Headquarters fully infommed as to their positions and whereabouts.

4. Capt.A.R.M.DARBY, M.C. will report to the G.O.C, 137th Infantry Brigade at Zero - 60 minutes to act as liaison officer.

5. O.C.'C' Company will arrange to advance East of the CANAL as soon as possible after the Infantry. Orders for the move forward of 'A' and 'D' Companies will be issued by Battalion Headquarters.

6. Several hundred filled belts will be sent up to Battalion dump on Y day and will be drawn from there by barrage batteries under arrangements to be made by Major H.S.WINDELER.

7. Watches will be synchronized at Brigade Headquarters at 10.0 p.m. on Y day.

8. Thirty two 'T' Bases will be delivered to Battalion dump on afternoon of 28th September. 'A' and 'D' Companies will arrange for the conveyance of these to the Battery positions.

9. Each Company will have its fighting limbers complete with pack-saddlery in a sheltered position within easy reach of Battalion dump.
   Transport Officers will report to the second-in-command at Battalion dump at Zero - 30 minutes. They will bring their horses and mounted grooms. If possible visual communication will be arranged between dump and transport. Two runners per Company will report to Battalion dump Zero - 90 minutes. They will be retained and must know the whereabouts of their Company Headquarters.

10. ACKNOWLEDGE within Battalion.

27/9/18.

[signature]
Capt & Adjt,
46th Battn.Machine Gun Corps.

Distribution.

x 1. 46th Division.	x 7. C.Coy.	13. Q.M.
x 2. 137th Inf:Bde.	x 8. D.Coy.	14. Signals.
x 3. 138th Inf:Bde.	9. T.O.'A' Coy.	15.)
x 4. 139th Inf:Bde.	10. T.O.'B' Coy.	/16.)War Diary.
x 5. A.Coy.	11. T.O.'C' Coy.	17)
x 6. B.Coy.	12. T.O.'D' Coy.	18) File.

x 2 Tracings attached.

S E C R E T.
****

Copy No 11

46th BATTALION MACHINE GUN CORPS ORDER No 64A.

Amendments and additions to Order No 64.

Armourers Shop.

1. Only 'B' and 'C' Company Artificers will be at the Advanced Armourers Shop.
'A' and 'D' Company Artificers will remain at Transport lines or as ordered by Company Commanders.

Advanced Cold Shoeing Depot.

2. 1 Cold Shoer will be at the Battalion Forward Dump.

Runners.

3. 4 (four) Cyclist Orderlies from Division rationed to 29th inclusive will be attached to Battalion from to-day and will be disposed between HUDSON'S POST and Advanced Battalion H.Q. as arranged direct with Signals.

Communication.

4. Every possible means must be taken for keeping up communications.
Bridges across the CANAL must be reconnoitred as soon as is possible and 'A' and 'D' Companies will send forward reconnoitering parties as soon as possible after 137th Brigade have crossed the CANAL and this party will act as guides to the Companies and will watch the progress and the bridging of the CANAL.
Company Commanders must send back reports

by any available means (runners, cyclists or mounted orderlies) through the relay post to Battalion Headquarters.

[signature]
Capt & Adjt,
46th Battn.Machine Gun Corps.

28/9/18.

Distribution.

1. A.Coy
2. B.Coy
3. C.Coy
4. D.Coy.
5. T.O.'A' Coy.
6. T.O.'B' Coy.
7. T.O.'C' Coy.
8. T.O.'D' Coy.
9. Q.M.
10. Signals.
11.)
12.)War Diary.
13.)
14.) File.

S E C R E T.
****

Copy No 7

46th BATTALION MACHINE GUN CORPS ORDER No 66.

Reference 46th Battalion Machine Gun Corps Order No 65.

Para.1. O.C.'B' Company will detail 4 (four) guns only for the defence of the left flank.

The Americans are attacking the ground on our left and the greatest care will be taken not to fire on them. The only firing done by this section will be at direct targets definitely established to be Germans.

Later on in the attack this section will be relieved by guns of 2nd Life Guards Battalion.

As soon as the section is in position a runner will be sent back to Battalion Dump. He will be retained as a guide for 2nd Life Guards.

If possible the Section Commander will establish communication with the Americans.

Orders for the disposal of this Section will be issued to O.C.'B' Company by battalion H.Q. when the attack has progressed.

ACKNOWLEDGE.

Issued at 1.15 p.m.

28/9/18.

B. Aitken
Capt & Adjt,
46th Battn.Machine Gun Corps.

Distribution.

1. A.Coy.
2. B.Coy.
3. C.Coy.
4. D.Coy.
5. 2nd Life Guards Bn.
6.)
7.)War Diary.
8. File. (6)

S E C R E T.
****

Copy No 14

46th BATTALION MACHINE GUN CORPS ORDER No 68.

1. The Batteries of 46th Battalion machine gun corps will move forward to their Battery positions as soon as the 137th Infantry Brigade is clear of G.28 central and open fire on their tasks as early as possible. Great care must be taken that the infantry are sufficiently advanced to be safe before fire is opened. Firing must cease if succeeding infantry waves pass through the battery positions and not re-open until the infantry are a safe distance in front of batteries. Firing will be continued on the 1st Task until Zero + 153 mins and on the 2nd Task until Zero + 350 mins.

2. On Y/Z night the 137th Infantry Brigade will form upon their original jumping off line and attack at Zero as previously arranged.

3. The Officers Commanding 2nd Battn.(Life Guards) Guards M.G. Regt and 100th Battn.M.G. Corps will arrange that their batteries are in position by 2.0 a.m. Y/Z night.

4. The Officers Commanding 2nd Battn.(Life Guards) Guards M.G. Regt and 100th Battn.M.G. Corps will report when their batteries are in position to 46th Battn.M.G. Corps advanced Headquarters.

5. When the supporting Brigades (138th & 139th) and 'A' and 'D' Companies of 46th Battalion M.G. Corps are East of G.28 central the 2nd Battn.(Life Guards) Guards M.G.Regt will consolidate in depth from the trenches running through G.28 central to our original jumping off line. 40 (Forty) guns will be sent to the forward trenches. Particular attention will be paid to the flanks.

6. After the 100th Battn.M.G.Corps has completed the barrage task the O.C. will arrange for two companies to be ready to move East of the CANAL on receipt of orders. Their role will be to protect the flanks of the 46th Division and to engage any targets that may be seen. The remaining two companies will "Stand by" in the vicinity of their battery positions.

7. The Headquarters of the 46th Divisional Machine Gun Officer will be at advanced Division Headquarters at R.3.b.5.5.

8. Representatives of 2nd Battn.(Life Guards) Guards M.G. Regt, 100th Battn.M.G.Corps will be at the Divisional Machine Gun Officer's advanced Headquarters at 10.0 p.m. Y/Z night to synchronise watches.

9. Zero hour will be notified later.

10. Two Supply Tanks will follow advance and will dump S.A.A. etc at LA BARAQUE G.29.c.8.2. if possible

11. ACKNOWLEDGE.

28/9/18.

H.F. Waters, Major
for Lieut-Colonel,
46th Divisional Machine Gun Officer.

Distribution.

1. 46th Division.
2. 137th Inf:Bde.
3. 138th " "
4. 139th " "
5. 100th Bn.M.G.Corps.
6. 2nd Bn.(Life Guards)Gds M.G.Regt.
7. 30th American M.G.Bn.
8. 1st Bn. M.G.Corps.
9. A.Coy
10. B.Coy
11. C.Coy
12. D.Coy.
13.)
14.)War Diary.
15. File (8)

S E C R E T.
****

Copy No____

46th BATTALION MACHINE GUN CORPS ORDER No. 67.

1. The times for firing the barrages and rates of fire will be as follows :-

100th Battalion Machine Gun Corps.

Group.	Task.	Times From	To.	Rates of Fire.
No I.	1st.	Zero	Z + 330	5 mins - 250 R.P.M. 10 mins - 150 R.P.M.
	2nd.	Z + 28	Z + 330	30 mins - 50 R.P.M. 285 mins - 20 R.P.M.
No II	1st(a)	Zero	Z + 15	250 R.P.M.
	(b)	Zero	Z + 12	250 R.P.M.
	2nd.	Z + 12	Z + 15	250 R.P.M.
	3rd.	Z + 15	Z + 100	(2 mins. 250 R.P.M. (10 " 150 " (30 " 50 " (43 " 20 "
No III.	1st.	Z + 30	Z + 100	5 mins. 250 R.P.M. 10 " 150 "
	2nd.	Z + 60	Z + 100	30 -" 50 " 25 " 20 "

2nd Bn.(Life Guards) Guards M.G. Regt.

Group.	Battery.	Task.	Times From	To.	Rates of fire.
No IV	1.	1st	Zero	Z + 6	250 rds per min.
		2nd.	Z + 6	Z + 14	250 " " "
	2.	1st	Zero	Z + 8	250 rds per min.
		2nd.	Z + 8	Z + 14	250 " " "
	3.	1st.	Zero	Z + 8	250 rds per min.
		2nd.	Z + 8	Z + 15	250 " " "
No V.	4.	1st	Zero	Z + 10	250 rds per min.
		2nd.	Z + 10	Z + 15	250 " " "
	5.	1st.	Zero	Z + 10	250 rds per min.
		2nd.	Z + 10	Z + 15	250 " " "
	6.	1st.	Zero	Z + 8	250 rds per min.
		2nd.	Z + 8	Z + 14	250 " " "
	7.	1st.	Zero	Z + 5	250 rds per min.
		2nd.	Z + 5	Z + 13	250 rds per min.

H. E. Walter, Major
for Lieut-Colonel,
46th Divisional Machine Gun Officer.

28/9/18.

Distribution.

1. 46th Division.
2. 137th Inf:Bde.
3. 138th : :
4. 139th : :
5. 2nd Bn.(Life Gds) Gds M.G.Regt.
6. 100th Bn.M.G.C.
7. 30th American M.G.Bn.
8. 1st Div.M.G.Battn.
9. A.Coy.
10. B.Coy.
11. C.Coy.
12. D.Coy.
13.)War
14.) Diary.
15.File (5)

S E C R E T.
****

Copy No 17

46th BATTALION MACHINE GUN CORPS ORDER No 69.

Battn.H.Q.

1. Battalion Headquarters close at VRAIGNES and open at R.8.b.6.6 at 6.0 p.m. this day. (and not 10.0 p.m. as stated in Order No 64).

Camp.

2. The Q.M. will remain i/c of the Camp.

Tanks.

3. It is now notified that two supply Tanks will follow advance and will dump at LA BARAQUE G.29.c.8.2 a total of :-

   200 Shovels
   100 picks
   100 boxes (S.A.A.) clip
   100 boxes (S.A.A.) bundle
   100 gallons water
   100 boxes No 23.

Transport.

4. Company Transport Officers will notify Battalion H.Q. location of their Company Transport lines as at 4.0 p.m. this day and will notify changes as they take place

Solidified Alcohol.

5. Companies will be issued with special allotment of solidified alcohol as follows :-

   'A', 'B' & 'D' Companies 60 each.
   'C' Company 70

   An issue of chewing gum will also be made.

Casualties.

6. Reference Order No 64 para.17. A new phase for reporting estimated casualties will open midnight 30th Sept/1st October, 1918.

   Any estimates after that date will not include those submitted before that date.

Barrels.

7. 30 (Thirty) barrels will now be at the dump.

[signature]

Capt & Adjt,
46th Battn.M.G. Corps.

28/9/18.

Distribution.

1. A.Coy.
2. B.Coy.
3. C.Coy.
4. D.Coy.
5. Q.M.
6. Signals.
7. T.O.'A' Coy.
8. T.O.'B' Coy.
9. T.O.'C' Coy.
10. T.O.'D' Coy.
11.)
12.)War Diary
13. File.

Headquarters,
46th Division.

Secret

46/21/60

Herewith War Diary of the Battalion under my Command for the month of October, 1918.

Blicke Capt. & Adj.

5/11/1918.

Lieut-Colonel,
Commanding 46th Battn.M.G.Corps.

146

Secret

VR 8

Oct

****

46th BATTALION MACHINE GUN CORPS.

W A R   D I A R Y.

OCTOBER 1918.

****

Instructions regarding War Diaries and Intelligence Summaries are contained in F. S. Regs., Part II. and the Staff Manual respectively. Title pages will be prepared in manuscript.

Army Form C. 2118.

WAR DIARY

~~INTELLIGENCE SUMMARY~~

(Erase heading not required.)

OCTOBER 1918.

46th BATTALION MACHINE GUN CORPS.

No 1 Sheet.

Place	Date	Hour	Summary of Events and Information	Remarks and references to Appendices
VENDELLES	1st.		Our Machine Guns assisted a further advance by co-operating with the guns of 32nd Battalion Machine Gun Corps. 4 Officers reinforcements. 21 O.Rs. reinforcements. Order No 70 issued (copy attached) 2 O.Rs.Evac: 9 O.Rs. ~~Killed~~ Wounded. 1 O.R.Killed 1 Officer Wounded.	O.No 70
	2nd.		Preparations for a further advance were made. Amendment to Order No 70 issued (copy attached). 1 O.R. Wounded.	O.No 70A.
	3rd.		Successful operation was carried out. Machine Guns Companies were attached to Brigades and received orders direct from Brigade Commanders concerned. 5 Officers Wounded. 3 O.Rs.Evacuated. 68 O.Rs. Wounded. 14 O.Rs. Killed. 1 O.R. reinforcement. 2 Off: Killed.	
	4th.		Exploitation of yesterday's attack. Battalion Headquarters moved to LA BARAQUE. Order X issued copy attached. 1 O.R. Evacuated. 22 O.Rs. Wounded. 5 O.Rs. Killed. 1 Officer Wounded.	X.
LA BARAQUE.	5th.		Machine Gun Battalion withdrawn to rest W. of the CANAL and E.of ASCENSION VALLEY in accordance with Divisional Order G.114 (copy attached) Order Y issued (copy attached) 2 Officers reinforcements. 23 O.Rs. reinforcements. 9 O.Rs. Wounded.	Y.
VENDELLES.	6th.		Companies resting, cleaning up & training. Lieut.E.G.Holden to M.G.T.C.,Grantham. 6 Officers reinforcements. 6 O.Rs. Evacuated. 3 O.Rs. Wounded. 20 O.Rs. reinforcements.	
	7th.		Companies resting, cleaning up & training. 8 O.Rs. Evacuated. 1 O.R. Wounded. 1 Officer Wounded.	
MAGNY.	8th.		Companies moved forward with Brigades. Battalion Headquarters moved forward to MAGNY LA FOSSE. 'B' & 'C' Companies attached to 138th Brigade. G.164 (copy attached). ~~[illegible]~~	G.164.

D. D. & L., London, E.C. (A8004) Wt W1771/M2031 750,000 5/17 Sch. 52 Forms/C2118/14

Army Form C. 2118.

WAR DIARY
or
~~INTELLIGENCE SUMMARY.~~

(Erase heading not required.)

Instructions regarding War Diaries and Intelligence Summaries are contained in F. S. Regs., Part II. and the Staff Manual respectively. Title pages will be prepared in manuscript.

OCTOBER 1918.

46th BATTALION MACHINE GUN CORPS.

Sheet No 2.

Place	Date	Hour	Summary of Events and Information	Remarks and references to Appendices
MAGNY.	9th.		Machine Guns sent forward guns to assist attack on FRESNOY RAILWAY in accordance with G.191 (copy attached). Advance Guard formed. G.206.(copy attached) Capt.L.R.G.Heins to M.G.T.C.,Grantham. 2 Officers reinforcements. 2 O.Rs. Evacuated. 50 O.Rs. reinforcements.	G.191 G.208.
FRESNOY.	10th.		Battalion Headquarters moved forward to FRESNOY from MAGNY. 2 Companies sent forward with 137th & 139th Infantry Brigades 2 Companies in reserve at Divisional Headquarters (G.244,copy attached). 1 Officer Returned after evacuation. 2 O.Rs. Evacuated. 10 O.Rs. reinforcements.	G.244.
	11th.		G.277 issued (copy attached) Defensive measures taken in accordance therewith. 2 O.Rs. Evacuated. 1 O.R. Wounded.	G.277.
	12th.		During the period 10/14th Companies occupied positions in the forward area before BOIS DE RIQUERVAL and were attached to Brigades. No active operations were carried out during this period. 1 Officer returned after evacuation. 7 O.Rs. Evacuated. 1 O.R. Wounded.	
	13th.		2 O.Rs. Evacuated.	
	14th.		4 O.Rs. Evacuated. 2 O.Rs. Wounded. 30 O.Rs. reinforcements.	
	15th.		Preparations for the major operation mentioned in Order No 71 were made and completed. 2 O.Rs. Evacuated. Lt.C.J.Highwood & 2/Lt.E.A.Cowley to M.G.T.C.,Grantham.	
	16th.		Order No 71 issued (Copy attached. ~~amendment to Order No 71~~) 46/12/638 issued (copy attached). Amendment to Order No 71. 46/12/639 issued (Amendment to Order No 71) copy attached. 11 O.Rs. Evacuated. 1 O.R. Wounded	O.No 71. 46/12/638. 46/12/639.

D. D. & L., London, E.C. (A8004) Wt W1771/M2031 750,000 5/17 Sch. 52 Forms/C2118/14

Instructions regarding War Diaries and Intelligence Summaries are contained in F. S. Regs., Part II, and the Staff Manual respectively. Title pages will be prepared in manuscript.

WAR DIARY

~~INTELLIGENCE SUMMARY~~

(Erase heading not required.)

Army Form C. 2118.

OCTOBER 1918. 46th BATTALION MACHINE GUN CORPS.

Sheet No 3.

Place	Date	Hour	Summary of Events and Information	Remarks and references to Appendices
FRESNOY	17th.		Successful attack launched. Machine Guns (64 Guns) rounds fired 460,000. 8 Officers reinforcements. 2 Officers Wounded. 7 O.Rs.Evacuated. 21 O.Rs. Wounded. 4 O.Rs. Killed. 76 O.Rs.reinforcements.	
	18th.		Our Guns withdrawn to the vicinity of FRESNOY to rest billets. Lt.D.S.Gay, Wounded at duty & to hospital. 2 O.Rs. Evacuated. 5 O.Rs. Wounded. 1 O.R.Killed.	
	19th.		Cleaning up etc and general overhaul of equipment and transport. 1 O.R. Evacuated.	
	20th.		Divisional Parade Service (Ceremonial), and March Past. 1 Officer returned after evacuation. 2 O.Rs. reinforcements.	
	21st.		Report on Operations 17th October issued. (copy attached marked Z. 3 O.Rs. Evacuated.	Z.
	22nd.		2 O.Rs. Evacuated. During period Oct.21/31st general training carried out in area I 4, 5, 10, 11. This included Tactical Schemes and field firing. Range Practices were also carried out.	
	23rd.		2 O.Rs. Evacuated.	
	24th.		6 O.Rs. Evacuated. 1 O.R. reinfrocement.	
	25th.		'C' Company on the range. MajorC.V.Rigby, M.C. to M.G.T.C. Grantham. 8 O.Rs. Evacuated.	
	26th.		'B' Company on the range. 4 O.Rs. Evacuated. 15 O.Rs. reinforcements.	
	27th.		Battalion Parade. (Divine Service). 4 O.Rs. Evacuated. 33 O.Rs. reinforcements.	

D. D. & L., London, E.C. (A8094) Wt W1771/M2031 750,000 5/17 Sch. 52 Forms/C2118/14

Army Form C. 2118.

Instructions regarding War Diaries and Intelligence Summaries are contained in F. S. Regs., Part II. and the Staff Manual respectively. Title pages will be prepared in manuscript.

WAR DIARY

~~or INTELLIGENCE SUMMARY~~

(*Erase heading not required.*)

OCTOBER 1918.

46th BATTALION MACHINE GUN CORPS.

Sheet No 4.

Place	Date	Hour	Summary of Events and Information	Remarks and references to Appendices
FRESNOY	28th.		'A' Company on the range. 9 O.Rs. Evacuated. 2 Officers reinforcements.	
	29th.		11 O.Rs. Evacuated.	
	30th.		'D' Company on the range. 2 O.Rs. Evacuated. 2 O.Rs. reinforcements.	
	31st.		4 O.Rs. Evacuated. 19 O.Rs. reinforcements.	

Blicke, Capt. & Adjt.
for Lieut-Colonel,
Commanding 46th Battn.Machine Gun Corps.

D. D. & L., London, E.C.
(A8064) Wt W1771/M2031 750,000 5/17 Sch. 52 Forms/C2118/14

SECRET. Copy No.______

46th BATTALION, MACHINE GUN CORPS ORDER No. 40

Ref: Sheet 62.B,
1/40,000.

1st October, 1918.

1. Should the operations of to-day against the BEAUREVOIR LINE be successful, the cavalry will be pushing through between LEVERGIES and JONCOURT.

2. The 46th Division will be prepared to follow up this advance.

3. Should this operation take place, the Division will march as shown in the margin.
The Advanced Guard will be commanded by the G.O.C., 139th Inf: Bde:

4. The Order of March of the Main Body will be as shown in the margin.

5. The general direction of the march will probably be, in the first instance, N.E. towards MONTBREHAIN. The BELLENGLISE - JONCOURT & BELLENGLISE - LEVERGIES Roads should be reconnoitred.

6. Company Transport will be re-organised to-day.

7. Companies must, therefore, arrange for ample ~~ammunition~~ communication with their C.Q.M.S's., who will be ready to move to join their Company Headquarters, at short notice.

8. Should this move take place each Company would have one supply wagon with supplies and H.Q. one wagon.
Presumably no other transport would be available.
CQMS's should therefore hand in any surplus stores which the Q.M. will dispose of together with his surplus stores.

9. ACKNOWLEDGE.

Issued at 5.15 p.m.

1/10/18.

[signature]
Capt & Adjt,
46th Battn.M.G.Corps.

Advance Guard.
H.Q.- 139th Inf: Bde:
1 Bde, RFA.
1 Fd. Co. RE.
139th Inf: Bde:
'A' Coy: 46th Bn. MGC.
1 Coy, 1st Monmouthshire R.
Detachment, Field Amb'ce.
Detachment, IX Corps Cyclists.
Div'l: Mounted Troops.

Main Body.
Remainder of Artillery.
Remainder of RE.
137th Inf: Bde:
138th " "
H.Q., 46th Bn: MGC. & 'B' C
Field Ambulances.

137th Bde Group.
"A" Bn, 137th Inf: Bde.
1 Fd. Co, RE.
'C' Coy: 46th Bn. MGC.
"B" Bn, 137th Inf: Bde.
Remainder RFA.
1 Section, 6" How:) If
RGA: 1 Section, 60) avail-
pdr. guns, RGA.) able.
"C" Bn, 137th Inf: Bde.
"B" Field Ambulance.

138th Bde Group.
"A" Bn, 138th Inf: Bde.
1 Fd. Coy, RE.
D.Coy, 46th M.G.Bn.
"B" Bn, 138th Inf: Bde.
"C" Bn, 138th Inf: Bde.
Remainder HA.
Remainder 1st Monmouthshire R.
1 Coy
"C" Field Ambulance
Remainder of "A" Field Ambulance.

Distribution.

1. A.Coy.
2. B.Coy.
3. C.Coy.
4. D.Coy.
5. Second -in-Command.
6. B.T.O.
7. Q.M. (to notify CQMS's).
8. Signals.
9. 46th Division.
10. 137th Inf: Bde.
11. 138th Inf:Bde.
12. 139th Inf:Bde.
13. File (3)
14. War Diary (2).

S E C R E T.
****

Copy No 14

46th BATTALION MACHINE GUN CORPS ORDER No.70A.

Amendments to Order No 70.

1. Delete in Main body "H.Q.,46th Battn.M.G.Corps and 'B' Company." and substitute Remainder 46th Battalion M.G.Corps.

2. After "Remainder 1st Monmouthshire Regt" in 138 Brigade Group Add 'D' Company 46th Battn.M.G.Corps.

3. 137th Bde Group. To "Remainder RFA" add "less DAC". Add "A" Coy, Div'l Train."

4. 138th Bde.Group. Add "DAC" "B", "C", "D" Coys, Div'l Train."

2/10/18.

Capt & Adjt,
46th Battn.Machine Gun Corps.

Distribution.

1. A.Coy.
2. B.Coy.
3. C.Coy.
4. D.Coy.
5. Second-in-Command.
6. B.T.O.
7. Q.M. (to notify CQMS's).
8. Signals.
9. 46th Division.
10. 137th Inf:Bde.
11. 138th : :
12. 139th : :
13. File (3).
14. War Diary (2).

X.

SECRET.

Following from Division 4/10/18.

Night of 5/6th 138 Inf: Bde with 1/Monmouths and 46th M.G.Bn attached will relieve 3rd Brigade under G.O.C. 137th Brigade from N. Divisional boundary to a line H.24.d.9.5. H.24 central H.28 central AAA 139 Bde with 2/Life Guards M.G.Battn. and 9 Corps Cyclist Battn. will relieve 14 and 97 Brigades of 32nd Division from above line to a line I.32.a.0.0 N.4.a.0.0 AAA 137 Bde will be in reserve in MAGNY area AAA arrangements to be made between Brigades concerned in consultation with 46th M.G.C. AAA All reliefs to be complete by 0600 6th October AAA Time of passing of Divl Comd notified later AAA Line to be taken over runs H.36.c.5.2 where in touch with French SUNKEN ROAD to H.36.a.5.5 H.30.d.0.5 SUNKEN ROAD to H.19.c.0.0 AAA On relief 3rd 14th and 97 Bdes will move under orders of their Divisions.

1. For information.

2. The 2nd Life Guards M.G.Regt will arrange M.G. relief with 32nd M.G. Battalion and 139 Inf: Bde direct.

3. The disposition within this Battalion night 5/6th will be :-

B.)
) Companies 16 guns each in 138 Inf: Bde Sector.
D.)

A.)
) Companies in reserve at MAGNY.
C.)

(Sd) R.DICKENS, Capt & Adjt,
46th Battn.Machine Gun Corps.

4/10/18.

Distribution.

1. 2nd Life Guards M.G.Bn.
2. 32nd M.G.Bn.
3. 139th Inf: Bde.
4. 46th Bn.M.G.C. (Advanced) (5).

Y.

Following from Division, 5/10/18.

139 Bde plus 2/Life Guards will take over SEQUEHART Sector tonight from 97 and 14 Bdes as already arranged AAA 138 Bde plus 46 M.G. Bn and Pioneers will be prepared to take over from 137 Bde AAA 137 Bde H.Q. will be relieved by 6th Div AAA On relief 3rd Bde will concentrate on MAGNY LA FOSSE and move as directed by 1 Div AAA Cyclists on relief will come under orders of G.O.C., 138 Bde and be moved into Bde Reserve AAA 137 Bde H.Q. will join own Bde on command passing AAA All reliefs to be reported.

Following from Division 5/10/18.

A Bde of 6th Divn and NOT the 138th Bde will now be relieving the 3rd Bde and H.Q. 137 Bde tonight AAA Orders later AAA 138 and M.G.Bn to be prepared to withdraw to area W. of CANAL and E. of ASCENSION VALLEY AAA.

Major G.A.Wade, M.C.
O.C.'A' Coy.
" 'B' "
" 'C' "
" 'D' "

1. For information.

2. Machine Guns will be relieved as follows and probably tonight :-

1 Company 1st Division by 1 Company 6th Division.
'B' & 'D' Companies 46th Div. by 1 Coy 6th Div. in such position as G.O.C, Brigade desires.

3. All details to be arranged between Company Commanders concerned.

4. Completion reliefs to be wired to Battalion H.Q. by code word 'SQUARE'.

5. 'C' Company remain with their Transport and arrange for 'D' Company's accommodation.

6. 'A' Company move vide minute 2 and arrange 'B' Company's accommodation.

7. Guides between Companies and rendezvous can be arranged direct.

8. Companies on arrival at destination will each send one runner conversant with their Headquarters to report to and remain at Battalion Headquarters (near cross roads) LA BARAQUE) to convey any orders etc.

5/10/18.

(Sd) R.DICKENS, Capt & Adjt,
46th Battn.Machine Gun Corps.

"A" Form

Army Form C. 2121
(In pads of 100.)

MESSAGES AND SIGNALS.

No. of Message..............

Prefix.............. Code..............m | Words. Charge. | This message is on a/c of: | Recd. at...........m.

Office of Origin and Service Instructions

SDR to 137
138
139
6 Div.

Sent
At..................m.
To....................
By....................

.... Service.

....
(Signature of "Franking Officer.")

Date..................
From..................
By....................

TO 137 138 139 Bdes. MG Bn. Signals. CRA. CRE. ADMS. DAPM. Q. GSO I. 6 Div. IX Corps. 47 Fr: Div. File. War Diary.

Sender's Number.	Day of Month.	In reply to Number.	AAA
* G.164.	8th.		

The 138th Inf: Bde will relieve the 16 Inf: Bde in the Line as far NORTH as the grid line through I 9 central I 12 central tonight AAA 16 Bde HQ are at PRESELLES H 17 c AAA 138 Bde will make HQ in same neighbourhood AAA 138 Bde will take over line as he finds it and obtain touch with French AAA Line believed to include BEAUREGARD and MARICOURT AAA French believed to be in FONTAINE AAA 6th Div attacks JONNECOURT I 6 early tomorrow morning and shells FRESNOY and trenches I 17 central commencing about 5 am AAA 138 will patrol forward towards FRESNOY in early morning AAA If found to be unoccupied will occupy line of Rly from J 8 a 2.0 to I 30 b 3.7 gaining touch with French on RIGHT AAA If occupied by enemy report to be sent to DHQ and attack will be arranged AAA Cav; Patrols will also be reconnoitring early morning AAA 137 Bde will move to PRESELLES Area 139 Bde will move to PRESELLES Area with one Bn N.W. of HILL I 19 b 0700 AAA 139 Bde will concentrate LEVERGIES Area tomorrow morning AAA MG Bn will place two companies in line with 138 Bde

From

Place

Time

The above may be forwarded as now corrected. (Z)

.... Censor.

Signature of Addressor or person authorised to telegraph in his name.

* This line should be erased if not required.

(4715) Wt. W3253/P511 1,113,336 Shts. 2/18 C. & Co. (8434)

"A" Form

Army Form C. 2121
(In pads of 100.)

MESSAGES AND SIGNALS.

No. of Message..............

Prefix.............. Code..............m | Words. | Charge. | This message is on a/c of: | Recd. at...........m.

Office of Origin and Service Instructions

Sent

At.....................m.

To.......................

By.......................

.... Service.

(Signature of "Franking Officer.")

Date...........

From ....

By ....

TO

Sender's Number. | Day of Month. | In reply to Number. | AAA

tonight and be prepared to assist in attack
on FRESNOY tomorrow AAA 138 Bde will report
relief complete when command of RIGHT Sector
will pass to GOC 46 Div AAA Artillery
arrangements later.

From 46 Div:

Place

Time 2110

The above may be forwarded as now corrected.

(Z)

(Sgd) CF.Jerram,Lt-Col.

Censor.

Signature of Addressor or person authorised to telegraph in his name.

* This line should be erased if not required.

(4715) Wt. W3253/P511 1,113,330 Sbts. 2/18 C. & Co. (2324)

"A" Form

MESSAGES AND SIGNALS.

Army Form C. 2121
(In pads of 100.)

No. of Message..............

Prefix.............. Code...............m | Words. Charge.

Office of Origin and Service Instructions

SDR or wire whichever quickest.

At...............m.
To...............
By...............

This message is on a/c of:

.... *Service.*

(Signature of "Franking Officer.")

Recd. at...........m.
Date...............
From...............
By...............

TO CRA. CRE. Signals. 137 138 139. 1 Monmouths MG Bn. AA & QMG. DAPM. Div:Observers. GSO Iw File. War Diary. IX Corps. 6 Div: 126 Fr.Div: 5 Tank Bn. Div: Cav'y (Greys). 2nd Life Gds.

Sender's Number.	Day of Month.	In reply to Number.	AAA
* G.191.	9.		

Ref:Sheet 62.B. 1/40,000 The enemy appears to be making a general retirement from S.QUENTIN to CAMBRAI AAA Forward boundaries of IX Corps and 46th Div are shown on Map "B" about to be issued AAA 138 Bde will organise an a one Bn front keeping two Bns in hand for attack AAA 138 will patrol to Rly I 30 J 19 and 13 occupy this line if no opposition push patrols towards BOIS D'ETAVES and J 15 a AAA Should Rly be held an attack will be organised AAA Present information shows 126 French Divn advancing on our RIGHT with little opposition AAA 6th.Divn immediately W. of Rly in their area AAA Touch to be maintained with both flanks and a platoon (Officers Comd) detailed to move with French LEFT platoon AAA Cable will be laid forward on the line MERICOURT BOHAIN ANDIGNY LES FERMES being run to MERICOURT at once AAA Bde HQ will advance on this line and will esyablish as close as possible to it AAA On Rly being occupied French will take over up to new forward boundary and 46th Divn will adjust

From
Place
Time

The above may be forwarded as now corrected.

(Z)

Censor.

Signature of Addressor or person authorised to telegraph in his name.

* This line should be erased if not required.

(4715) Wt. W3253/P511 1,113,376 Shts. 2/12 C. & Co. (2884)

"A" Form
MESSAGES AND SIGNALS.

Army Form C. 2121
(In pads of 100.)

No. of Message..............

Prefix.......... Code..........m	Words. Charge.	This message is on a/c of:	Recd. at..........m.
Office of Origin and Service Instructions	Sent	.... Service.	Date..........
	At..........m.		From ....
	To..........		
	By..........	(Signature of "Franking Officer.")	By ....

TO (2)

Sender's Number.	Day of Month.	In reply to Number.	AAA
*			

accordingly AAA Two sections Tanks will move to Valleys about I 14 & 15 two sections remaining PRESELLES advanced section to be prepared to operate against FRESNOY in first instance and subsequently B. D'ETAVES and SEBONCOURT AAA 46 MG Bn will move guns to support attack on FRESNOY Rly AAA Artillery will prepare to put down barrage on Rly AAA Heavies on trenches in BOIS D'ETAVES and on W. side of SEBONCOURT AAA Other Units of Divn will remain for present in area now occupied except to move as directed by Q to get Divn into own area AAA On Rly being captured 138 Bde will organise an Ad. Guard on one Bn front composition HQ 138 Bde 1 troop Cavalry 1 Bde RFA DET.RE. 138 Inf: Bde 1 Supply Tank 1 MG Coy DET.F.Amb. AAA RE for purpose of road and water reconnaissance and repair of bridges J 13 b 9.3 J.13 B 9.9 J 2 a AAA CRA is arranging to place one Bde RFA at disposal 138 Bde at once AAA On Rly being taken 137 will move one Bn about MERICOURT two Bns MANNEQUIN HILL HQ to MARICOURT AAA Reports to Cable Head MERICOURT.

From 46 Div.
Place
Time 1230

The above may be forwarded as now corrected. (Z)

Censor.

(Sd) C.F.Jerram,Lt-Col.GS.
Signature of Addressor or person authorised to telegraph in his name.

* This line should be erased if not required.

(4715) Wt. W3253/P511 1,113,336 Shts. 2/18 C. & Co. (2684)

"A" Form

Army Form C. 2121 (In pads of 100.)

MESSAGES AND SIGNALS.

No. of Message............

Prefix...... Code......m	Words. Charge.	This message is on a/c of:	Recd. at......m.
Office of Origin and Service Instructions	Sent	.... Service.	Date........
Priority	At........m.		From ....
138.	To........	(Signature of "Franking Officer.")	By ....
	By........		

TO MG Bn.

Sender's Number.	Day of Month.	In reply to Number.	AAA
* G.208	9.		

Form Advanced Guard as in G.191 AAA Push patrols forward general direction of advance road J 2 a 8.8 – BOHAIN – D 22 d – ANDIGNY – WASSIGNY AAA One platoon cyclists on arrival in Divn will be attached 138 AAA Supply Tank ordered to rendezvous about I 15 c RE RAMC and MG's will report under arrangements made by CRE ADMS and Div: MG Comdr AAA Patrols should not get mixed up with organised resistance AAA Should such be met with an attack will be organised AAA 138 Bde will take over from 16 Bde line of Rly up to N. Div'l Boundary patrols being pushed to Northwards along Rly at once AAA If not possible in daylight relief will take place tonight AAA 6 Div supporting troops are along roads I 12 a & c.

From 46 Div.

Place

Time 1545

The above may be forwarded as now corrected.

(Z)

.... *Censor.*

(Sgd) CF.Jerram, Lt-Col.

Signature of Addressor or person authorised to telegraph in his name.

* This line should be erased if not required.

(4715) Wt. W3253/P511 1,113,336 Sbts. 2/18 C. & Co. (2884)

"A" Form
MESSAGES AND SIGNALS.

Army Form C. 2121
(In pads of 100.)

No. of Message..............

Prefix.............. Code..............m | Words. | Charge.

Office of Origin and Service Instructions

Sent
At....................m.
To......................
By......................

This message is on a/c of:
GOC
GSO I Service.
File (2)
War Diary (2).
(Signature of "Franking Officer.")

Recd. at...........m.
Date..................
From..................
By.....................

TO CRA. CRE. Signals, 137 138 139 Bdes.
1/Mons: R. MG.Bn: AA & QMG. ADMS. DAPM.
Div'l Observers. Det. Corps Cyclists.
5 Tank Bn. IX Corps. 6 Div: 126 Fr: Div.

Sender's Number.	Day of Month.	In reply to Number.	AAA
* G.244.	10th.		

Brigade groups for purposes of movement will be formed forthwith AAA Adv.Gd.Group is already formed AAA CRE ADMS & MG Bn. will attach to 137 & 139 Bdes one Fd.Coy one Fd.Ambce.and one MG Coy respectively AAA Remainder RE RAMC & MG will move with DHQ or as arranged with Gen:Staff AAA Objective for the day ANDIGNY LES FERMES & Ridge running N. & S. AAA Outposts to be placed E. of this Ridge AAA Line of resistance on Ridge AAA Objective of French is MENNEVRET AAA Dispositions to be taken up by dark AAA 138 Bde Group outposts HQ REGNICOURT if objective is taken AAA 137 HQ FRESNOY one Bn on Rly N. & well clear of Stn which is believed mined two Bns about FRESNOY Loading Bn ~~xxxRlyxN.~~ to be prepared to assist Adv.Gd in case of enemy attack AAA 139 Bde HQ FRESNOY Bde disposed about MERICOURT BEAUREGARD AAA DHQ to FRESNOY opening 1800 AAA Tanks and Divl Supply Tank to LANDRICOURT J 9 c AAA Artillery to keep close touch with situation and move so as to cover Outpost Line and enemy approaches E. of it AAA RE & Pioneers remain under CRE for work except those with Adv.Gd. and move will be arranged so far as possible not to interfere with work AAA CRE will place all labour possible on clearing the MERICOURT FRESNOY Road and the Road at J 2 a 9.8 AAA At latter place first work is to make diversion 100 yds N. of bridge.

From 46 Div.
Place
Time 1400

The above may be forwarded as now corrected. (Z)

(Sgd) CF.JERRAM, Lt-Col.
General Staff.

Censor. Signature of Addressor or person authorised to telegraph in his name.

* This line should be erased if not required.

(4715) Wt. W3253/P511 1,113,356 Sbts. 2/18 C. & Co. (2884)

"A" Form

MESSAGES AND SIGNALS.

Army Form C. 2121
(In pads of 100.)

No. of Message..............

Prefix.............. Code...............m

Office of Origin and Service Instructions

Words. Charge.

Sent

At...................m.

To.......................

By.......................

This message is on a/c of:

.... *Service.*

(Signature of "Franking Officer.")

Recd. at...........m.

Date..............

From ....

By ....

TO MG.Bn.

Sender's Number.	Day of Month.	In reply to Number.	AAA
* G.277	11th.		

Following defensive arrangements will be made AAA M.G.Coys one with Ad Guard one to road ~~J 4 d 2.8 AAA One to railway J 13 8 and 2~~ one in Reserve FRESNOY AAA Guns to be in position and lines of fire laid out and sufficient crews ~~at guns to man them in case of attack AAA 138~~ ~~Bde in event of attack will move one Bn to~~ x road J 4 d 2.8 and 2 Bns to road J 13-8 and 2 AAA 139 be prepared to counter attack AAA Artillery ~~will continue closely to support outpost line.~~

From 46th Div.

Place

Time 19.10

The above may be forwarded as now corrected.

(Z)

.... *Censor.*

(Sd) C.F.Jerram, Lt-Col.

Signature of Addressor or person authorised to telegraph in his name.

* This line should be erased if not required.

(4715) Wt. W3255/P511 1,113,336 Shts. 2/18 C. & Co. (2834)

S E C R E T.
****

Copy No 18

46th BATTALION MACHINE GUN CORPS ORDER No.71.

Reference accompanying Maps "A".

1. (a) The 46th Division will attack in a S.E. direction with objective the Road running through squares E.13.b. - 14 - 9 - 10 - ANDIGNY-LES-FERMES E.11.a.0.7 on October 17th with two Brigades, 139th Infantry Brigade on the right, 138th Infantry Brigade on the left, 137th Infantry Brigade holding present line.
The attack is being continued on our left by the 6th Division and the French are attacking from the South. The 138th Infantry Brigade will be prepared, on receipt of orders to join hands with the French along the MENNEVRET - ANDIGNY Road. The 1st Division is following the 6th Division and exploiting success EASTWARD.

(b) Men must be warned that the Forest has been gassed and must be prepared to adjust their gas masks on moving through it.

(c) The Western edge of the Artillery Barrage Zone is a line D.12.a.C.7 - E.13.d.0.5.

(d) Divisional H.Q. will remain in its present location.
138th Inf:Bde & 139th Inf:Bde H.Q. will be together at D.11.b.5.0.

(e) On attached map are shown :-

(a) Jumping Off Line GREEN.
(b) Divisional Boundaries BROWN.
(c) Inter Brigade Boundary. YELLOW
(d) Line held by us at present. RED.
(e) Objective. BLUE.

The infantry will consolidate with their advanced posts well to SOUTH of the Road.

(f) One Section of three tanks has been allotted to the Division; they will move forward with the supporting infantry to the Strong Point about E.1.d. They will move along the line of trenches to E.13.b.7.0, when one will continue along the trench to D.19.b.9.5, the other two moving EAST to assist in the mopping up of REGNICOURT & ANDIGNY-LES-FERMES.

(g) Aeroplanes will call for flares at C plus one hour thirty minutes.

(h) Six Brigades R.H.A. & R.F.A. will put down the barrage.
General principle of the barrage will be :-

(1) A thick 18 pdr barrage with one round smoke per lift.
(2) A 4.5 How. barrage beyond the 18 pdrs.

The 4.5 Hows. will fire in the barrage until such time, as the infantry reach the crest on the line of the BOHAIN - ANDIGNY Road, when they will lift on to the N. edge of the FORET D'ANDIGNY and fire smoke shell.

(i) Dummy Tanks & Dummy Figures will be placed in position during Y/Z night so as to be apparent at dawn, and simulate an attack on the BOIS DE RIQUERVAL from a Westerly direction.
A special Rolling Barrage will come down at ZERO on a line at safety distances from our Advanced Posts and will move through the BOIS DE RIQUERVAL in an EASTERLY direction at the rate of 100^x in 4 (four) minutes.
On reaching the open space E.26.a. - E.20.c.& a, the barrage will rest until the main barrage replaces it, or, in the case of the SOUTHERN Portion, until the main barrage ceases.

(j) The forming up line will not be taken over from the 6th Division. The 138th & 139th Infantry Brigades will be in position by ZERO - 1 (one) hour.
The reserve Battalion of the 139th Infantry Brigade will take up a position about D.18.a. avoiding the Valley in D.18.b. 12.d.

(k) A large proportion of entrenching tools will be carried by the Infantry and Machine Gun Personnel.

/over

Action of Machine Guns.

(2) (a) Two companies of the 2nd Life Guards M.G.Battn and one company of the 6th Battn.M.G.Corps will assist the Division by placing a barrage in accordance with the attached Fire Organization Orders, and as shown on attached map.

(b) 'A' Company is detailed to assist the 139th Infantry Brigade and will arrange details with G.O.C., 139th Inf:Bde.

'B' Company is detailed to assist the 138th Infantry Brigade and will arrange details with G.O.C. 138th Inf: Bde.

'C' Company is in the line with 137th Infantry Brigade and will have a dual role (a) To defend the original Divisional Front by direct fire if necessary.

(b) To barrage RIQUERVAL WOOD in accordance with attached Fire Organization Orders.

'D' Company will send forward 8 (eight) guns as soon as possible after the barrage to the high ground about E.7.b.central to fire at intense rate 0 - 72 on ANDIGNY - LES - FERMES in support of our advancing infantry. These guns will remain here and be ready to fire again if called upon.

The remaining 8 (eight) guns of 'D' Company will be in reserve at NORTH EAST end of BOHAIN ready to move instantly with limbers.

'D' Company will move to assembly positions at dusk Y/Z night.

(c) A dump of 500 boxes of S.A.A. has been formed at D.12.a.00.50. This is available for the use of companies of 46th Battn.M.G.Corps and also Companies of the 2nd Life Guards M.G.Battn. and 6th Battn. M.G.Corps who are assisting 46th Division.

(d) Company Commanders of 'A', 'B' & 'D' Companies will be at Brigade Headquarters at ZERO and will arrange for runners from Sections to report there.

(3) ACKNOWLEDGE.

Note. In view of the number of civilians in the area it is more than ever important that these operations should be kept SECRET.

Issued at 12.00

[signature]

15/10/18. Major,
46th Battn.Machine Gun Corps.

Distribution.

* 1. 46th Division.	* 10. A.Coy.
* 2. C.R.A.	* 11. B.Coy.
* 3. C.R.E.	* 12. C.Coy.
4. 137th Inf:Bde.	* 13. D.Coy.
5. 138th Inf:Bde.	14. D.T.O.
6. 139th Inf:Bde.	15. Signals.
* 7. 2nd Lige Gds M.G.Bn (10)	16. Q.M.
* 8. 6th Bn.M.G.Corps (5)	17. File (2)
9. 1st Bn.M.G.Corps.	18. War Diary. (2)

Maps only sent to those marked *

S E C R E T.

File

40TH BATTALION,
M. G. CORPS.
46/12/639

O.C. 'A' Coy.
" 'B' "
" 'C' "
" 'D' "
" 2nd Life Guards M.G.Battn.
" 6th Bn. M.G.Corps.

Reference 46th Btn.M.G.Corps Order No 71.

1. ZERO hour will be 05.20 1[illegible]/10/18.

2. ZERO for the Machine Gun Barrage will be the moment the Artillery Barrage commences.

3. ACKNOWLEDGE.

16/10/18.

A. K. Darby Capt
~~Major~~
for Lieut-Colonel,
Commanding 46th Battn. M.G.Corps.

S E C R E T.

FIRE ORGANIZATION ORDERS. ATTACK BY 46th DIVISION. Issued at 11.00 16/10/18.

Ref: Maps 62.B.N.E. 1/20,000

UNIT.	No of Guns.	Approximate Position.	Tasks to be as near as safety will allow to following points:-	Rate of fire.	Times Zero Plus.	Remarks.
46th Btn.	4	J.6.c.62.82	E.25.c.40.70 to E.25.c.30.80 to E.19.d.85.60 to E.20.c.05.45.	250 p.m.	0 to + 5	Fire on this
M.G.Corps.	4	J.4.b.90.20	E.25.c.30.45 to E.25.a.00.35 to E.25.a.60.70 to E.25.d.05.60.	100 per	5 to 123	target in
'C' Coy.	4	J.5.a.82.95	E.19.c.75.50 to E.19.c.52.82 to E.19.b.30.45 to E.19.b.55.00	minute.		case of S.O.S
	4	D.28.d.72.50	D.30.b.80.40 to D.30.b.70.85 to E.19.c.95.30 to E.25.b.10.60.			or disturbance after + 123.
2nd Life Guards.	8	D.12.c.	(1) E.19.b.30.45 to E.13.d.70.60 to E.14.c.15.40 to E.19.b.65.10	do	0 to 123	And in case of S.O.S. or disturbance after + 123
	8	do	(2) E.7.b.20.10 to E.1.d.25.10 to E.1.d.80.55 to E.7.b.80.30	100 p.m.	0 to 20	
	16	do	(3) Trench E.1.d.55.30 to E.2.b.1.4.	100 p.m.	0 to 21	
	24	do	(4) E.7.d.20.45 to E.7.d.20.80 to E.7.d.85.75 to E.7.d.80.55	100	21 to 33	
	24	do	(5) E.7.d.20.20 to E.7.d.20.40 to E.8.c.20.50 to E.8.c.20.20	do	33 to 42	
	16	do	(6) E.13.b.50.60 to E.7.d.50.15 to E.8.c.20.30 to E.14.a.15.45	do	42 to 48	
	8	do	(7) E.14.c.00.55 to E.14.c.10.90 to E.14.c.40.80 to E.14.c.30.45	do	42 to 60	
	16	do	(8) E.14.a.50.55 to E.14.a.60.85 to E.14.b.10.85 to E.14.b.05.30	do	48 to 60	
	12	do	(9) E.14.d.80.35 to E.14.d.95.90 to E.15.c.05.25 to E.15.c.20.85	do	60 to 123	And in case of S.O.S. or disturbance after + 123.
	12	do	(10) E.20.a.95.00 to E.20.b.44.90 to E.20.b.80.70 to E.20.d.25.30	do	60 to 123	
6th Bn.	16	D.18.b.	(a) E.8.a.60.60 to E.8.a.40.85 to E.2.b.70.25 to E.3.d.05.90	do	0 to 30	
M.G.Corps.	16	do	(b) E.8.a.90.20 to E.8.a.70.45 to E.3.c.20.70 to E.3.c.50.35	do	30 to 42	
	16	do	(c) Road E.14.a.70.50 to E.9.d.30.60	do	42 to 60	
	8	do	(d) Valley E.15.a.10.20 to E.15.a.10.60 to E.15.b.40.80 to E.15.b.50.30	do	60 to 123	& S.O.S.) or
	8	do	(e) E.21.a.30.00 to E.15.c.70.10 to E.15.d.30.00 to E.21.c.90.80	do	60 to 123	& S.O.S.) disturbance after + 123.

C. A. Wade [signature]

Major,

46th Battn. Machine Gun Corps.

SECRET.

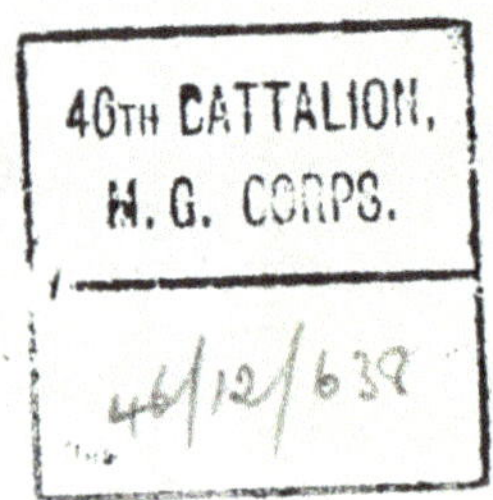

O.C. 'A' Coy.
" 'B' "
" 'C' "
" 'D' "
" 'C' Coy., 6th Bn.M.G.Corps.
" 2nd Life Guards M.G.Battn.

1. The Artillery barrage will now lift from the protective barrage line at ZERO + 105 and will continue on S.O.S. Line till plus 123 minutes.

2. The following alterations are therefore made in the Machine Gun Barrage :-

Task I.

8 (eight) guns will fire on area E.19.b.50.45 to E.13.d.70.60 to ; E.14.c.15.10 to E.19.b.65.10 from ZERO to Plus 60 and will then lift to area E.20.c.70.15 to E.20.c.40.45 to E.20 central to E.20.d.25.30 and will fire till Plus 123 and in case of S.O.S.

'C' Coy, 6th Battn.M.G.Corps.
Task 'D'

Valley E.15.a.10.20 to E.15.a.10.60 to E.15.b.40.80 to E.15.b.50.30 will be fired on from ZERO + 60 to ZERO + 103 and all guns will then traverse 10° right bringing barrage on to area E.15.c. & d. which will be fired on till + 123 and in case of S.O.S.

"C" Coy, 46th Battn.M.G.Corps

Battery firing on area
E.19.c.75.50 to E.19.c.52.82 to E.19.b.50.45 to E.19.b.55.00 will fire on it from ZERO till ZERO + 103 and will then switch 10° right on to area in E.19.d. which will be fired on till ZERO + 123 and in case of S.O.S.

3. Care must be taken to ensure that no one passes across the front of guns whilst firing. Sentries will be placed on flanks for this purpose.

4. Fire will not be opened at ZERO till Artillery barrage comes down.

5. ACKNOWLEDGE.

19/10/18.

Major,
for Lieut-Colonel,
Commanding 46th Battn.M.G. Corps.

Z

Report on Operations on October 17th, 1918.

1. The role of the machine guns was as follows :-

One Company was allotted to each of 137th, 138th & 139th Infantry Brigades and one remained in reserve.

Two Companies of the 2nd Life Guards Machine Gun Battalion and one Company of the 6th Battalion Machine Gun Corps were allotted to the 46th Division, for Barrage Purposes.

2. The company attached to the 137th Infantry Brigade had a dual role
(1) To defend by direct fire, if necessary, the original Divisional area West of RIQUERVAL WOOD.
(2) To barrage the Wood in E.25.a., b & c, and in E.19 from ZERO till ZERO + 125.

Four guns were placed at each of following positions :-

J 6 c 82.82	J 8 a 82.95
J 4 b 90.20	D 28 d 70.50

This company expended 82,000 rounds in the latter task, two sections having to fire for ¾ of an hour in box respirators on account of Green Cross Shells which fell about J 6 b & d.

At 07.45 the Officer Commanding the Section at J 6 c 82.82 reported that the enemy was shelling the wood in E 25 c & d.

This information was forwarded to the 137th Infantry Brigade and patrols were sent into the Wood.

One patrol returned at about 09.30 having penetrated to the clearing in E 20 c & 26 a.

At 14.00 the 137th Infantry Brigade ordered two sections forward to support a battalion of infantry in E 14 & 20.

One section was sent to about E 26 a 40.80 and another to about E 13 d 90.20.

The remaining two sections were disposed for direct fire on to Western edge of the BOIS DE RIQUERVAL, one section at J 6 b 2.4 and one at D 29 c 1.3.

3. The Machine Gun Barrage lasted from Zero till Zero + 123 minutes. It progressed by bounds in front of the advancing infantry and was carried out in accordance with the Fire Organization Orders issued with 46th Battalion Machine Gun Corps Order No 71 of 16/10/18, slight alterations being made in the lifts to conform with alterations in the "artillery barrage".

Four hundred and sixty six thousand rounds were expended.

4. The Company operating with the 139th Infantry Brigade had tasks as follows :-

No 1 section was to assemble in rear of left company 8th Battalion Sherwood Foresters and to follow to objective E 9 c 3.2.

No 2 section was to assemble in rear of 'B' Company, 8th Battalion Sherwood Foresters and was to follow them through E 7 d, E 8 c and REGNICOURT consolidating on objective ORCHARD E 14 a.

No 3 section lined up in rear of 'C' Company 8th Battalion Sherwood Foresters and was to assist in consolidation of wood E 14 c.

No 4 section assembled in rear of 'D' Company 8th Battalion Sherwood Foresters and was to occupy embankment E 13 b.

Sections advanced at ZERO + 9 minutes.

No 1 Section proceeded towards high ground E 7 b. At 05.50 the officer & N.C.O. were wounded by close range Machine Gun Fire and the section halted 100x in rear. Two gun teams then moved to high ground D 6 d. where they joined No 4 section. The remaining sub-section was placed by Major Rigby of 'B' Company in trench E 7 b 7.7

<u>No 2 Section.</u>

At 07.00 approximately three guns were at E 13 a 9.5 and were moved by the Company Commander and placed with the infantry along embankment E 13 b 30.15.

The infantry were forced to withdraw at 08.00, one gun team went with them. Reinforcements almost immediately reoccupied the embankment and the section officer moved the two guns to high ground E.13.b.7.7.

No 3 Section.

In the mist the section lost touch with the infantry but moved forward and posted two guns in embankment E 15 b 7.6 and two guns in trench in front.

At 11.30 the section again advanced and dug in on spur E 14 c 6.6.

No 4 Section, proceeded up valley E 1 c, E 7 a & d where they were fired on by enemy Machine Guns in the clearing. Section came into action and were about to engage enemy when an infantry officer arrived, stating that his own troops were mopping up the clearing.

Troops of the 1st Division then came up from the rear, firing on the section and finally charging them. The Section Officer showed them where they were and they then moved off through E 7 b.

Owing to the wood not being mopped up the section withdrew under fire to D 6 d, being joined there by two gun teams of No 2 Section, previously mentioned, and by two of No 1 Section.

Four strong teams were organized and the remaining guns etc were sent to Company Headquarters at D 6 c 00.25.

At 10.00 the section pushed forward on to high ground E 9 c on the forward slope, but was forced back on to the reverse slope by artillery and Machine Gun fire.

At 19.00 reinforcements arrived and two gun teams with guns were sent up to Nos 1 & 2 Sections, 16 (sixteen) guns being in action at 20.00.

5. The Company operating with the 138th Infantry Brigade had orders to push two sections forward with the infantry battalions and to get two guns into each of the posts to be established at :-

E 10 b 5.6.
E 10 d 1.9.
E 9 c 9.3.
E 9 c 7.2.

Two sections were to watch the left flank and ANDIGNY-LES-FERMES in case of attack not succeeding, or in case of counter attack.

The Company formed up on the East side of the road from W 25 c 2.0 to W 26 b 8.5.

Teams were small and each section took two pack mules carrying belt boxes.

Teams and mules were in place by 00.46.

The guns moved forward at Zero as closely as possible in support of the infantry.

At 15.00 their disposition was as follows :-

2	guns	E 10 b 5.8.
2	:	E 10 d 1.9.
2	:	E 9 c 9.3.
2	:	E 9 c 7.2.
4	:	E 9 a 8.5.
4	:	E 3 a 7.8.

The guns remained in these positions till withdrawn on evening of 18th.

6. Eight guns of the reserve company advanced close behind the barrage with orders to support the advance of the infantry by direct overhead covering fire from the high ground in E 7 b. on to ANDIGNY-LES-FERMES. When they advanced to this position they found that it was strongly held by the enemy who greeted them with machine gun fire. The sections withdrew and waited till the trenches had been mopped up. It was then too late to afford covering fire so the sections took up defensive positions to deal with any counter attack.

7. Owing to the mist no favourable targets were seen but had the enemy counter attacked heavily at any time he would have found our machine guns in great strength and amply supplied with ammunition.

8. Our casualties in this operation were :-

Officers	3
O.Rs.	32.

Major,

Commanding 46th Battn.M.G.Corps.

21/10/18.

Instructions regarding War Diaries and Intelligence Summaries are contained in F. S. Regs., Part II. and the Staff Manual respectively. Title pages will be prepared in manuscript.

46TH BATTALION. M. G. CORPS.

Army Form C. 2118.

No 46/2/1 14-1-19.

WAR DIARY

~~or INTELLIGENCE SUMMARY.~~

(Erase heading not required.)

NOVEMBER 1918.

46th BATTALION MACHINE GUN CORPS.

Sheet No 1.

Vol 19

Place	Date	Hour	Summary of Events and Information — Ref: Sheet 57.B. & 57.A. 1/40,000	Remarks and references to Appendices
BOHAIN.	1st.		Commanding Officer inspected all Transport. 7 O.Rs. Evacuated sick. 1 O.R. rejoined from Third Army Worskhops.	
	2nd.	10.00 11.00	Order No 74 issued (copy attached) Order No F/1 issued (copy attached). 8 O.Rs. Evacuated sick. 2 O.Rs. reinforcments.	O.No 74 O.No F/1.
	3rd.		Order No F/2 issued (copy attached) 3 Companies guns detached for duty with 1st Division proceeded to the line and dug in West of Sambre - Oise Canal. 1 Coy was in immediate support. 8 O.Rs. Evacuated sick. 1 Officer wounded. 1 O.R. reinforcement.	O.No F/2.
L'ARBRE de GUISE.	4th.	05.45 10.30	3 Companies guns fired in the barrage prior to the 1st Division attack on the SAMBRE-OISE CANAL. 20,000 rounds were fired. Guns ceased to come under orders of 1st Division,and 3 Coys joined their Infantry Brigades, which passed through the 1st Division after the crossing of the Canal. 'A' Coy went into Divisional Reserve. 2 O.Rs. evacuated sick. 12 O.Rs. wounded. 6 O.Rs. reinforcements.	
	5th.		No 148842 L/Cpl.(now Cpl) G.Webb awarded M.M. 10.000 rounds fired indirect fire on to supposed minor opposition in the advance. 2 O.Rs. wounded.	
	6th.		Battalion Headquarters moved from L'Arbre de Guise to CATILLON M.19.b.10.50 10,000 rounds fired harassing fire on tracks at night. 1 Section guns engaged successfully hostile movement near HAUT LIEU. 2 O.Rs. Evacuated sick.	
	7th.		Battalion Headquarters moved from CATILLON to PRISCHES. 1 O.R. Wounded. 2 O.Rs.Evac:sick.	
	8th.		The advance continued with little opposition from the enemy and only occasionally were pairs or sections of guns required to engage targets.	
	9th.		ditto ditto. 2 O.Rs. Evacuated sick.	

D. D. & L., London, E.C.
(A8:04) Wt W1771/M2031 750,000 5/17 Sch. 52 Forms/C2118/14

Army Form C. 2118.

Instructions regarding War Diaries and Intelligence Summaries are contained in F. S. Regs., Part II. and the Staff Manual respectively. Title pages will be prepared in manuscript.

WAR DIARY or ~~INTELLIGENCE SUMMARY.~~

46th BATTALION MACHINE GUN CORPS

NOVEMBER 1918.

(Erase heading not required.)

Sheet No 2.

Place	Date	Hour	Ref: Sheet 57.B. & 57.A. 1/40,000 Summary of Events and Information	Remarks and references to Appendices
	10th.		The advance continued with little opposition from the enemy and only occasionally were pairs or sections of guns required to engage targets. 1 O.R. Accidentally wounded.	
	11th.	08.00 11.00	Battalion Headquarters moved from PRISCHES to SAINS DU NORD. A R M I S T I C E came into force.	
	12th.		Training commenced. Major G.A.WADE, M.C. awarded Bar to M.C. Major W.T.BOUGHEY) " H.S.WINDELER) Awarded M.C. Lieut.W.H.HOFF) 3 O.Rs. Evacuated sick.	
	13th.		2 O.Rs reinforcements.	
	14th.		Battalion Headquarters moved from SAINS DU NORD to BOUSIES. 33 O.Rs. reinforcements. 1 Officer returned from M.G.T.C., Grantham.	
	15th.		1 O.R. Evacuated sick.	
	16th.	11.00	Battalion inspected by the Divisional Commander who presented immediate award M.M. to O.Rs. of this Battalion. 1 Officer to M.G.T.C., Grantham. 34 R.Rs. reinforcements. 3 O.Rs. Evacuated sick.	
	17th.	10.30	Divisional Parade Divine Service at LANDRECIES. Divisional Commander presented M.C. to Major W.T.BOUGHEY and Croix de Guerre to Sgt.Abbott.	
	18th.		Commanding Officer inspected Battalion Transport. 1 Officer Evacuated sick. 2 O.Rs. Evacuated sick.	
	19th.		1 O.R. Evacuated sick. 2 O.Rs. Reinforcements.	
	20th.		1 O.R. Evacuated sick.	

D. D. & L., London, E.C. (A8094) Wt W1771/M2031 750,000 5/17 Sch. 52 Forms/C2118/14

Army Form C. 2118.

WAR DIARY
or
~~INTELLIGENCE SUMMARY.~~
(Erase heading not required.)

Instructions regarding War Diaries and Intelligence Summaries are contained in F. S. Regs., Part II. and the Staff Manual respectively. Title pages will be prepared in manuscript.

NOVEMBER 1918. 46th BATTALION MACHINE GUN CORPS.

Sheet No 3.

Place	Date	Hour	Ref:Sheet 57.B. & 57.A. 1/40,000 Summary of Events and Information	Remarks and references to Appendices
	21st.		Battalion commenced Salvage work on the MORMAL Forest.	
	22nd.		Continued with Salvage work. 3 O.Rs. Evacuated sick.	
	23rd.		Continued with Salvage. 3 O.Rs. Evacuated sick. 4 O.Rs. Reinforcements.	
	24th.		ditto 1 Officer to Ministry of Labour.	
	25th.		ditto 32 O.Rs. Reinforcements.	
	26th.		ditto 2 O.Rs. Reinforcements.	
	27th.		Battalion Transport by Companies marched past the Divisional Commander. 9 O.Rs. Reinforcements.	
	28th.		Continued with Salvage. 15 O.Rs. Evacuated sick.	
	29th.		ditto 38 O.Rs. to U.K. Coalminers. 7 O.Rs. to Base Depot.	
	30th.		ditto 1 Officer to Base from Hospital.	

[illegible] Capt. & Adjt.
for Lieut-Colonel,
Commanding 46th Battn.Machine Gun Corps.

D. D. & L., London, E.C.
(A8004) Wt W1771/M2031 750,000 5/17 Sch. 52 Forms/C2118/14

S E C R E T.
****

Copy No _____

46th BATTALION MACHINE GUN CORPS ORDER No. 74.

OPERATION F.

Reference WASSIGNY 1/40,000

1. On a date Z the IX Corps is attacking the SAMBRE - OISE CANAL in conjunction with the XV French Corps on the Right and the XIII British Corps on the Left.

2. The 1st Division is attacking on the Right of the Corps Front. The 32nd Division is attacking on the Left.

3. The 46th Division will be in Reserve and will be prepared to relieve the 1st Division after its capture of the final objective and exploit success to the Eastward.

4. 'A', 'C' & 'D' Companies will take part in the initial barrage under the orders of the 1st Division. Companies will ensure their teams are well dug in.
'B' Company will work with 138th Infantry Brigade.

5. 'C' Company on completion of their barrage will work with 139th Infantry Brigade.
'A' and 'D' Companies on completion of their Barrage will move into Divisional Reserve about MAZINGHIEN.

6. Subsequent Moves. (a) 138th Inf: Bde will be prepared, on receipt of orders, to move to the line of the road X 11 b - R 30, with a view to :-

(i) Supporting the 1st Division, if required to do so.
(ii) Relieving the RIGHT Brigade of the 1st Division.

(b) 139th Inf: Bde will be prepared to move so as to bring its head on the cross roads R 28 d, with a view to relieving the LEFT Brigade of the 1st Division.

(c) 137th Inf: Bde will be prepared to move to the LA LOUVIERE Area E. of the R 33, 34 Grid, to be in Divisional Reserve after the relief of the 1st Division.

7. Advanced Battalion Headquarters will be established at MOLAIN W 16 c. (with Advanced Divisional H.Q.) by 08.00 Z day.

8. Battalion report centre for all messages will open at Brigade Signal Office L'ARDRE DE GUIZE (W 6 b.) at 18.00 Y day. Advanced Battalion Headquarters will be in telephonic communication with the Report Centre.

9. 137th, 138th & 139th Infantry Brigade Headquarters will be at L'ARDRE DE GUIZE from 08.00 Z day.

10. Should the 1st Division be relieved approximately on the Red line:- Battalion Headquarters will be at L'ARDRE DE GUIZE (W 6 b.) with Advanced Divisional Headquarters.
Brigades in line at BOIS DE L'ABBAYE (M 32 c).
Reserve Brigade at LA LOUVIERE (R 35 c).

11. An Intelligence Map showing Artillery Barrage of 1st Division and bridging arrangements for crossing the Canal has been issued to Companies. The main Traffic route for advance on Z plus 1 day will be MAZINGHIEN - S 9 c. - FESMY - LE SART - PRISCHES - CARTIGNY Road Bridges in 32nd Division area will not be used by 46th Division unless it is required to support the 32nd Division.
As soon as Bridges are capable of taking wheeled Traffic they will be so labelled.

/Over.

12. For the initial Barrage tho 1st Machine Gun Battalion are making S.A.A. dumps at :-

X 4 d 7.2 (Estaminet in REJET DE BEAULIEU)
X 5 a 2.2 (Farm)
X 18 c 3.8 (Side of Track).

13. Tho usual aeroplane signals will be used.
Other light signals boing :-
S.O.S. RED - RED - RED.
Succoss. WHITE - WHITE - WHITE.

14. The Battalion Signal Sgt and Cpl, also 4 (four) Hoadquarters runnors will bo at Roport Contro (W 6 b) for work back to Battalion Hoadquartors. X With 2 R.E. Signallers.

Companies will each send 1 cyclist runnor to tho Report Contro by 18.00 Y day for delivoring to Companies. These runners will be changed immediately any move of Company Hoadquartors is mado and a runner conversant with now location sent to replace.

The Report Contro will as far as is possible move forward with Infantry Brigade Headquarters.

15. As soon as a Company Hqrs, Transport lines etc is decided upon, ostablished or changed the location must be at once sent to Battalion Hoadquarters.

Periodical Operation reports stating dispositions, targets engaged etc etc will be sent to onsure Battalion Hqrs are constantly in touch.

16. Ammunition supply will bo maintained normally by Companies from a Company dump or mobile roservo,and in the latter case this must be at onco replacod.

Large dumps can where necessary be made by Battalion on application, in which caso a guide should where nocessary be sont and the ammunition will be delivered by Lorry or S.A.A. Section Wagons.

17. Battalion Q.M. Storos will for the present romain at BOHAIN.
Men for leave will roport to Q.M.
Surplus Stores can be dumped at Q.M. Stores.

18. Companies to acknowledge.

Issued at 22.00

2/11/18.

[signature]
Capt & Adjt,
46th Battn.Machine Gun Corps.

Distribution.

1. A.Coy.	9. 46th Division.
2. B.Coy.	10. 137th Inf:Bde.
3. C.Coy.	11. 138th : :
4. D.Coy.	12. 139th : :
5.)	13. 1st Bn.M.G.Corps.
6.)Filo.	14. Q.M.
7.)	15. Filo.
8.)War Diary.	16. Signals,46th Division.

O.C.'A' Coy.
" 'B' "
" 'C' "
" 'D' "
Q.M.
****

SECRET.
****

F/1

46th Battn.M.G.Corps ~~46/12/08I.~~ 2nd November, 1918.

Reference 46th Battalion Machine Gun Corps Order No 74. F/1.

S.A.A. Section move 3/11/18 to X 13 a.if possible or near to this. We have to use Mobile Reserve and then full up from S.A.A. Section who will deliver on any Officers' signature if indent is marked "URGENT"

Food Containers, should where possible be brought into use.

Packsaddlery - additional to establishment can be issued if required and demanded at once.

Wire Cutters - additional to establishment can be issued if required and demanded at once.

Supply Railhead - from 5/11/18 at VAUX AUDIGNY.

Rum Issue - ½ issue per day for fighting Troops.

½ issue twice weekly for other Troops.

Extra Rations - send in a supplementary indent when men report who are rationed for 1 or 2 days.

Trench Shelters - Further 8 (eight) per Company have been applied for.

[signature]
Capt & Adjt,
46th Battn.Machine Gun Corps.

S E C R E T.
****

O.C. 'A' Coy.
" 'B' "
" 'C' "
" 'D' "
Q.M.
****

Reference 46th Battn.Machine Gun Corps Order No 74.

F/2.

---

1. Synchronisation Watches. Company Commanders concerned will synchronise watches under arrangements to be made with 1st Battalion Machine Gun Corps.
If desired watches can be synchronised at Brigades at 13.00 and 19.00 on Y day.

2. Co-operation with R.A.F. (46 Div: G 117/51)

(a) As so many fresh reinforcements have recently been received, who are not familiar with the procedure of lighting flares, it is very necessary that all ranks should be carefully instructed therein beforehand. They should be informed that, failing the Regulation Signals, the display of any bright object, or even the waving of their arms, will help to indicate their position to the contact plane, whose task will be particularly difficult owing to the enclosed country through which the operations will be conducted.

(b) In the event of a hostile counter-attack being threatened, the contact plane will drop white parachute lights over the centre of the hostile troops.

3. Tracing 'A'. showing boundaries and objectives is issued herewith.

4. Command. During the initial operation and until additional orders are issued 'D' Company will work and move under the orders of Major H.S.Windeler (O.C.'A' Company).

5. Artificers. Only 2 (two) are at present with the Battalion and normally 'A' Company will use 'D' Company's Artificer and 'C' Company will use 'B' Company's as is necessary under arrangements to be made direct between Companies.

6. Tommy Cookers. 20 (twenty) per Company will be issued to-morrow 4/11/18.

3/11/18.

Capt & Adjt,
46th Battn.Machine Gun Corps.

Instructions regarding War Diaries and Intelligence Summaries are contained in F. S. Regs., Part II. and the Staff Manual respectively. Title pages will be prepared in manuscript.

Army Form C. 2118.

WAR DIARY

~~or INTELLIGENCE SUMMARY~~

(*Erase heading not required.*)

DECEMBER 1918.

46th BATTALION MACHINE GUN CORPS.

Sheet No 1. Vol 10

Place	Date	Hour	Ref: Sheet 57.B. & 57.A. 1/40,000 Summary of Events and Information	Remarks and references to Appendices
BOUSIES	1st.		3 O.Rs. Evacuated sick.	
	2nd		Each morning Salvage work at the MORMAL Forest was carried out by the Battalion. In the afternoon football matches were played. 5 O.Rs Evacuated sick.	
	3rd.		A few men received special Boxing Training. All ranks spent much time on making watertight and improving their billets. 1 O.R. Evacuated sick. 1 Officer Evac:to U.K.	
	4th.	10.00	Lecture to the Battalion by the Rev.H.E.Ridsdale, C.F., subject "The State & the Individual" Really a lecture leading up to Educational Training which was splendidly delivered and fully appreciated by all ranks. Capt.Pirkis appointed the Battalion Demobilization & Educational Training Officer. 3 O.Rs. to M.G.T.C. Grantham. 5 O.Rs. Reinforcements. 1 O.R. on Educational Course.	
	5th.		Salvage work continued. Football in afternoon. 2 O.Rs. Evacuated sick. 1 Officer to M.G.T.C.,Grantham.	
	6th.		Orders Nos. 75 & 75A. issued (copies attached) Educational Training commenced in the Battalion and continued each morning and evening throughout December. Football in afternoon.	O. 75 & 75A.
BOHAIN.	7th.	08.00	The Battalion marched from BOUSIES to BOHAIN without any hitch and arrived at 14.30 hours. 4 O.Rs. evacuated sick.	
	8th.		Educational Training recommenced & continued every weekday morning throughout December with the exception of December 25th. Salvage work carried out every weekday morning in the BOHAIN area with the exception of December 25th. Almost every afternoon in December Football and Sport was played in the Battalion. 21 O.Rs. Reinforcements.	
	9th.		2 O.Rs. to M.G.T.C.,GRANTHAM. 1 O.R. Miner to U.K..	
	10th.		---	
	11th.		11 O.Rs. Miners to U.K.. 1 O.R. to Etaples for transfer to Home Establishment.	

D. D. & L., London, E.C.
(A8004) Wt W1771/M2031 750,000 5/17 Sch. 52 Forms/C2118/14

Army Form C. 2118.

Instructions regarding War Diaries and Intelligence Summaries are contained in F. S. Regs., Part II. and the Staff Manual respectively. Title pages will be prepared in manuscript.

WAR DIARY

~~or INTELLIGENCE SUMMARY.~~

(*Erase heading not required.*)

DECEMBER 1918.

46th BATTALION MACHINE GUN CORPS

Sheet No 2.

Place	Date	Hour	Ref: Sheet 57.B. & 57.A. 1/40,000 Summary of Events and Information	Remarks and references to Appendices
BOHAIN	12th.		Battalion Route March. 13 O.Rs. Reinforcments. 12 O.Rs. on Educational Course.	
	13th.		Major J.JOYCE, D.S.O., M.C. reported for duty as Second-in-Command of the Battalion.	
	14th.		4 O.Rs. Miners to U.K.. 10 O.Rs. Reinforcements.	
	15th.		Battalion Boxing Competition. 5 O.Rs. Miners to U.K.	
	16th.		1 O.R. Evacuated sick.	
	17th.		2 O.Rs. Evacuated sick. 3 O.Rs. Reinforcements.	
	18th.		Battalion Xmas Cards in Bulk arrived and issued to the men. 2 O.Rs. Evacuated sick. 1 O.R. to report to Dispersal Centre for Demobilization.	
	19th.		All mares in the Battalion inspected by D.A.D.R. 11 O.Rs. Miners to U.K.	
	20th.	17.30	Battalion Boxing Competition. 2 O.Rs. Evacuated sick. 13 O.Rs. Miners to U.K. 2 O.Rs. on Educational Course.	
	21st.		Semi-final Div.T.Ass.F.C. Battn.Hqrs versus Div'l Signals, result 1 - 1. 1 O.R. to U.K. Pivotal man. 2 O.Rs. reinforcements. Lieut.Ackland appointed A/Q.M. vice Capt & Q.M. M.J.SOMERFIELD to U.K. on leave.	
	22nd.		------	
	23rd.		15 O.Rs. to U.K. Miners. 2 O.Rs. Reinforcements. 13 O.Rs. returned from Education Course for Xmas.	
	24th.		Semi-final Div.T.Ass.F.C. Battn.Hqrs versus Div'l Signals. Result Bn.H.Q.3 - Signals 1.	
	25th.	17.00 18.00	Xmas Dinners were excellently prepared and served. Concerts arranged for the evenings for most of the men. The last Xmas in France passed very enjoyable & satisfactory. 1 O.R. Miner to U.K.	

D. D. & L., London, E.C.
(A8004) Wt W1771/M2031 750,000 5/17 Sch. 52 Forms/C2118/14

Instructions regarding War Diaries and Intelligence Summaries are contained in F. S. Regs., Part II. and the Staff Manual respectively. Title pages will be prepared in manuscript.

Army Form C. 2118.

WAR DIARY

~~or~~ ~~INTELLIGENCE SUMMARY.~~

(*Erase heading not required.*)

DECEMBER 1918. 46th BATTALION MACHINE GUN CORPS.

Sheet No 3.

Place	Date	Hour	Summary of Events and Information — Ref: Sheet 57.B. & 57.A. 1/40,000	Remarks and references to Appendices
BOHAIN.	26th.		-----	
	27th.		1 O.R. on Educational Course.	
	28th.		~~Final D.T.A.F.C. C/230 Bde. R.F.A.~~ 1 O.R. to U.K. Pivotal man. 1 O.R. Miner to U.K. 2 O.Rs Reinforcements.	
	29th.		Battalion Band Instruments arrived & practice commenced. Lack of Flue Players who were applied for at once. 1 O.R. on Education Course.	
	30th.		1 O.R. Evacuated sick.	
	31st		Lieut.E.G.Holden appointed Acting Assistant Adjutant.	

Eric G. Holden Lt for Lieut-Colonel,
Commanding 46th Battn.Machine Gun Corps.

D. D. & L., London, E.C. (A8204) Wt W1771/M2031 750,000 5/17 Sch. 52 Forms/C2118/14

Copy No.......7.

46th BATTALION MACHINE GUN CORPS ORDER NO.75.A.

Reference Order No. 75.

1. As much work as possible on making present billets clean will be done to-night.

Latrines must be clean before marching off to-morrow.

Trench latrines must have a top of earth.

2. Two lorries will be at the Church BOUSIES at 06.00 hours to-morrow and the Quartermaster will detail a guide to guide them as follows :-

1. to Q.M.Stores to pick up Company Guides, thence to 'C', 'D', 'B' and 'A' Companies in order stated to pick up Stores. Only ½ lorry is allotted to each Company and 1 man per Company can travel on the Lorry.

1 to Battalion Orderly Room, thence to Q.M. to carry Q.M.Stores, forms, tables, etc etc.,

3. Men marked excused marching by the Medical Officer will be ordered to report to 1/2nd Field Ambulance BOUSIES by 07.50 hours to-morrow to be conveyed by ambulance.

4. On arrival at destination Company Commanders will arrange a foot inspection.

5. Companies wires will be reeled off by the Battalion Signal Sergeant at 07.30 hours to-night.

The line from Battn. Signals will be reeled in by Brigade Signals after 08.00 hours to-morrow.

6/12/1918.

Blicke
Capt & Adjt.,
46th Battn. M.G.Corps.

Distribution :-

1. O.C. 'A' Coy.
2. " 'B' "
3. " 'C' "
4. " 'D' "
5. Q. M.
6. M. O.
7.) 8.) War Diary.
9.(10.(File.

Copy. No. 10

46th BATTALION MACHINE GUN CORPS ORDER NO. 75.

Reference VALENCIENNES & ST.QUENTIN. 1/100,000

Reference Warning Order within Battalion.

1. The Battalion will proceed by march route from BOUSIES to BOHAIN on the 7th inst.
2. March table on reverse. Order of march 'A', 'B', 'C', 'D' Companies Battalion Headquarters in column of route "action not expected".
3. Dress :- Battle order, soft caps worn, steel helmets carried.
4. Packs, Blankets etc will as far as is possible be carried on limbers. Any stores wich Companies cannot carry will be dumped at Quartermaster's Stores by 16.00 hours to-day properly labelled.
5. The strictest march discipline will be maintained throughout the march. Clock hour halts will be observed.
6. The Medical Officer will ride in rear of the column.
7. Billeting Certificates will be rendered by Companies and Quartermaster vide B.R.O. No. 2406.
8. The Quartermaster will arrange that all Sports Kit in use is available at once on arrival at BOHAIN and will have all stores which cannotbe carried properly dumped and left i/charge of a party from Headquarters which party he will attach to the 138th Inf. Bde. for rations. All forms, tables etc, issued to or made by Companies will be handed in this morning and the Quartermaster will have these dumped with any wood etc, so that these can be brought along later if required and if transport can be arranged.
9. Sick parade on the 7th will be at 06.00 hours. Reveille 05.00.
10. Battalion Headquarters will close at BOUSIES at 08.00 hours the 7th inst and will open at BOHAIN on arrival.

Acknowledge within the Battalion.

[signature]

6/12/18.

Capt & Adjt.,
46th Battn. M.G.Corps.

Distribution :-

O.C. 'A' Coy.
" 'B' "
" 'C' "
" 'D' "
Q. M.
M. O.
46th Division 'A',
46th Division 'G',
War Diary, (2).
File. (2)

MARCH TABLE to accompany 46th BATTN. M.G.CORPS.ORDER No. 75.

Company.	Time to pass Road Junction F.28.c.10.00.	Route.
'A'	08.00.	CROIX - LE CATEAU - HONNECHY STN - BUSIGNY.
'B'	08.05.	
'C'	08.10.	REMARKS.
'D' with B.H.Q.	08.15.	1. Dinners from Kitchen at 11.50 halt. 2. Battalion Headquarters will have dinners from 'D' Coy. Kitchen and rations will be arranged accordingly by the Q.M. 3. O.C. 'D' Coy. will issue orders re time of parade for B.H.Q. with R.S.M. 4. Teas will be taken immediately on arrival at BOHAIN.

Instructions regarding War Diaries and Intelligence Summaries are contained in F. S. Regs., Part II. and the Staff Manual respectively. Title pages will be prepared in manuscript.

JANUARY. 1919.

46 Battn M.G.

Army Form C. 2118.

WAR DIARY
or
INTELLIGENCE SUMMARY.
(Erase heading not required.)

Vol 11

Place	Date	Hour	Summary of Events and Information	Remarks and references to Appendices
	1		Salvage work.	
		14.00 to 18.00	Men of this Battalion subscribed together and gave tea and presents to 650 children of BOHAIN. This was preceeded by a Cinema Performance in the Fancies Theatre. 2 Other Ranks proceeded on Education Courses.	
	2.		Salvage work. Semi-Final of section matches. No.4 Section 'A' Coy. 5 goals. Transport 'D' Coy. 1 goal.	
	3.	17.30	Salvage work. 1st Divisional Concert Party kindly gave a performance in the Fancies Theatre. 1 Other Rank proceeded to Second Army H.Q. as Interpreter.	
	4.		Salvage work. Final of Divisional troops Group Corps Football Competition. 46th Battn. M.G.C. 'HQ' 0. V C/230 Bde. R.F.A. 1 goal. Final of Battalion inter-section Matches. No.4 Sec. 'A' Coy. the winners. 2 Other Ranks to U.K. as Miners.	
	5.	12.30	Battalion Race Meeting held. Copy of programme attached. 7 Other Ranks Demobilized.	
	6.		Salvage Work. 1 O.R. returned After Evac. 5 O.Rs. Demobilized. 1 O.R. Sick.	
	7.		Salvage work.	
	8.		Salvage work. Battalion Boxing Show held in Boxing Ring, Rue de la Republique, BOHAIN. 3 O.Rs posted from Base Depot. 2 O.Rs. Sick.	
	9.		Salvage continued. 1 O.R. proceeded on Education Course.	
	10.		Salvage continued.	

D. D. & L., London, E.C. (A8204) Wt W1771/M2031 750,000 5/17 Sch. 52 Forms/C2118/14

Instructions regarding War Diaries and Intelligence Summaries are contained in F. S. Regs., Part II. and the Staff Manual respectively. Title pages will be prepared in manuscript.

WAR DIARY
or
INTELLIGENCE SUMMARY.
(Erase heading not required.)

Army Form C. 2118.

Place	Date	Hour	Summary of Events and Information	Remarks and references to Appendices
	11.		XIII Corps Race Meeting held at CAUDRY. Salvage continued. 1 O.R. posted After Evac. 1 O.R. proceeded on Education Course.	
	12.		1 O.R. proceeded on Education Course.	
	13.		Salvage continued. 20 O.Rs proceeded to CAMBRAI pending Demobilization.	
	14.		Salvage continued. 1 O.R. sent to Prison. 3 O.Rs proceeded on Education Course. 1 Officer, 22 O.Rs proceeded to CAMBRAI pending Demobilization.	
	15.		Salvage continued. 1 O.R. proceeded on Education Course.	
	16.		Salvage continued. Divisional Commander inspected the Billets of the Battalion. 1 O.R. returned from Education Course.	
	17.		Salvage continued. A.D.M.S. inspected billets, sanitation and cookhouses. 1 O.R. Demob. whilst on leave. 1 O.R. Evac C.C.S. (Dental) 19 O.Rs proceeded to CAMBRAI pending Demobilization.	
	18.		Salvage continued. Capt. G.C.M.L.Pirkis appointed Battalion Demob. Officer. Lieut. C.R.G.Heath appointed Ass. Demob.Officer. Lieut J.M.Beeley appointed Battalion Education Officer. 1 O.R. Evac Sick. 33 Reinforcements from Base Depot. 3 O.R Retd after evac. 1 O.R. retd from absence without leave. 1 Officer and 3 O.Rs proceeded to CAMBRAI pending Demobilization.	
	19.		1 Officer & 54 O.Rs proceeded to CAMBRAI pending Demobilization.	
	20.		Salvage continued. 2 O.R.s Sick. 1 O.R. Demob. whilst on leave. 9 O.Rs proceeded to CAMBRAI pending demobilization.	

D. D. & L., London, E.C.
(A8004) Wt W1771/M2031 750,000 5/17 Sch. 52 Forms/C2118/14

Army Form C. 2118.

Instructions regarding War Diaries and Intelligence Summaries are contained in F. S. Regs., Part II. and the Staff Manual respectively. Title pages will be prepared in manuscript.

WAR DIARY
or
INTELLIGENCE SUMMARY.

(Erase heading not required.)

Place	Date	Hour	Summary of Events and Information	Remarks and references to Appendices
	21.		Battalion Parade for Company and Arms Drill. 1 O.R. retd After Evac. 23 O.Rs proceeded to CAMBRAI pending Demobilization.	[illegible]
	22.		Salvage continued. 1 O.R. demobilized whilst on leave.	[illegible]
	23.		Salvage continued. Captain S.E.Moore M.G.C. lectured on Demobilization and Reconstruction. A very good lecture and much appreciated by all. 1 O.R. retd from Education Course. 1 O.R. demobilized whilst on leave.	[illegible]
	24.		Salvage continued. 26 O.R.s proceeded to CAMBRAI pending demobilization.	[illegible]
	25.		Salvage continued. 1 O.R. sick. 7 O.Rs posted from Base Depot. 1 O.R. proceeded on Education Course. 7 O.R.s proceeded to CAMBRAI pending Demobilization.	[illegible]
	26.		3 O.Rs proceeded to CAMBRAI pending demobilization.	[illegible]
	27.		Salvage continued. 23 O.Rs Demobilized. (Off strength). 1 O.R. from Base Depot. 1 Officer 16 O.Rs proceeded to CAMBRAI pending demobilization.	[illegible]
	28.		Salvage continued. 1 O.R. Sick. 12 O.Rs proceeded to CAMBRAI pending demobilization.	[illegible]
	29.		Salvage continued. 2 O.Rs posted from Base.	[illegible]
	30.		Salvage continued. 137th Inf.Bde. Concert Party performed in Fancies Theatre, being much appreciated. 2 O.Rs posted from Base Depot.	[illegible]
	31.		G. O. C. inspected Battalion in billets, he expressed his appreciation of the work done on billets by all ranks. 4 O.Rs proceeded to CAMBRAI pending Demobilization.	[illegible]

D. D. & L., London, E.C.
(A8o64) Wt W1771/M2031 750,000 5/17 Sch. 52 Forms/C2118/14

46th Division.M.G.Battalion., Lieut-Colonel E.M.Lannowe, D.S.O.
Commanding

A flat race meeting will be held on Sunday January 5th, 1919, when the following events will take place.
Entries close midnight 31/12/1918.

1st Race 12.30
THE VICKERS HANDICAP. 6 furlongs - Open to all Officers of the 46th Division M.G.Battalion - 12 Stone or over.
Entrance fee 10 francs.

2nd Race 13.00.
THE ANDIGNY PLATE, 5 furlongs. Open to all N.C.Os. and men belonging to the 46th Division.
Winner 100 francs, Second 50 francs. Third 25 francs.

3rd Race. 13.30.
THE BOHAIN TOWN HANDICAP. 1 mile - Open to all officers of the 46th Division.
Entrance 20 francs. 12 stone 7 lb or over.

4th Race. 14.00.
MULE DERBY. Open to all, 5 furlongs.
Winner 50 francs, Second 30 francs, Third 20 francs.

5th Race. 14.30
THE P.B.I.PLATE. Open to Infantry and M.G.C. Officers of the 46th Division. (Captains and Subalterns only).
Entrance 10 francs. Weight 12 Stone or over.

6th Race. 15.00
THE BELLENGLISE PLATE. 5 furlongs. Open to N.C.Os. and men of the 46th Div.M.G.Battalion.
Winner 50 francs. Second 30 francs. Third 20 francs.

7th Race. 15.30.
CONSOLATION RACE. (Officers) 6 furlongs. Open to any horse of the 46th Division which has never won a race.
12 Stone or over.
Post Entries. Entrance 10 francs.

SPECIAL NOTES.

In events 2 & 6, horses must be N.C.Os. or mens' mounts and not Officers Chargers.

All riders are asked to ride in Colours, which should be declared with entries.

All entries with fees to reach the Hon.Secretary, Capt.G.Moody, 46th Div.M.G.Battalion by last D.R. December 31st, 1918.

The course will be at about 62B.N.E. D.16 central and will be flagged.

The Hon.Secretary will arrange upon notification, stabling for those desiring to send their horses two days prior to the Races - Groom rations & Forage for Horses should be sent with them.

The Totalisator & Bookmakers will be in attendance.

Jockeys to be weighed out at least 20 minutes before each race otherwise will be considered as non-starters.

Number cloths (which must be returned immediately after each race) will be provided at the weighing in enclosure.

D.A.G.
3rd Echelon,
G.H.Q.

7

SECRET

46th Battn. M.G.Corps. 46/2/4.
****

Herewith original Copy of the War Diary of this Unit for the month of February 1919 forwarded in accordance with G.R.O. 1598.

Tha. G. Holden capt. .

5/3/19.

Major,
Commanding 46th Battn. M. G. Corps.

FEBRUARY. 1919.

Instructions regarding War Diaries and Intelligence Summaries are contained in F. S. Regs., Part II. and the Staff Manual respectively. Title pages will be prepared in manuscript.

WAR DIARY
or
INTELLIGENCE SUMMARY.
(Erase heading not required.)

46 Bn M G Corps

Army Form C. 2118.

Place	Date	Hour	Summary of Events and Information	Remarks and references to Appendices
BOHAIN.	1		Salvage Work. Educational Training carried out comprising instruction in French, Shorthand, Book-keeping and elementary mathematics. Capt. & Adjt. R.DICKENS returned from leave to PARIS. 17 O.Rs Demobilized. 1 O.R. Retd After Evac. 1 Officer Demob. 9 O.R.S proceeded to CaMBRIA for Demob. or Re-enlisted for New Army.	
	2.		2 O.Rs Demobilized. 14 O.Rs. proceeded to CAMBRAI for Demob.	
	3.		Salvage work and Educational Work carried out. 11 O.Rs Demobilized.	
	4.		Salvage work and Educational training carried out. Major H.S.Windeler and Capt. T.A.N. Walker returned from leave to COLOGNE. The Whizz-Bangs Concert Party (46th Div) performed nightly from 4th to 8th inclusive. A very good show, greatly appreciated by all. 1 O.R. proceeded on Educational Course.	
	5.		Educational training and salvage work carried out. Lt. R.L.Griffin and Lieut S.A.Parkes returned from leave to YPRES and district. Major J.JOYCE D.S.O. M.C. appointed Second-in-Command of this Battalion. 1 O.R. from Base Depot. 12 O.Rs proceeded to CAMBRAI for demob.	
	6.		Salvage work and Educational Training carried out. Lieut S.A.Parkes proceeded to U.K. for Demobilization. 10 O.Rs proceeded to CAMBRAI for Demob. 10 O.Rs demobilized.	
	7.		Salvage work and Educational training. 9 O.Rs proceeded to CAMBRAI for Demob. or re-enlistment. 1 O.R. demobilized.	
	8.		Salvage work and Educational Training. Capt. T.A.N. Walker proceeded to U.K. for Demob. also 10 O.Rs. 12 O.Rs. Demobilized.	
	9.		10 O.Rs. Demobilized.	
	10.		Salvage work and Educational Training. Pte. Jones of South African Brigade lectured to 200 men on South Africa. 8 O.Rs Demobilized. 2 O.Rs proceeded on Educ. Courses.	

D. D. & L., London, E.C. (A8094) Wt W1771/M2031 750,000 5/17 Sch. 52 Forms/C2118/14

Army Form C. 2118.

Instructions regarding War Diaries and Intelligence Summaries are contained in F. S. Regs., Part II. and the Staff Manual respectively. Title pages will be prepared in manuscript.

WAR DIARY
or
INTELLIGENCE SUMMARY.

(Erase heading not required.)

Place	Date	Hour	Summary of Events and Information	Remarks and references to Appendices
BOHAIN.	11.		Lieut. H.W.Rudland. proceeded to CAMBRAI for duty with XIII Corps Concentration Camp. 12 O.Rs Demobilized. 2 O.Rs retd from Educ. Courses.	[initials]
	12.		Salvage work and Education. Capt & Adjt. R.Dickens proceeded to U.K. for Demob. Lieut E.G.Holden. (Royal Berks Regt. (M.G.C.)). took over the duties as Adjutant, vice Capt. R.Dickens. 1 O.R. retd After Evac.	[initials]
	13.		SAlvage work and educational training. 1 Officer and 8 O.Rs demobilized. 6 O.Rs proceeded to Cambrai for Demobilization.	[initials]
	14.		4 O.Rs Demobilized. 2 O.Rs from Base Depot, 3 O.Rs retd from Courses. 1 O.R. proceeded to CAMBRAI for demobilization.	[initials]
	15.		Salvage work and Educational Training. 10 O.Rs Demobilized. 4 O.Rs proceeded to CAMBRAI for demobilization.	[initials]
	16.		Capt. M.J.Somerfield and Lieut. H.A.Spendlove struck off strength of Battalion. Lieut. E.G.Holden appointed A/Capt. whilst employed as Adjutant. 1 O.R. demobilized whilst on leave. 1 O.R. from Base Depot.	[initials]
	17.		The Commanding Officer inspected the Battalion. 2/Lt. W.T.Thornton proceeded on 14 days Ordinary leave to U.K. 2/Lieut. W.G.Oncken died at No. 12 C.C.S. BUSIGNY of Pneumonia. 8 O.Rs Demobilized. 1 Officer Demobilized.	[initials]
	18.		Salvage work and Educational Training.	[initials]
	19.		Salvage work and Educational Training continued.	[initials]
	20.		Salvage work and Educational Training Continued. 2/Lt. A.E. Francis proceeded to DOULLENS on duty.	[initials]

D. D. & L., London, E.C.
(A8304) Wt W1771/M2031 750,000 5/17 Sch. 52 Forms/C2118/14

Army Form C. 2118.

WAR DIARY
or
INTELLIGENCE SUMMARY.

(Erase heading not required.)

Instructions regarding War Diaries and Intelligence Summaries are contained in F. S. Regs., Part II. and the Staff Manual respectively. Title pages will be prepared in manuscript.

Place	Date	Hour	Summary of Events and Information	Remarks and references to Appendices
BOHAIN.	21.		1 O.R. Detached pending demobilization. Lt. P.Deehan proceeded on leave to U.K.	[initials]
	22.		Salvage work and Educational Training continued. 1 O.R. proceeded to CAMBRAI for demob.	[initials]
	23.		1 O.R. Proceeded to CAMBRAI for demobilization. Capt. G.Moody 1/5th Lincolns (M.G.C.) promoted T/Major. 2 O.R. Evac C.C.S.	[initials]
	24.		Salvage work and Educational Training continued. 2/Lt. A.R.Lorimer returned from leave to U.K 2/Lt. A.E.Francis returned from DOULLENS. 1 O.R. returned from Education Course.	[initials]
	25.		Salvage work and Educational Training Continued. 1 O.R. returned from Prison.	[initials]
	26.		2 O.Rs returned from Leave.	[initials]
	27.		All Ranks worked on getting ready for moving to INCHY. Major Witty H. and Capt. N.McVie. proceeded to PARIS on duty.	[initials]
	28.	10.00 14.30.	The Battalion marched out from BOHAIN. Battalion arrived at INCHY. 9 O.R. proceeded to CAMBRAI for Demob. or Re-enlistment.	March Table attached. [initials]

D. D. & L., London, E.C.
(A8004) Wt W1771/M2031 750,000 5/17 Sch. 52 Forms/C2118/14

46th BATTN. MACHINE GUN CORPS. ORDER No. 76.

Reference :- Valenciennes & St. Quentin 1/100.000

1. The Battalion will proceed by march route from BOHAIN to INCHY on the 28th instant.

2. March table on reverse. Order of march, B.H.Q. ; 'A', 'B', 'C' and 'D' Companies ~~of rout~~, action not expected.
~~Details of B.H.Q. in front of 'A' Company.~~

3. Dress :- Battle order, soft caps worn, steel Helmets carried.

4. Packs, blankets, etc. will as far as possible be carried on limbers. ~~Any stores which Companies cannot carry. will be dumped at Quartermasters Stores by 12.30 hours to-day properly labelled.~~

5. The strictest march discipline will be maintained throughout the march. Clock hour halts will be observed.

6. The Medical Officer will ride in rear of the column.

7. Billetting Certificates will be rendered by Companies and Q.M. vide B.R.O. 2406.

8. The Quartermaster will arrange that all stores which cannot be carried is properly dumped and left in charge of a party.

9. All forms and tables which have not already been moved to INCHY will be moved there by lorry on 28th instant.

10. Sick parade on 28th instant will be at 07.30 hours as usual and Reveille at 06.30 hours.

11. Company Orderly Officers will render to Battalion Orderly Room at 09.30 hours a certificate that all billets have been left in a clean and sanitary condition.

12. All limbers not proceeding with the column to be packed in 'B' Company's yard. Major Moody will take charge and arrange for their transport to INCHY on March 2nd.

13. Battalion Headquarters will close at BOHAIN at 10.00 hours on 28th inst. and will open at INCHY on arrival.

14. ACKNOWLEDGE within the Battalion.

27/2/19.

R. G. Holden
Capt & Adjt.,
46th Battn. M. G. Corps.

Distribution.

O.C. 'A' Coy.
" 'B' "
" 'C' "
" 'D' "
Q. M.
M. O.
46th Div. 'G'.
46th Div. 'A'.
War Diary (2).
File. (2).

MARCH TABLE to accompany 46th BATTN. MACHINE GUN CORPS' ORDER No. 76.

COMPANY.	D.22.a.00.70.	ROUTE.
B.H.Q. 'A' Coy. 'B' Coy. 'C' Coy. 'D' Coy.	10.00 hours. (facing east. (Head of 'A' (Coy. to be (50 yards (short of (cross roads (D.22.a.00.70.	BUSIGNY - HONNECHY REUMONT . TROISVILLE.
DETAILS.	Transport will be in rear of Battalion under the senior Transport Officer.	REMARKS. 1. Dinners at 12.50 hrs halt. 2. B.H.Q. will have dinner from 'D' Coy. kitchen and rations will be arranged, accordingly by the Q.M. 3. Band at head of 'A' Coy.

Page 1.

MARCH 1919.
****

Instructions regarding War Diaries and Intelligence Summaries are contained in F. S. Regs., Part II. and the Staff Manual respectively. Title pages will be prepared in manuscript.

WAR DIARY or INTELLIGENCE SUMMARY.

(Erase heading not required.)

8 M.G.C. 46 Bn M.G.C. Vol 13

Army Form C. 2118.

Place	Date	Hour	Summary of Events and Information	Remarks and references to Appendices
INCHY	1		All Ranks worked on improving Billets which were in a very dilapidated condition. 9 Horses and 9 Mules were sold to the French at LE CATEAU.	
	2	11.00	Divine Service. 2 O.R's returned from Hospital.	
	3		Work was continued on Billets. 1 O.R. returned after Evacuation.	
	4		Educational Training re-commenced. Work continued on billets.	
	5		Educational training carried out. Work continued on billets. 3 O.R's struck off strength under G.R.O.3396	
	6		Educational training carried out. Work continued on billets.	
	7		Battalion bathed at CAUDRY. 2/Lieut W.T.Thornton returned from leave to U.K.	
	8		Work continued on billets. 'C' Company held a whist drive. 26 Light Draught Horses marked 'X' proceeded to DIEPPE under 2/Lieut A.W.Cantello.	
	9	11.00	Divine Service.	
	10	09.45	The Battalion carried out a Route March. Lieut. C. Brockis proceeded on leave from 12th March 1919 to 26th March 1919.	
	11		Two Companies worked under own arrangements. One Company did physical training. One Company had their guns etc. inspected by Armourer Staff-Sergeant. Work done on sanitation of Billets. 3 L.D. Horses and 1 charger went to PRISCHES for sale.	
	12		Parades as for 11th instant. 3rd M.A.C. Concert Party performed.	
	13		As for 11th and 12th instant. Definite information received that this Battalion goes to RHINE as a unit. Major H.S.Windoler M.C. proceeded to ENGLAND to rejoin Newfoundland Regt. Capt, W.D.Colley proceeded on leave to U.K. 15th March 1919 to 29th March 1919	
	14		Parades as for 13th instant.	

D. D. & L., London, E.C. (A8-04) Wt W1771/M2031 750,000 5/17 Sch. 52 Forms/C2118/14

Instructions regarding War Diaries and Intelligence Summaries are contained in F. S. Regs., Part II. and the Staff Manual respectively. Title pages will be prepared in manuscript.

WAR DIARY
or
INTELLIGENCE SUMMARY.
(Erase heading not required.)

Army Form C. 2118.

Place	Date	Hour	Summary of Events and Information	Remarks and references to Appendices
INCHY	15		'A' 'B' and 'C' Companies went for Route March under Major W.T.Boughey M.C.. Major G.Moody and Lieutenants C.E.Sheffield and A.W.Harrison were detached pending Demobilization. 1 L.D. and 7 Riding Horses were sent away for sale to the French. 5 O.R's were struck off strength and posted to XIII Corps Concentration Camp. 1 O.R. on strength after Evacuation.	
	16	10.00	Ceremonial Church Parade. Major-General G.F.Boyd C.B.,C.M.G.,D.S.C.,D.C.M., addressed the Battalion after the Service. Farewell address. Lieut F.Russell proceeded on leave to U.K. 18/3/1919 - 1/4/1919, Lieut Simpson and 141 Other Ranks proceeded to U.K. for Demobilization. 155 'X' Mules and 24 'X' Chargers taken on strength of Battalion.	
	17		All ranks worked on getting limbers and animals ready for a move. A draft consisting of 1 Sgt. 9 Cpls. 5 drivers and 113 gunners arrived from 50th Batt. M. G. Corps.	
	18		Work on transport and limbers continued. 3 'X, Chargers received from R.E's. Lieut. T.S.Rees died at No.19 C.C.S. CAUDRY of Broncho-Pneumonia following influenza.	
	19		'A' 'B' and 'D' Companies went to bath at CAUDRY. 18 O.R's. detached pending demobilization.	
	20		Companies worked under own arrangements. The funeral of the late Lt. T.S.Rees was held at CAUDRY at 15.00 hours.	
	21		'C' Company went to bath at CAUDRY. 'A' 'B' and 'D' Companies worked under Company arrangements Lieut C.R.G.Heath went on leave to U.K. from 23/3/19 - 6/4/19. 1 O.R. on strength after Evac.	
	22		Work carried on under Company Arrangements. 1 O.R. on strength after Evacuation. 1 O.R. struck off strength on transfer to XIII Corps Concentration Camp.	
	23		Divine Service.	
	24		All Companies on Route March. 16 O.R's detached pending demobilization. 15 Officers from 50th and 102nd Battalions reported for duty. Lieut A.H.Morrison, Lieut F.E.Hyde, 2/Lieut A.C.Heggs, Lieut H.W.Rennison Lieut R.J.King, 2/Lieut J.Fife, 2/Lieut T.G.Lloyd, Lieut W.H.Butt 2/Lieut E.L.West, Lieut P.W.Simpson, 2/Lieut F.Walker, 2/Liwut J.Wilson 2/Lieut S.Stevens, 2/Lieut N.B.Fox, 2/Lieut M.T.J.Keens	

D.D. & L. London, E.C. Wt. W. 771/M2031 750,000 5/17 Sch. 52 Forms/C2118/14

Instructions regarding War Diaries and Intelligence Summaries are contained in F. S. Regs., Part II. and the Staff Manual respectively. Title pages will be prepared in manuscript.

WAR DIARY
or
INTELLIGENCE SUMMARY.
(Erase heading not required.)

Army Form C. 2118.

Place	Date	Hour	Summary of Events and Information	Remarks and references to Appendices
INCHY	25		Companies worked under Company arragements. Lieut R.J.Wheeler and Capt J.W.Pooley joined for duty from 59th Batt. M.G.Corps. 1 O.R. Evacuated to C.C.S. No.5 Section 46th Divisional Signals joined prior to moving to Ar,y of Occupation. Lieut G.D.Bray M.M. proceeded on leave to U.K. from 27/3/19 - 10/4/19.	[initials]
	26		'A' and 'B' Companies did physical training. 'C' and 'D' Companies worked under Company arrangements. Draft of 84 men joined for duty from 50th Batt. M.G.Corps.	[initials]
	27		Companies worked under Company arrangements, with the exception of 'B' Company, which did Salvage work in the vicinity of INCHY-BEAUMONT.	[initials]
	28		The Battalion bathed at CAUDRY. The D.A.D.V.S. 46th Division inspected all the animals in the Battalion. 1 O.R. evacuated to C.C.S.	[initials]
	29		'A' Company did Salvage work. Remaining Companies worked under Company arrangements. Wire received that the Battalion entrains at CAUDRY for the RHINE. 6 O.R's posted from 59th Batt. M.G.C. 1 O.R. returned from Hospital. 1 O.R. struck off strength under G.R.O.3396.	[initials]
	30		All Companies worked on preparing for the move. 5 O.R's posted from 50th Batt. M.G.C.	[initials]
	31		All Companies worked on preparing for the move.	[initials]

D. D. & L., London, E.C. (A8094) Wt W1771/M2031 750,000 5/18 Sch. 52 Forms/C2118/14

D.A.G.,
British Army of the Rhine.
****

Herewith War Diary of the Battalion under my Command for April 1919.

E.W. G. Holden Capt & adj

6th May 1919.

for Major,
Commanding 46th Battn. M.G. Corps.

Instructions regarding War Diaries and Intelligence Summaries are contained in F. S. Regs., Part II. and the Staff Manual respectively. Title pages will be prepared in manuscript.

WAR DIARY
or
INTELLIGENCE SUMMARY.
(Erase heading not required.)

APRIL. 1919.

Army Form C. 2118.

Place	Date	Hour	Summary of Events and Information	Remarks and references to Appendices
	1		Battn.Headquarters, 'B' and 'D' Companies entrained at CAUDRY for the RHINE. Left CAUDRY at 18.30 hours.	
	2.		Journey to RHINE. 'A' and 'C' Companies entrained at CAUDRY.	
	3.		Battn. H.Q. 'B' and 'D' Companies arraived at MECHERNICH. 1 O.R. Off strength to U.K.Demob.	
	4.		'A' and 'C' Companies arraived at MECHERNICH. 2 Officers on Strength. 2 O.Rs Off strength to U.K. Demob. 1 O.R. on Strength from 50th Bn.	
	5.		Companies under own arrangements.	
	6.		Divine Service.	
	7.		Under Company arrangements. 2 Officers on strength from Base. 1 O.R. to U.K. Demob.	
	8.		Under Company arrangements.	
	9.		Companies under own arrangements. 3 O.R.s off strength under G.R.O. 3396.	
	10.		As for the 9th.	
	11.		As for the 9th and 10th.	
	12.		Battn. Parade for Battn. Drill under Major W.T.Boughey MC. 1 O.R. struck off strength under G.R.O. 3396. 1 O.R. on strength from After Evacuation.	
	13.		Divine Service. 1 O.R. Struck off strength under G.R.O. 3396.	
	14.		Companies under own arrangements. 1 O.R. Struck off strength under G.R.O. 3396.	
	15.		As for the 14th. 1 O.R. struck off strength under G.R.O. 3396. 1 O.R. Retd after Evac.	

D. D. & L., London, E.C.
(A8104) Wt W1771/M2031 750,000 5/17 Sch. 52 Forms/C2118/14

Army Form C. 2118.

Instructions regarding War Diaries and Intelligence Summaries are contained in F. S. Regs., Part II. and the Staff Manual respectively. Title pages will be prepared in manuscript.

WAR DIARY
or
INTELLIGENCE SUMMARY.
(Erase heading not required.)

Place	Date	Hour	Summary of Events and Information	Remarks and references to Appendices
	16.		As for the 14th and 15th. 3 Officers on strength from Base.	
	17.		Under Company arrangements.	
	18.		Preparation for Inspection by Corps Commander.	
	19.		The Battalion paraded for inspection at 11.00 hours by Lieut.General Sir Walter Braithwaite. KCB. Commanding IX Corps. He expressed his satisfaction on the good turnout and steadiness of the men on parade. 1 Officer posted from Base. 10 O.Rs. on strength from the 38th Battn.	
	20.		Divine Service.	
	21.		This date was recognised as a holiday instead of Good Friday. 2 Officers posted from Base. 2 O.Rs returned after Evacuation.	
	22.		Under Company arrangements.	
	23.		Under Company arrangements. 1 O.R returned after Evacuation.	
	24.		Under Company arrangements. 1 Officer posted from 50th Battn.	
	25.		Under Company arrangements. A Library was opened on this date for the use of all ranks in the Battalion.	
	26.		Companies paraded independently and carried out Machine Gun Drill.	
	27.		Divine Service.	
	28.		Under Company arrangements. 1 O.R. posted from Base. 1 O.R. returned after Evac.	

D. D. & L., London, E.C.
(A8004) Wt W1771/M2031 750,000 5/17 Sch. 52 Forms/C2118/14

Instructions regarding War Diaries and Intelligence Summaries are contained in F. S. Regs., Part II. and the Staff Manual respectively. Title pages will be prepared in manuscript.

WAR DIARY
or
INTELLIGENCE SUMMARY.
(Erase heading not required.)

Army Form C. 2118.

Place	Date	Hour	Summary of Events and Information	Remarks and references to Appendices
	29.		Under Company arrangements. 3 O.Rs posted from IX Corps.	
	30.		Under Company arrangements. 1 O.R. off strength to U.K. Serving Soldier.	

D. D. & L., London, E.C.
(A8 c4) Wt W1771/M2031 750,000 5/w Sch. 52 Forms/C2118/14

46th BATTN. MACHINE GUN CORPS. **WAR DIARY** *or* **INTELLIGENCE SUMMARY.** MAY 1919. Army Form C. 2118.

(*Erase heading not required.*)

Instructions regarding War Diaries and Intelligence Summaries are contained in F. S. Regs., Part II. and the Staff Manual respectively. Title pages will be prepared in manuscript.

Place	Date	Hour	Summary of Events and Information	Remarks and references to Appendices
MECHERNICH.	1		From midnight April 30th / May 1st to reveille May 2nd, each Company held one section, with guns in a state of immediate readiness for any trouble and disorder which might result during the holiday of Labour Demonstration by the Civil population. No further action was needed.	
	2.		Under Company arrangements. 2 Other Ranks to Cooking Course IX. Corps.	
	3.		Under Company arrangements.	
	4.	11.30	Divine Service.	
	5.		All Gas Respirators were inspected by the IX. Corps Chemical Adviser. 2 Other Ranks to Pigeon Flying Course.	
	6.		Under Company arrengements. All animals of the Battalion were inspected by the A.D.V.S. IX. Corps.	
	7.		Under Company arrangements.	
	8.		Under Company arrangements.	
	9.		Under Company arrangements.	
	10.		Under Company arrangements.	
	11.	11.30	Divine Service.	
	12.		Machine Gun Training carried out under Company arrangements 09.00 hrs to 11.00 hours. At 11.15 hrs Lieut. Reilly (South Staffs Regt). lectured the Battalion on :- " (a) His treatment and experiences whilst prisoner of war in Germany.". " (b) The tale of his attempted escape. 2 Officers to Hospital. 2 Other Ranks to Pigeon Flying Course.	

D. D. & L., London, E.C. (A8001) Wt. W1771/M2031 750,000 5/17 Sch. 52 Forms/C2118/14

Army Form C. 2118.

Instructions regarding War Diaries and Intelligence Summaries are contained in F. S. Regs., Part II. and the Staff Manual respectively. Title pages will be prepared in manuscript.

WAR DIARY
or
INTELLIGENCE SUMMARY.

(Erase heading not required.)

Place	Date	Hour	Summary of Events and Information	Remarks and references to Appendices
MECHERNICH.	13.		Machine Gun Training under Company arrangements. 1 O.R. On strength after evac.	
	14.		Machine Gun Training under Company arrangements.	
	15.		Machine Gun Training under Company arrangements.	
	16.		Machine Gun Training under Company arrangements. 1 O.R. to U.K. Serving Soldier.	
	17.		All Companies on Route March. 1 O.R. to the M.G.T.C. Grantham.	
	18.	10.00	Divine Service.	
	19.		Machine Gun Training under Company arrangements. 1 O.R. Posted to Home Service. 2 O.Rs. to Pigeon Flying Course.	
	20.		Machine Gun Training under Company arrangements.	
	21.		Machine Gun Training under Company arrangements.	
	22.		Machine Gun Training under Company arrangements. 113 O.Rs. Posted to 1st Bn. 109 O.Rs. Posted to 6th Bn. 1 O.R. Off Strength.	
	23.		Machine Gun Training under Company arrangements. 1 O.R. to U.K. Demob over age. 2 O.Rs from Pigeon Flying Course.	
	24.		Under Company arrangements. 1 O.R. Off strength under G.R.O. 2795. 1 O.R. From Pigeon Flying Course.	
	25.		No Parades.	
	26.		Under Company arrangements.	
	27.		Under Company arrangements. All equipment and Stores of the Companies were handed into the Q.M.Stores in preparation for the disbanding of the Battalion.	

D. D. & L., London, E.C.
(A5031) Wt. W1 71/M2031 750,000 5/17 Sch. 52 Forms/C2118/14

Instructions regarding War Diaries and Intelligence Summaries are contained in F. S. Regs., Part II. and the Staff Manual respectively. Title pages will be prepared in manuscript.

WAR DIARY
or
INTELLIGENCE SUMMARY.
(Erase heading not required.)

Army Form C. 2118.

Place	Date	Hour	Summary of Events and Information	Remarks and references to Appendices
MECHERNICH.	28.		All animals of the Battalion were entrained and despatched to the Veterinary Evacuating Station, COLOGNE. 10 Officers Off Strength to U.K. (Demob).	
	29.		Under Company arrangements. Captain E.G. Holden , Royal Berkshire Regiment relinguished the post of Adjutant to the Battalion and proceeded to England to report to the War Office regarding his transfer to India. 1 Officer Off. strength.	
	30.		Under Company arrangements. 1 O.R. Off Strength whilst on leave. Admitted into Hospital.	
	31.		Under Company arrangements.	
		18.00	A farewell dinner was given to all men remaining in the Battalion before being disbanded. Afterwards, a very successful concert was held, and everyone spent a most enjoyable evening.	

J.E. Hyde Lieut. r.a.d.i.
for Major,
Commanding 46th Battn. M. G.Corps.

D. D. & L., London, E.C.
(A8094) Wt. W1-71/M2031 750,000 5/17 Sch. 52 Forms/C2118/14

www.ingramcontent.com/pod-product-compliance
Lightning Source LLC
Chambersburg PA
CBHW080920230426
43668CB00014B/2165

* 9 7 8 1 4 7 4 5 2 1 2 9 1 *